Healing the Hurt
Behind Addictions
And
Compulsive Behaviors

To Homer —
many blessings,
Carol

Also By Carol M. Howe

Homeward To An Open Door;
Exploring Major Principles Of
A Course In Miracles

Emergency Procedures
For Regaining Peace Of Mind
(English, Spanish, And German)

Children As Teachers Of Peace
(Co-editor)

Video And Audio Tape Sets

Healing the Hurt
Behind Addictions
And Compulsive Behaviors

By
Carol M. Howe

Healing The Hurt Behind Addictions
And Compulsive Behaviors

January, 2000

Copyright © 2000 by Carol M. Howe

ISBN: 1-889642-20-7

Cover design by Jane Harrington

Production and typography by Cathy Sanders

CAROL M. HOWE
P.O. BOX 151456
ALTAMONTE SPRINGS, FL 32715

Table of Contents

Acknowledgments

So many deserve deep gratitude for the blessings in my life, that recounting them is quite impossible. Suffice it to say that each encounter has left an imprint and, without that influence, my present life could not have come to pass. Primary among those whose lives have changed mine forever are my sons, Gregory and Nelson, who have always been my inspiration, my greatest teachers, and provided the motivation for my own soul-searching. And, to them, this book is dedicated with love and thanksgiving.

I am forever indebted to my spiritual partner and colleague, Robert White, whose breadth and depth of talent is second to none. His suggestions for improving this book were brilliant and, as always, right on the mark. And, he cooked quite a few meals while I was buried in mountains of paper from successive revisions and changes!

With great affection and delight, I applaud the following brave souls who have turned their lives around, freeing themselves from the tyranny of their own addictions, and who have chosen to share their insights through this book: Bo and Thais Abernethy, Becky Bailey, Jasper Becker, Kathy Becker, Jack B., Skip Brennan, Larry Cavallaro, Tom Corkhill, Daphne Cronin, Cathy Darnell, Toni Furbringer-Long, Dave Harkins, Keith Lashley, Rebecca Lindsay, Debbie Lundberg, Joan Mangani, Lori McPadden, Susan Miller, Kate O'Neil, Glendon Perkins, Bryan T., Gary and Nancy Troxell, Margarita Villoch, John and Lisa Wells, and Robert White.

No creative work comes together in isolation and I am deeply grateful for the thoughtful suggestions and specific help offered by so many. Margarita Villoch played a pivotal role by transcribing the addiction workshop tapes for her own use, which sparked the idea of a book in the first place. Katherine Bracewell was instrumental in the early stages of this enterprise with her excellent initial edit of the workshop transcriptions and Cathy Darnell spent long hours transcribed many of the original taped interviews. Toni Furbringer-Long and Marty Hunt provided valuable insight and editing suggestions for the workshop transcriptions. The final manuscript had to pass muster with Linda Corkhill who did a superb job of reading with her heart as well as with her very incisive intellect. My dear friend and fellow traveler, Sarah Whalen, has contributed far more than her superb editing skills. She has been a life-long friend, present and available through all of life's "triumphs and tragedies," and for her I am forever grateful. And last but certainly not least, special thanks go to Cathy Sanders, whose expert services as a graphic designer have been so essential, and to Jane Harrington, artist extraordinaire, whose cover design so aptly portrays the oneness of both problem and solution.

Preface

If, twenty years ago, someone had predicted I would be writing a book on the subject of addictions, I would have dismissed the idea as preposterous. In the first place, if I thought of them at all, addictions seemed entirely unrelated to my life, and in the second place, my college degree is in mathematics, which certainly did not include emphasis on such subjects. Fresh out of college, I taught secondary-level mathematics for a few years, then went to work for IBM as a systems engineer. The opportunity to work with computers seemed to occur quite by chance, for, at the time, I knew nothing about them, nor was I even interested. Now I recognize that I was led by an inner guidance, which I experienced as a sense of enthusiasm or fullness, or the feeling of "yes!"

That job proved to be a perfect one, requiring my strongest skills and providing an excellent arena to expand beyond my recognized limits. In particular, I experimented with an ability that has served me very well ever since—to know that I can accomplish any task to which I commit regardless of prior knowledge or experience. Those days, which I recall with great fondness, prepared the way for the next chapter of my life; in 1970 we began our family and the next round of self-discovery began in earnest.

In much the same unexpected way I found myself working for IBM, my current position as consultant, lecturer, and facilitator in the field of personal growth and transformation occurred as a natural consequence of my quest for meaningful answers, rather than from career planning or specialized training. As a young adult, I never intended to be a consultant or facilitator, or to be involved in group work of any kind—certainly not in the field of addictions. In the early 1970's, motivated primarily by a desire to raise my children the best I could, I began to explore psychological and spiritual matters beyond the bounds of conventional interests. At first, it was a welcome exception to meet individuals involved with similar searches, for I knew very few at the time who seemed to be genuinely interested in self-discovery. Now, I find that virtually all those in my personal universe have made it their purpose to live authentically, doing their own inner work, pursuing their own inner direction, and healing their own minds. From them I have learned so very much and to them I am forever indebted! That ever-trustworthy inner guidance has continued to orchestrate the crossing of our various paths, enriching our lives and encouraging the profound discoveries documented herein.

Several years ago, I was invited to present a workshop at a conference for women in traditional addiction recovery programs, primarily from alcohol, drugs, and food. It was an extraordinary experience for all of us, with many participants spending much of their free time exploring the perspectives offered in this workshop about the true cause of their addictions. Long into the night, we examined these challenging, yet liberating ideas, very new to most of them, and one person characterized the response as a "feeding frenzy." For the first time, many opened their eyes to a viewpoint they intuitively felt was true, personally useful, and fundamentally different from those with which they were familiar.

I presented a similar program in Florida a year or so later that, once again, proved to be particularly helpful and enlightening, and friends urged me to transcribe and publish the workshop's curriculum. Part way through the transcribing process, several individuals with whom I was doing private consulting made crucial discoveries about their own addictions and the need for addressing their fundamental cause. It for millions of people, participating in or watching sporting events truly is an addiction, which is not at all amusing.

So, what is an addiction anyway? The *American Heritage Dictionary* defines an addict as "one who devotes or gives oneself habitually or compulsively." We would redefine an addict as one who uses any substance, activity, or way of relating to the world to obscure fear, pain, terror, loneliness, and feelings of inadequacy and alienation. Addictions serve one purpose: to attempt to feel better and to prevent awareness of our distress and pain, thus obscuring the need for healing. We must be clear that it is this common purpose of masking pain that allows so many varied elements to be categorized as addictions. (The word *pain*, used throughout this book, refers to all disturbance or lack of comfort and peace of mind, whether physical, emotional, or undifferentiated. It also refers to lack of joy and fulfillment, safety and certainty.) In fact, as we shall see, almost everything we do and almost all the plans we lay serve that single goal of distracting us from a fundamental feeling that something is irrevocably and forever wrong with us.

Hear this more specifically. If we are ever to live in safety and in peace, we must look carefully and without defense at the ways we spend our time, the activities in which we engage, and the matters that preoccupy us. The activities of this world are basically neutral. They include all that make up our daily lives—jobs, schooling, hobbies, relationships, raising families, leisure pursuits, religious ceremonies, and our varied searches for meaning and understanding. Because our culture has indiscriminately applauded those who work long hours, constantly drive toward higher goals, or seek additional information, we have failed to notice there are always two significantly different motivations for what we do, accomplish, or seek. The motivation for the activity, not the activity itself, determines whether it shares the common purpose of all addictions. The simple question we rarely address is, "What is my purpose for engaging in these activities?" For many, this is a disturbing or, at least, puzzling question because it makes us aware of our lack of purpose, our deliberate decision not to examine the contents of our minds, or the belief that those contents are entirely unrelated to the feelings and circumstances of our lives. We don't notice our motivations because we don't wish to do so. We choose to stay unaware of our thinking, choices, and habits in order to avoid responsibility, interpreting responsibility as blame or too much to deal with. Our motivations and purpose are like the proverbial elephant in the middle of the room that everyone studiously avoids acknowledging.

Now, if we define an addict as someone who uses substances, people, or situations as a way to avoid inner turmoil or pain, it should be immediately obvious that we all fall into this category. Basically, all of us are addicted to something or engage in obsessive or compulsive behaviors to some degree, because all of us retain some patterns of thought and belief that result in emotional, physical, or mental pain. This pain, hidden in the recesses of our minds and left to grow and fester, is the fundamental cause of our constant need for more and greater addictions.

If, on hearing of this one universal cause behind addictions, you find yourself upset, that is very telling. It is also excellent, because once in touch with our own distress, we can move on to the next step of healing. You cannot heal what you refuse to allow into awareness. Remember the old adage, Where there's smoke, there's fire. Where there is upset, there lurks a belief, masquerading as truth, that our basic nature is flawed and unworthy. This book challenges that belief and presents the one generic process required by all, benign and helpful and gravely misunderstood. The need to be free of our hurt is universal, and the process for freeing ourselves is already established, awaiting our acceptance, not our invention.

A blanket statement that we all have some unfinished business initially sounds insulting or disturbing, particularly when we have worked so hard to appear totally "together" in the eyes of the world. At this point, many declare, a bit too hurriedly, that they certainly do *not* have any upset feelings stored within, so this work does not apply to them. I guarantee those feelings are there. Why should it be so surprising to find we are out of touch with them when one of our highest priorities has been to be out of touch? We have worked very hard to stay unaware of our feelings and assumptions, believing it was in our best interests to do so. It is essential that everyone look more carefully than ever at the objections to exploring these topics and hasten to the point of *feeling* the feelings, rather than just thinking about them. For if we deny the presence of pain to the point of unawareness, we delay the time for healing but never eliminate the need for it. Again, some of you may tell yourselves you are not in pain and this has nothing to do with you. Think again. Here is denial at work. It is not an accusation or an insult to hear we are holding onto pain, because pain is merely an indicator, an attention-getting signal. It indicates with unerring precision that we are choosing not to love ourselves or others, a choice that obscures our birthright of happiness, and if we are willing to pay attention, the pain caused by that unhelpful choice can clear up with a change of mind and heart.

After my father died and my mother developed Alzheimer's disease and was placed in a nursing home, my brother and I were cleaning out our family home. As we pored over boxes and files, we came across some of our mother's diaries and journals. She was a great one for keeping records of everything, and her private thoughts were no exception. We found a journal entry written when I was five and my brother three years old. She wrote about the basically satisfactory nature of her life and marriage but ended with the sentence, "But I must constantly guard against introspection." What a telling statement and how true of most of us! Even when I was small, I had the feeling my mother was driven by something, so much so that if she ever stopped her relentless busy-ness, some unknown threat would overtake her. By the world's standards, she was quite a success. She was very active in church and civic affairs, ran her own business, stayed very involved with our school events, and presided over a large home that was always the center of interesting activity. Everyone liked coming to our house because it was a lively, busy place where the unusual was the norm. Still, she was typical of millions who don't dare take time out to be quiet or contemplative. As I grew older, I would sometimes ask her why she could not just sit and rest. She never gave an explanation, rather an excuse about how much she had to do. She clearly bought into her own programming. Like her, most of us refuse to acknowledge the obvious: that we create our busy-ness because it keeps us preoccupied and unable to be acquainted with the contents of our minds—contents, by the way, that greatly influence the quality of our lives. By her own admission, she feared intro-spection. She has lots of company.

To bring this topic closer to home, what do we fear will happen if we start to examine our thoughts or our feeling nature? Most of us never find out, because we have given the world and all its activities the purpose of avoiding this essen-tial introspection. What are these feelings that we find so fearful and so powerful? What is it we so desperately try to hide? Having worked with so many men and women, I have found one common denominator in every case: upset feelings are associated with an assessment of worthlessness. We mistakenly assume that inner disturbance is a true barome-ter of fact. It is not. Lack of peace is actually a barometer of a mistaken but all-consuming belief that the self-talk in which we all engage and the attendant upset is accurate or inevitable. We listen to the inner chatter that speaks endlessly of our inferiority or wickedness or lack of value. Our single problem is that we listen to it indiscriminately and never ask the one essential question, Is this assessment of myself true? Notice how that question has never been asked and, even as you read these words, seems suspect.

Since we have asked the wrong questions and therefore not recognized the answers right in front of us, we feel besieged and hassled, knowing our way of life is very unsatisfactory but not understanding where things have gone wrong. They have gone wrong primarily in our own minds, and it is only there that we will find the answer. Do you hear that? *Only in our minds.* Now you may rage, "My problems are not in my mind! They are with my kids, my boss, my finances, my race, my age!

These have nothing to do with my mind!" Well, this is the time for a heart-to-heart talk, the time to hear that, whether we know it or not, all experience begins, grows, and ends in our own minds. And it does indeed spill out into, and is reflected in, the tapestry of our very complex and varied daily lives. This in no way negates the fact that all experience begins in one's own mind. If you find that upsetting, then we are on our way. If you find that a comfort, we are still on our way. We are all on our way home, and we will all get there through the same generic, helpful process.

The first predictable step in this process involves bringing all the feelings we have deliberately ignored into unavoidable awareness. Here is the place in the process where major healing can occur and peace of mind can be restored. Unfortunately, this is also where our unexamined and erroneous assumptions are allowed the upper hand. At this first point, so easily translated into the next healing step, most of us quickly thwart the inborn healing process by denying these disturbing feelings. We mistakenly back away from them and rush to our addictions—both to the commonly recognized substances and the socially acceptable, even culturally encouraged ones—in order to shove them out of awareness. And the closed loop of pain and the attempts to medicate it continues.

As we commence our exploration, it is crucial to note that no matter what we discover about our beliefs and opinions or all those uncomfortable feelings we have fought so diligently to repress, we are still valuable, worthy, and able to change even the worst of circumstances. We have a basic right to be here and be listened to. Our addictive behaviors do not make us wrong!

Many people who come for an initial private appointment are surprised at how little time we spend on the specifics of their problems. That is intentional, because our joint purpose is to move on to the solution as quickly as possible. Everyone really wants peace of mind, and most of us don't have the faintest idea how to attain it. All the resources and help we need to change our minds, and therefore to heal, are always present and available. Down through the ages, in both myth and reality, people have searched the world over for what would satisfy, make them happy—the Answer, only to find that what they were looking for was right before them. Our situation is actually simple because everything needed is here now: you are loved, you have a right to a happy life, you are supported more than you possibly know, and you have a meaningful contribution to make. Notice that this seems to say nothing about addictions; however, it says everything about the solution to them.

Perhaps many have heard of these ideas but not yet taken them seriously, nor put them into practice. If we truly want to change the quality of our lives, individual and collective, we must be willing to examine our own minds and move past our beloved notions and opinions, rather than incessantly blaming others. In so doing, we discover our own goodness and all we truly have to offer. This book is not about intellectually interesting but unworkable theses. It presents proven, predictable processes, embraced by courageous men and women everywhere, some of whose stories and comments appear throughout this book. Our joint purpose now is to unhook the association between addictions and genetics or events and to reestablish a connection between our assessment of ourselves, painful feelings, and the need to obliterate them. If we are willing to experience those feelings, take responsibility for their existence, and accept a proven, simple process for allowing them to be transformed, our troubles—and addictions—can be over.

Part 1

The Workshop

To derive the most benefit from this book, you are invited to participate fully in the workshop presented here and to see yourself as one of us, because you are! I am not speaking to you as an expert from on high but as one who teaches what she wants to continue to reinforce in herself. From my earliest days at IBM, I have been a diagnostician. Whether it's finding the errors in computer programming logic or the errors in our own human programming, seeing what impedes an individual's happiness or fulfillment is my strong suit and one I offer to you. Anyone familiar with computers knows that a single, simple logic error in programming can have major and far-reaching consequences. In the same way, a simple error in the way we view ourselves or erroneous ideas we may hold can cause great pain and disastrous results. In both cases, a simple correction can allow the otherwise correct logic to prevail and everything, for both computer and individual, works as flawlessly as a Swiss watch. We all can walk together on the same quest—to look for the errors in our thinking and correct them—and thus allow our own harmony and peace of mind to be restored.

My own fears, unrecognized for a long time, were ones common to millions of us. From my earliest years, the behavior patterns that were rewarded were to please everyone at all costs, gain approval, avoid conflict, and bury upset feelings as part of the "peace at any price" syndrome. Although rarely stated verbally, the requirement to be agreeable and say "yes" resulted in my becoming a master in the arts of bargaining, compromise, and negotiation. I hoped everyone else would be a mind reader when it came to my needs, so I would not be required to ask for them. Despite my many accomplishments, I harbored the notion that something about me, if revealed, would somehow "give me away." Had I been asked to be specific about my fears or what I thought was wrong with me, I could not have done so. Does this sound familiar? Also, the unstated, but dreaded, possibility of being rejected slammed the door shut on honest communication. My crippling inability to say no and the attendant requirement to be perfect kept me extremely busy, to say the least. My endless, self-imposed need to prove myself as okay and worthwhile was paradoxical and contradictory because I kept getting all the positive confirmation anyone could possibly need to prove self-worth. Yet I continued.

I was not alone. Most of our society's institutions model for us that being genuine about how we feel must be discarded as we "mature" and that feelings should be locked away as unwholesome and unwanted aberrations. This modeling in forming our basic perspectives about feelings and the accompanying, unspoken assumptions are more powerful than millions of words. They are not, however, more powerful than our ability to make probing inquiry and change our minds. I look back on the ways I formerly confined myself and am amazed that I acquiesced without questioning for so long.

As a result of those subtle, but chronic feelings that something was missing, I started exploring, always searching for how life worked and usually feeling frustrated with my lack of answers. Some vital piece of information, the key, seemed deliberately withheld or just beyond my reach. My highest wish is for you to know that nothing you need will be withheld. Your curriculum is tailor-made for you, and you need hunt no further than your own daily life for specific help in knowing how to proceed. As one of my earliest teachers often said, "The secret is there is no secret." Take that to heart and join with us to end the unnecessary emotional self-abuse most of us have endured thus far.

You are now invited to take part in our addictions workshop. The date is February 17, 1996 and the place is Winter Park, Florida. Visualize the setting as you enter a small, brightly-lit reception area furnished with a table, two chairs, a bookshelf, and announcement boards on the walls. You can already hear a buzz of conversation in the adjoining meeting room, as some have come quite early for coffee and conversation with friends. You can sense a warm friendliness as you enter the classroom, a space with about sixty-five chairs set up in semicircular rows, most of which will be filled. Many original paintings and beautifully illustrated calligraphy posters with inspirational quotes fill the walls. The overall light is soft and inviting, with several spotlights highlighting the paintings. The recording equipment is set up in one corner with plants and small tables filling in the others.

Many of today's participants in this daylong event are "regulars" who attend all my classes and seminars. For them, this day is part of a larger, ongoing inquiry, but for others this is a first exposure to a new way of looking at this topic. A few in the group have come with friends and are merely curious. Others felt drawn to attend and have no idea what they are in for. To add to the mix, some have successfully changed their minds and altered their behaviors and others are still held in the grip of their addictions. In addition to the various levels of sophistication about this topic, there is a wide range in age, educational and socioeconomic backgrounds, and types of careers and talents. However, because the atmosphere is open and inviting, everyone quickly becomes part of a cohesive group. I never cease to be amazed at the courage so many people display as they start their explorations!

Many of humankind's common fears and objections are given voice through the following questions, comments, and discoveries. The topics may seem random, but these excerpts are the faithful transcriptions of a live, unrehearsed workshop and are presented in the order they occurred. Although not specifically identified, the various responses are made by many different people who come from all walks of life and different levels of experience. These selected highlights represent almost everyone's confusion, doubt, and misunderstanding related to addictions, their basic cause, and their ultimate solution. In addition to the fears and objections, many observations reveal great wisdom, insight, and willingness to see addictions in a very different light.

Therefore, please take a seat in our workshop, perhaps in the back if you are uncomfortable with these new ideas or right in the middle if you feel more courageous. To join in, simply decide you are among friends, immerse yourself in the ambient energy, listen with an open heart and mind, and be part of the process. Notice your reactions, how you would answer any given question, or any upset you feel. Consider yourself very welcome and fully included!

[February 17, 1996   9:00am
Workshop begins after coffee, registration and general conversation.]

Last week, I spoke with a dear, lovely lady who is going through a big trauma in reshaping her family, including a divorce, moves to other cities, and the relocation of her children. She told me, "You know, sometimes I have the feeling I'm addicted to guilt." I congratulated her enthusiastically on her insight. She is not a full-time student of psychology or metaphysics and came to that realization not through an intellectual process but by recognizing she seemed to be stuck in a quagmire of guilt, unable to get out. We will return to her discovery about guilt addiction, for it applies to almost all of us.

Prior to all my workshops, I always ask myself, What wants to happen here? not daring to presume ahead of time that I know. While always aware of the major topic, I'm fascinated, after years of presenting, to watch how a specific, different subtopic arises every time. One might call it the "slogan for the day." In contemplating today's gathering, a thought kept repeating in my mind, "Very simple, very deep." This unique gathering jointly decided it's time to take a next step of commitment, to move out of the intellectual study of addictions into a real experience of the underlying process at work. Collectively, though perhaps unknowingly, we have asked that these very simple concepts be addressed.

In my mind's eye, I keep seeing the *V* in the word *very* with the open part reducing to the point at the bottom of the letter. With that visual image in mind and in keeping with the idea of "very simple, very deep," here are three ideas we will spend the rest of the day investigating. The first is that the true, invisible Spirit essence of us, with which we are scarcely acquainted, is the source of all contentment, all joy, all abundance, and all security. In the experience of this, our own Presence, lies our freedom and our peace. This Life, the essence and truth that animates us, is one unbroken, unbounded, invisible element or power. To most of us, these sound like mere words, theoretically correct but not "owned" by us. To bring clarity to this matter, please consider this. If, suddenly, that invisible, animating Life or essence vanished and in these chairs sat many dead bodies, you would very clearly know what we are talking about when we refer to Life essence or energy, as compared to the *form* of a body. There is not a person here who doesn't know exactly what we are talking about. Has everyone here seen a dead body? It appears the majority of you have. It is very clear that the form of a body, without any Life manifesting through it, is a most uninteresting thing. Therefore, Life—that invisible Spirit essence of who and what we are—holds and has built into it every experience of joy, serenity, abundance, and creativity that we can possibly imagine. And it is happening and available right now. So, here is Life, ever available, eternal beyond our comprehension, overflowing with all that satisfies, and yet, it is not the major focus of our attention on a moment-to-moment basis.

Our second idea concerns form, physical, three-dimensional form—not only forms we can touch but intangible forms of beliefs, notions, opinions, and all the perceptions we swear are true and accurate that coincide with the world of form. We are greatly attached to these forms, giving them tremendous importance and focusing most of our attention on them. We are taught the world of form is the primary reality and, therefore, requires and deserves most of our concern and focus. We take for granted and do not question the primary importance of this world of forms, perceptions, and interpretations. We move through our daily lives with mostly unquestioned allegiance to the conventional wisdom of the world, not daring to ask the blasphemous question, Is this really the ultimate experience possible, now? We will definitely make it our business here to question this idea.

The third category, stated as simply as possible, is that we have choice about where to place our attention, choice about what we term desirable or necessary. The specifics we consider important vary greatly by culture, age, or century. The physical conditions or possessions deemed good by a person living in the desert would be very different from those of someone living in a large modern city. Is this simple so far? These are the only three elements we need to consider: Life, form, and choice. We will discover that at every second our attention and desire is focused on Life (Spirit), or form, one or the other, in the broadest sense. At any moment, we are either interested in Life or we are preoccupied with the world of form, and all its corollary beliefs. We are investing our very precious resources of attention and intent, purpose and goals, in one camp or the other. You might object and say it's not "or," but "and," that you are really interested in a combination of the two. In fact, we try to make a mishmash of the two and pretend we are unbiased in our allegiance, but we are actually focusing our attention on and paying attention to one or the other at any given moment. In any given day or hour, our focus constantly vacillates back and forth between the two, Spirit or form. We do so 100 percent by our choice and our desire. Nobody—and listen to this carefully—*nobody* makes us focus our attention in a way we choose not to. We may pretend others "make us do it," but that is only an excuse for not taking responsibility for what is happening in our current affairs. It is always 100 percent our choice. What we pay attention to and what goals we set directly and specifically create our inner as well as outer experience. Therefore, they are a crucial element in the exploration of addictions.

With this topic, "Healing the Hurt Behind Addictions" I intend to make clear, once and for all, that everyone is addicted to something. This program is not only for those who are associated with and have found comfort in organizations such as AA and other twelve-step groups. All of us are addicted, even though we may not recognize it. If not to a particular substance, we are all addicted to form, to control, to the way things are supposed to be, and we are all addicted to underlying guilt. We will return to this enormous statement as we proceed. So, this class is basically for everyone on the planet and not just a select few. There are no unfortunate or inferior groups that have it less together than others. Do you hear that? We're all in the same boat, as we shall see.

It should be self-evident, although it is often overlooked, that addictions, or cravings, the currently popular euphemism, do not appear out of nowhere or for no reason. Addictions serve one purpose, which we will look at unflinchingly, and that is to deal with pain, be it physical or emotional. They serve the purpose of distracting our attention from this pain, to sidestep it, deny it, or fix it. We are taught to medicate our pain, as is obvious from the enormous sums spent on prescription and over-the-counter drugs and their advertising, rather than to explore its deeper significance. It goes without saying, as millions have discovered, that our distractions do not solve a problem. They only prolong the inevitable time when we stare our distress in the face, with no place left to turn or hide. Many successfully numb their pain or deny its existence for a while, perhaps a lifetime, but the price for that numbness is lack of joy, lack of fulfillment, lack of a sense of individual worth, and a nagging feeling that something is missing. In the extreme, unresolved pain or upset results in violent or excessive behavior.

At this point, note that we believe three things: 1) pain is bad or undesirable, and recognition of it should be resisted at all costs, as it means something is wrong with me; 2) something or someone caused it some time ago, it's not my responsibility, or it just happens; and 3) there is nothing I can do about it anyway, except cope or resign myself.

If these statements were true, then our denial and frantic attempts to hide from pain would make sense. However, what if they are not true, not one of them? What if pain, rather than being interpreted as categorically undesirable were seen as a warning signal, much as your automobile has built-in signals to warn you when you need gas or when a system may be failing or malfunctioning. Drivers don't decide those warning lights mean they themselves are not okay, only that corrective measures must be taken with the car. In the same way, pain calls for a correction in our attitudes and perspectives about ourselves and others, not more punishment. To interpret pain in any other way is to accept an idea without examining it to see if makes any sense. Therefore, allow any sense of being wrong about any upset or distress you may be aware of to fade away. After all, you are in charge of your interpretations, and you can change them at will. I was perhaps forty years old before it occurred to me to ask the simple question, What is really the matter with feeling upset? I recognized my need to accept that this is an orderly and trustworthy universe and, if distress were present, to assume there is a benign and helpful way of experiencing it. Pain or lack of peace is a warning signal, not a pronouncement of defeat.

In addition to looking at the possibility of pain serving a useful function, we must also examine the thesis that we are the authors of our own distress. This is not an indictment but a very liberating and exciting possibility. If we are the source of our own upset, but don't understand how we create the hurt from which we then try to distract ourselves, we will unknowingly keep generating it. It is crucial to know where pain comes from and how we continue to bring it on ourselves. Contrary to popular belief, there is not a reservoir of hurt that started filling up when you were young, which you keep trying to empty. People sometimes say they have worked so hard, and discovered and let go of so much that they don't know how there can still be more—as if there were a five-gallon drum of hurt we think we have been draining away. That's not how it is. Any hurt we experience today is generated today, not in the past. Whatever we experience at any given time is caused at that moment. Therefore, we would be wise to find out how this happens, so we can stop. I promise that when the hurt, the sense of pain or emptiness, or the itch that can't be scratched is laid to rest, then our addictive or compulsive behaviors will vanish automatically. When there is nothing to hide, cover up, or compensate for, it's very easy to let go of any particular kind of behavior. In fact, you don't even think, I'm now going to let this go. It simply doesn't occur to you to choose that behavior anymore, and it loses its appeal as other thoughts and activities become more satisfying. Do you understand the simplicity of this so far? Does this make sense? Now, our immediate task is to see how we're unwittingly "shooting ourselves in the foot." Our interest is not in behavior modification, or tricky new ways to overcome various urges, but to see how the three ideas of Life and form and choice all come together. The challenge is so simple it doesn't require any education, learning, reading, or experience you cannot readily access this very moment. What we are talking about today is not beyond the grasp of one single soul—certainly not beyond anyone at this workshop.

[Everyone present is very caught up in the proceedings and listening with rapt attention. Note: students' responses are presented in *Italics*.]

To make this personally relevant, I will ask for your cooperation. Think of a person, situation, thing, or condition you hate, that drives you crazy, that you wish would go away, or you would dearly love to escape from. Say out loud the first thing that comes into your mind, whatever it is.

Rejection.
Fear.
Not being in control.
The need to have somebody else, other than who I've got!
Feeling deprived.

Okay, we have all experienced those. What about a specific person or condition, or a place that drives you crazy, which you can't stand. Truly begin to get a sense of your upset with someone or something, so you can become as deeply aware of chronic discomfort as possible. Who would you not like to see walk in this door? Does anyone come to mind causing you to think you would not like for him or her to come in and sit next to you?

> *My ex-wife.*
> *His stepmother.*
> *In-laws, parents.*

Can everyone here identify with the fact that there is someone you would prefer not to have walk in here, to look at, to talk to, or be with? Maybe it's not a person, but a situation. It may not even be someone you know personally but a person or group you've seen on television. It may be an age group, a race of people, a member of a certain profession. If you truthfully examine the canvas of your life, I suspect everyone can think of something or someone you would rather not deal with. What feeling do you experience in that person's presence, or in thinking about that person or situation? Allow yourself to get in touch with why you don't like being with that person or in that situation. What happens within you? Do you feel yourself shut down?

> *If the person is very judgmental, I don't want to be around him or her, and I feel myself shut down.*

So, your response is to shut down. Notice that before you shut down, you decided you needed to do so. What are you feeling that causes you to think, Oops, I'd better shut down?

> *There's a threat, a feeling of anxiety.*

The range of feeling may be very great—anxiety, panic, or nervousness—combined with a fear of being exposed or "found out" in some way. We then erroneously interpret those feelings to mean we are a "second-class citizen." Can you identify with that? Perhaps going to a specific location brings a sense of valuelessness or nervousness into awareness. Many years ago, while living in Colorado, we regularly went skiing in Aspen, and I remember feeling I was in the wrong town. I would walk down the streets feeling out of place, thinking this place was for "world-class" people and I wasn't world-class. Therefore, sometimes it's a place or circumstance, not necessarily a particular person, that evokes the sense of not belonging or the fear that someone will find out I'm not as okay as all the others who vacation in Aspen. That sense of not being okay, however you describe it, and deeper fears and pain underneath the surface of awareness, drive us to shut down. You can feel your entire body contract, withholding at all levels. Not only do we contract emotionally and physically, but we also indulge in certain behaviors in order to solidify our armoring. What are some of the things we do to avoid experiencing upsetting feelings? How about eating comfort foods, watching too much TV, working sixteen hours a day? These are socially acceptable distractions. Continual romance or relationships with a high drama level, when not exceeding a critical level of violence, also fall into the broad range of "normal" or socially acceptable behaviors.

Everyone feels upset or without value sometimes, especially when being honest in the process of healing, which we are doing here. Many people accept such lack of value or worth all the time, or they feel very alien and apart in this world, presuming they don't know how to "do" life, but believing everyone else does. Endlessly and secretly, we all believe the same thing. The realization that we all hold common misperceptions is comforting in itself. Have you ever thought your life hasn't started yet? You're still making preparations, waiting, trying to find out whatever is required to do life successfully. After speaking with enough people over many years, I realized everyone is in the same dilemma, walking around thinking we're the only ones who feel out of the loop. Everyone else seems to have received a *Life Instruction Book,* while ours was left out. All of us are muddling around trying to do this on our own, while believing everyone else is in another boat marked for success. One of the great values of doing this work is to find out we are not the only ones having this experience, which allows a great and immediate sigh of relief.

I want to back up a second. I seem to be able to track myself on lots of my own thinking here, but I'm having difficulty distinguishing between the category of feeling uncomfortable about being found out and another category of, I just don't want to do this anymore. Is that some kind of disguise for the first category? Is there a difference?

Give me a specific.

The specific is going back to work at the university after my sabbatical. The craziness in that environment is still there. I think at one point it served a purpose in my life, and I could get into the drama and craziness, but now I don't want to do it anymore.

So you're saying you don't want to be involved with the craziness and chaos anymore?

I seem to do a bit of it, but not in that form. Right.

When you say, "I don't want to do that anymore," the "that" you're referring to is being in a chaotic work situation-correct?

Right. Am I somehow kidding myself, and it's the fear of being found out in another disguise?

Let me see if this brings clarity. What you don't like is the feeling of chaos and being out of control in your work environment. Is that it? If you find yourself experiencing a chaotic work situation, the chaos does not exist completely independently of you. You are bringing some chaos along with you. You may very well find, after being away for six months and doing your own shifting, changing, and growing, that when you return to the work situation with a greater sense of peace, it will be a very different ball game.

Now it just seems like the "same old, same old."

In other words, you also don't like the idea you are going nowhere, spinning around in circles.

That's it. You're saying I take my circle spinning with me?

[A full-length mirror stands against the front wall of the meeting room.]

Yes. To demonstrate this, I stand here in front of this mirror, and I'm going to put on a jacket. Now I take it off and put on a hat. I decide I don't like this outfit, so I'm going to put on a different shirt. How much input does the mirror have in all of this clothes changing? None! It has no input whatsoever. If someone came along and, looking into the mirror reflection, asked what happened to the plaid jacket in the mirror, you would consider him a bit nuts. Obviously, the reflection went away when I took off the jacket. The reflected jacket is not kept somewhere; there is no place where reflections are collected and stored. I can stand here, change clothes, take off items and put on new ones, and the mirror has zero percent to say about it. It cannot prevent my choices; it has no say in what it reflects. It instantly reflects differently as I change my clothes in front of it. If I wore a blue jacket for four hours and then took it off, this mirror won't object to reflecting a peach blouse instead. It does not have input into our experience in the world. Our three-dimensional physical experiences, as well as our inner feeling ones, just like this mirror, are faithfully reflecting back to us the choices we continuously make.

Remember this very simple fact: we can focus on Life or we can focus on form, and each of us makes the choice. And the conditions in our lives—the condition of our houses, work, bodies, all facets of our experience, our exact state of mind—reflect back to us at every moment throughout our day, throughout our lives, the choices we are making now. Here is a very important point about a mirror: it reflects what I am currently wearing as I stand in front of it, not what I wore yesterday, or when I was two years old. This is very good news! Because if I don't like what I am feeling or experiencing now, I can rest assured that whatever is being reflected in my life is my current state of mind. And nobody can make the condition of my mind be anything other than what my choice dictates. We choose to be loving or fearful, open or defended, compassionate or blaming. What does that indicate?

We're in charge.

One hundred percent.

Why don't we feel that we are?

Because of some confusion we are going to clear up.

> *I like the mirror example because, when I look at the mirror of my surroundings sometimes I see things not as though I've created them, but as if they already existed on their own. Therefore, I don't always see my part in creating my daily life. I see people's behavior and events and situations as if they were there independently. We wonder what we have to do with our life experience and forget we have everything to do with it.*

That is an answer to Marilyn's question. She doesn't want to go back into a chaotic work situation, as if the chaotic work situation existed independently of her. Conventional belief gives her two options: either go back into it and suffer or go back more heavily armored, so she will not feel it as much. Happily, there is another option that actually satisfies. The very important point is that she gets to decide whether her experience is going to be chaotic or not.

> *I want to make sure I'm not off base here. You asked us to think about that person we wouldn't want to come in the door. Basically, the person I would hate to have come in the door would be someone who reflects the part of me I hide. And if that person were to come sit down here, being blatantly obvious we have something in common, I would feel incredible shame.*

Exactly.

The way I would avoid that is to isolate myself, to avoid intimacy, and to do whatever I could to prevent being exposed.

You see, you are right on track with everyone else. The reason we don't want that person or condition in our lives is that we hate experiencing the feelings we associate with them. So we do what we think we must to avoid those feelings—shut down, isolate, avoid everyone, eat, drink, work, or play golf fourteen hours a day. In other words, we habitually respond to that sense of shame, alienation, pain, anxiety, or terror in a broad range of ways, some of which are considered (very artificially I might add) not acceptable and others as quite acceptable, even desirable or virtuous. For example, if you work hard or endlessly engage in philanthropies, that is considered very appropriate. Please note that an entire spectrum of behaviors or activities can serve a common purpose, which is to keep us distracted from those distressing feelings.

I'm trying to pick up what you were saying with Marilyn in the chaos scenario. In that university there may indeed be a lot of chaos, and therefore, it's hard for her to get grounded because they organize the department, she tries to align with that, they reorganize it, and she tries to realign with that. So, in fact, there is chaos that she is trying to deal with. It may not be a reflection of her at all.

I hear what you're saying. Many of our worldly institutions are basically chaotic and meaningless and insane, to be perfectly extreme about it. But the point is that we, individually, are not at the mercy of the status quo. As we keep changing our minds and attitudes and deciding what to experience now, we bring points of light into an otherwise darkened, chaotic place and begin to reorder it. We may not, at any given moment, completely clear out everyone else's experience of chaos, but in an amazing, miraculous way, impossible for us to understand, our experience will be more peaceful. We must realize we do influence our experience and are not at the mercy of the prevailing system. The whole point is to realize that, as we keep changing our minds, we exert enormous influence, not only on our own experience but also on that of the people around us. Don't forget this. Truth and peace, lovingness and contentment have a power that chaos does not have. Chaos and peace are not equally powerful options, so one person's decision to be peaceful can prevail over a much larger range of chaos around her. Remember that when you ask how one person can make a difference. Look at the many instances in our own personal or collective lives where one person has made a difference.

> *It's not about being an island of sanity in a sea of chaos. The chaos is caused by everyone's unquestioned acceptance of a belief in his or her own inherent unworthiness, and we're all trying to compensate for that and lay it off on somebody else. Therefore, the only thing of value you can offer anyone—or yourself—is the conviction of unconditional worth. In any situation, when you focus on worthiness, you receive for yourself and offer to everyone else what you and they are specifically looking for, whether they know it or not. In chaotic situations, people don't know their value, so you remember it on their behalf, offering them the only thing there is of value— a reminder of their inherent worth.*

Everyone is trying to escape from that pronouncement, "I'm not okay."

> *When my buttons get pushed, which continues to be less and less, I now am able to stay proactive, not overreacting but asking what is it that he just did, or what in this situation is my "stuff"? I may not be able to deal with it immediately. I may just have to be silent and take care of the business at hand, but I will deal with it. That's a commitment I've made to myself.*

That's specifically what's called for, because in our growing-up years, we learned to avoid a situation, person, or condition we didn't like. Usually, we do not realize it's the way we feel with that person or in that situation that motivates us to remove ourselves. How we feel becomes the basis for categorizing "enemies" and "friends" or places to avoid and places to go. We divide everything into two camps—what we resist and what we accept—because in one case we feel uncomfortable and in the other we feel fine, or at least less disturbed. Most of us have sought escape from what we associate with distress—get divorced, throw the kids out, or move to another city. In other words, the only option we knew was to remove ourselves from the person, place, or condition, presuming it was the causative agent, or resign ourselves to it. We don't try to escape unless we really think the cause of our upset or anger is "out there," and we are at its mercy, believing the best we can do is to run from it. If running away is not possible, then both we and the other person or condition might stay physically in place, but we shut down or distract ourselves through all the ways previously mentioned. This finger pointing and abdication of responsibility is a constant theme in novels, newspapers, TV, or movies, which endlessly promote the "you made me do it" or "it's your fault" worldview. Therefore, it is a gigantic step to choose this path of introspection, to have the courage to tell yourself when you feel uncomfortable in a situation, I have no idea where this discomfort comes from, but I'm going to own it as mine and recognize that the other person is only triggering it. The key word for the day is "triggering." The people and events we hate bring discomfort into our awareness, but they do not cause it.

> *And the postscript is that you can look at whatever discomfort you experience with the person as a gift, and then proceed with greater peace of mind to your next learning experience.*

No question about every difficult encounter being a gift. You remember Robert's favorite phrase, "The SOBs were sent to save you!" We try to stay within our comfort zone, in order to avoid any thing, place, or situation that might bring into awareness our sense of shame, discomfort, alienation, or lack.

Many people live very circumscribed lives, privately thinking, I don't dare do that, go there, say this, or ask for what I need. They believe they must stay severely confined to make certain they don't get too far out and allow that discomfort to come up. And yet, I'm telling you, if we are to be free of addictions and compulsions, the discomfort must come up to be healed. I can promise that for everyone here who has expressed, in one form or another, the wish to be free or to be who you are, or has said, "I want life to work better" or "I'm getting to the bottom of my own addictions or compulsions and finding out what makes me tick," the discomfort level has increased.

Listen carefully: We are all in the midst of a generic, inevitable process. No one is exempt, getting to skip this step of recognizing our responsibility for our discomfort and pain. We may strenuously object to this statement and exclaim we have no intention of deliberately placing ourselves in what seems to be harm's way, or embarking on a process of getting in touch with and owning our own upset. That would be antithetical to everything we've learned about avoiding pain at all costs, having never asked, What's so terrible about discovering my own pain? We don't have to remain in our discomfort long, although most of us have done so, but we can shorten this step immeasurably. When we say, "I want to be free," we are effectively stating, "I really want to experience my life and the essence of who I am; I want to be able to walk out my door and know I am going to take my peace and contentment with me wherever I go." As soon as we indicate our desire to live with freedom and certainty, one by one, all the stumbling blocks we have put in our way start to show up. Not the blocks that parents or the church or anyone else supposedly supplied, but our very own collaborations begin to arrive.

Now I'm putting this together, as this is a really recent idea for me and I'm processing this. I've been thinking of my head as a magnet, and if I'm thinking more positive thoughts, focusing on the positive things I want such as harmony and a happy heart, my head magnet attracts those desirable things. If I'm thinking about negative things, focusing on what I don't want, like pain and sufferings, then those things actually show up in my life. So when I get that uncomfortable feeling inside and think, Oh God, I have this feeling and this is horrible, I could think, Okay, this is signaling me. This is actually a guide or my friend, helping me see that I'm focusing on what I don't want.

Exactly.

So whatever I focus on, my magnet will attract to me, and the people, events, and situations that are attracted become my mirror "out there," showing me my focus.

Our world of time and space is the perfect mirror for our state of mind and always reveals what we are focusing on. This is a law we can be unaware of, but cannot change. I want to alter your analogy a bit. The magnet, to use your word, drawing the reflection back to you is not what we know intellectually, but what we actually believe and feel. Many of us think, Of course, I want happiness and peace and blessing and prosperity. So how come I'm not getting it since that's what I'm thinking about?

It is imperative to note that the magnet that attracts people or events actually starts with signals that go out from beliefs and subsequent feelings, from whatever is hidden, perhaps a feeling of shame about not being a first-class citizen. The signals don't originate from the intellect, or what we theoretically know. That feeling, growing out of a belief in our insignificance, runs the show, which is why many people are confounded. They speak affirmations and say they want sweetness and light, but for some reason it doesn't show up. Your world does not mirror your intellectual affirmations but always what you really believe and feel is true.

It's like the feelings have the energy. They actually are the magnets.

Yes, they are, and that's why the feeling of being unworthy is not an intellectual construct. When you feel humiliated, this is not just an idea or theory racing around in your head. You simply *feel* awful.

Let's take, for example, a book about positive thinking. I could buy the book because I want my life to be better. I could start making affirmations and thinking positively, but I'm really only going to change the superficial form aspects of my life because, hidden underneath, is a big magnet, a powerhouse of feelings still driving me—a gut magnet rather than a head one. I may temporarily alter some circumstances in my life, but until I can get to the source of pain underneath all that, I really can't make a permanent change.

Precisely! Affirmations, for some, are really only another distraction, another addiction, another layer to cover up this feeling. We believe that if we layer over it, ignore and hide it enough, it won't be there. Nothing could be further from the truth.

I need to go back a bit because I have been confused. A Course in Miracles states that when I ask for peace and understanding, I will know joy immediately. What I hear you say right now is that when I make a commitment to experiencing joy and peace, then upsetting things will start coming up. But, they are really showing me what is blocking me, what I truly believe, what I take for granted. Therefore, I can now look at those experiences as the first stages of finding my joy?

Absolutely!

I don't need to look at them as proof I'm doing something wrong.

Correct. Our vision is too narrow. It's the proverbial problem of looking through the slot in the fence and seeing only part of the elephant. As we broaden our vision, which is our purpose today, we see there is a generic path every one of us follows. At some point, we get down on our knees and declare, "I've had it! I'm not going to live this way anymore!" We become increasingly aware that the way our world is manifesting is not fun. More and more, we realize it doesn't work to our satisfaction and there is something wrong. Basically, the foundation of our world is insane. Perhaps a tragedy occurs wherein we lose something precious. I have spoken with so many who experienced the death of a child or a great reversal in their lives and then began to ask different questions. Recently, I saw a television interview with a well-known singer whose young son was killed in an automobile accident. She was driving the car. To paraphrase her statement, "No more phoniness, no more living in the glitter of things, it's time to be real because life is too short." At some point it dawns on each of us, I'm living a charade, the world is nuts, I'm not doing this anymore. And when we make that statement, the first phase of real healing commences.

When I was younger, I was unaware of this inevitable, yet kindly process. Therefore, my desire is to help you comprehend the process that is unfolding, so that when you do go through some painful times, you will do so with a different perspective and avoid thinking you have failed. Absolutely, you have not failed. You have taken the first step in becoming free, and you don't have to experience pain very long. This process is not about wallowing in pain but finally acknowledging its presence, realizing acknowledgment is the first step to getting in touch with that gut magnet. When we realize the process is to release us, rather than to punish, we can welcome it instead of running away. We might spend forty years being addicted to something, running away from those feelings and beliefs. It is amazing to realize we might be in some discomfort for a few days or weeks and then pass through it, in contrast to running from it for forty years and getting nowhere. The situation is rather like receiving an immunization for a disease. The shot is painful for a few moments but certainly preferable to having a deadly disease.

This idea about possibly experiencing difficulty is not very welcome at this point, but I guess that's where my willingness to look at this differently comes in.

Exactly! You say you want peace and often get a big mess

instead. This is the typical first step in clearing out all that blocks our peace. At this point, many declare they are not about to start a process that will bring pain into awareness after working so hard to keep it at bay for so long. Please note that we have no choice about this. We are being led inexorably by a loving and all-knowing guidance to a place of awareness, which leads to peace of mind and all the happy experiences that are our birthright. We would be wise to stop fighting so hard against our own liberation.

My true addiction, then, is to my magnet feelings, not to drugs, work, or anything else. Also, when the singer lost her son and experienced, perhaps for the first time, the feelings associated with that kind of loss, was that a gift?

Of course, those types of events are wake-up calls. She finally let her distress come up from underneath all the distraction.

It's just occurring to me that what I find most frightening is the power, the almost gravitational pull, of my own dark habits. It feels like that power is almost insurmountable, and what I am just realizing as I sit here is that power is actually my power. My own power is creating the trance that is so strong and has so much pull.

That's wonderful! You are echoing, in essence, an earlier comment. Remember my friend who thought she was addicted to guilt? Very likely, she intended to be facetious, but she was actually correct in that guilt is that magnet buried in unawareness, the feeling, as you say, of that power of darkness. You are correctly realizing darkness has no power of its own; it is always your own power, misdirected.

Those gut magnets you're talking about, can I call those beliefs?

You certainly can call them beliefs. We are confused because we think a feeling of unworthiness is not a belief but the truth.

Otherwise, we would not have such a response to it. We actually have been deluded into thinking unworthiness is the truth about us.

We have been discussing a specific target, person, or situation we would hate to see or encounter. Whether it's seen as another person or ourselves, it's an artificial distinction, because it is always yourself you hate.

So this is always true, whether it shows up in the form of another person or whether you acknowledge it is in your form, it's always something about ourselves we have a problem with?

Yes, always yourself.

I don't know if I understand correctly or if I missed something, but it seems to me the dark feeling that comes up within me, and the negative things that are within me, I don't recognize. Do I understand I have to know where those feeling are coming from, or can I just counteract them with a positive thought?

The first step is to know where they come from, and when I say "where they come from," I am not talking about traumas that may have occurred in your life or your past history, which must be sorted out. Traditionally, we have required historically based reasons for our addictions, however we do not have to uncover specific events. That's what is different about today. To say we need to know where a distressing feeling comes from means we must recognize what choice we are making this moment that is generating the feeling now. Today, now, this instant. We are talking about choosing what is important to us today and, therefore, becoming aware of where we put our attention today. Do you see this is very different from exploring events long since past? This is an enormous distinction.

So what you are doing, then, is removing the blame. We can ask, What am I thinking and doing and where is this coming from within me? and not go back to the past. This can lead to an awareness that you don't have to blame anyone or any circumstance.

Definitely, there is no one to blame, including ourselves, and it is so much more empowering to assume responsibility for our own circumstances. If we are altering our own inner and outer experience *today*, because of our attitudes and choices and beliefs *today*, is this not greatly more empowering than believing my present experience is because of what happened ten years ago? How frustrating that would be! How are you going to proceed if you're convinced the feelings you have today are caused by what happened a long time ago? How could we alter what is over and finished? However, if my feelings today reflect today's gut magnet beliefs, *those beliefs* I have choices about.

Okay. If I think these unwanted feelings I'm having today are associated with an incident that occurred when I was two, which is not the truth at all, then it's a big distraction and delay tactic to believe in this past association? The truth is that I feel unhappy because I feel separated from God, or goodness.

You're right on! To make this point, see if you can imagine a time line drawn across the front wall. The left side of the time line represents life when you were two. If life at two was unsatisfactory, that experience was based on a belief in guilt when you were two. It matters not the least that you may not have conscious recall of that belief in guilt. There is a law, always in operation, that what you truly believe about yourself is translated into your everyday life and feeling experience. If you move along your time line and life is still dissatisfying at age twelve, it was not the circumstances at age two that caused the twelve-year-olds's upset, but the unexamined acceptance of unworthiness still alive and well at age twelve. And continuing across the line from left to right, if you still have faith in your undeservedness at age ninety-nine, you will continue to experience upset at ninety-nine, but it is not caused by the events of the previous ninety-eight years. No matter where you stand in the chronology of your life, your present-day beliefs will be exactly mirrored in your life. Wherever an assessment of guilt, unworthiness, or not being okay appears in life, the feelings and events associated with that assessment occur then and there. In other words, the same uninterrupted feeling of unworthiness travels along with us through years. Yet, it is not yesterday's attitude that reflects as today's life any more than yesterday's clothes reflect in today's mirror. Because we have carried such a consistent attitude of unworthiness down through the years, our lives *seem* to have been consistent. So we erroneously conclude that life is bad today because of what happened then, which does nothing whatsoever to uncover what is actually going on.

Well, I have had a consistent attitude of shame. That is my primary magnet belief, and I was born with it. That's what brought me here.

Then the addictions are just a way of covering up the upsetting feelings stemming from that belief?

If we focus only on the addictive behavior, we are missing the real problem. It's just a cover-up. The real task is to go to the source, to handle the pain or terror or nervousness we are keeping out of awareness with the addictive behavior.

Yes, and how many people have controlled one addiction only to go right on to the next one and others after that, because the underlying hurt was not addressed? It is just a cover-up, and we do nothing to heal the hurt by switching from one addiction or distraction to another.

Sometimes I have a wonderful realization, and everything will be very satisfactory for a while. And yet, lo and behold, the pain continues to manifest, and I'm saying to myself, Please don't take me for a tumble, but it does. I recognize it, I can transcend it and have the peace, but the form is still there.

The form of what, a house, marriage, a job?

> *No, a situation, whatever it may be. Well, I guess patience and time generally handle it.*

May I stop you right there and say it is *not* patience and time that handle it. A lot of us think if we just wait long enough, it will get better. How many of us have been in a job, a house, or a marriage or relationship that wasn't working and said, "I don't understand why it's this way, but if I just hang in here a while longer, maybe something will be different"?

> *My mind is now aware of this situation, exposing my confusion, and I am allowing my Higher Power to be there, and yet my ego still has a way of taking me for a trip. Isn't my intent apparent enough? Do I really have to continue to experience the rest of it?*

I'm really glad you brought this up. Begin to realize that some choice for conflict is still operating. It's impossible to have an upsetting, difficult situation in your life unless you still prefer conflict, at least in part of your life. It is impossible to want only peace of mind now and still have on-going conflict. If you choose to be specific about this, I can walk you through it.

> *Okay. I have a daughter who is ten and perfectly innocent. She has been sheltered from all sorts of addictions and is a very healthy, beautiful child. However, I am an alcoholic, sober for four and a half years, and my seventeen-year-old son has had his share of difficulties. When the three of us are together, somehow, all of a sudden, the topic of drugs will start coming up with this little cutesy-type, candy-type, frivolous sort of attractiveness, and I think, Oh my God, please remove this, please remove all this now!*

Are you saying this is attractive from her perspective?

> *No, it's not, but this topic comes up. I really don't want to interpret*

this, but the children will be singing together, and my son will bring up crack cocaine, which is my worst fear.

For her?

Yes, for her. I have never had a problem with crack and neither has my son. Why it comes up in this playful way, I don't know. It's my worst fear for this beautiful child. Of course it would be, since both my son and I have very great addictive tendencies, yet she has been very protected from the drug issue by her father. I guess there's a lot of fear about if she's with me, is she going to be harmed? There is such confusion on my part. Of course, as a mother I want my children to be together, but should she be with him, or us? I feel I must save my child, whichever one it is!

Remember I told you we would go deeply into this topic, not staying at the theory or surface level? This is what I am talking about. I sense this is the time. Somewhere within you is guilt—fear you have harmed yourself, your son, and potentially, your daughter. Would that be fair to say?

Absolutely.

The bottom line driving our hurt is the fear that we have harmed others or ourselves. The things we are addicted to are the tips of the iceberg. We are really addicted to the idea and feelings of guilt. Now, I am going to make a really shocking statement because that is today's purpose. It is shocking, and why not? Why not be radical? You can be ordinary someplace else. What if you heard that feeling guilty about the ability to harm yourself or others is really very arrogant?

I like that.

Let me tell you why it's arrogant, and the rest of you, hear this! Until it is finally addressed, everyone carries this feeling of guilt to one degree or the other, whether it is in awareness or not.

What guilt infers is that the behaviors of my body, the words that come out of my mouth, the actions or thoughts related to my form, including the intellect and rational mind—all the elements that relate to my personhood—are so powerful they can override other people's choices, which means they override and destroy the oneness of Creation. Guilt asserts that form— my body and what it says or does, the roles I play with it such as mother, wife, or worker, all those ways we define ourselves— is greater than Love itself. Do you understand that's what guilt says? It says, "I am so bad, I am so flawed, the actions 'caused by' my badness are so great that I have wreaked havoc on everything, or I might, or I will!" You certainly can harm a body, but not the Spirit. That's the important distinction and one that will increasingly make sense. Now, along comes the truth, demonstrating guilt is merely ridiculous, not harmful. The truth, the oneness, the Life, the essence of us is not open to being harmed. In other words, guilt is nowhere near to being as strong as the power of Love. There is not even a chance your guilt can irrevocably harm yourself or anyone else. Hear this with as open a heart as possible. You have not hurt your son or your daughter, and you will not hurt your daughter, because the forms of our behavior can never alter our basic spiritual, invisible nature with its truth, purity, essence, innocence, and unity with All That Is.

Remember that we spoke earlier of our choice between allegiance to form or to Life. Allow the sense of distress to drain out of you. If your son and daughter go through experiences that seem to be difficult, hear these two things. There is no way you can intervene between their own sense of guilt, which they may choose for a while, and the unpleasant but tempo- rary consequences of that choice. You have no ability to override their gut beliefs, if you will, and the reflective experi- ences that inevitably manifest from them. Even if we could, we do not want to interfere, because how many of us here, who have had our own dark nights of the soul, would undo the awareness, the learning and compassion that developed out of those? Since we would not, why would anyone else? Certainly, these children have come into your life and are part of your process, since you have signaled your desire to be free, whatever it takes. You have children who, earlier rather than later, are coming to experience the consequences of wrong choices in their beliefs about who they are. But you have not hurt them nor have they hurt themselves permanently, and ultimately, everyone is safe.

I am understanding this exactly, and yet my mind still thinks I have to protect. I feel the same need to protect them from their stepmother; even though she is now out of the picture, the protector in me is still there.

Let me tell you a story I trust you can relate to. All of you hear this, because even though you may not be mothers, you will understand its relevance. I have two grown sons, and when they were very young, I sometimes thought I was an incompetent mother. My children, one in particular, seemed to be chronically discontented, and I took this very personally. I presumed if I were a good mother, no one would be unhappy.

Amen!

Have you ever taken another's upset personally? I did. I clung to my guilt and, I assure you, as a result I found myself in some very difficult, potentially dangerous situations where my life seemed to be at stake. Those several incidents included a near drowning in a boating accident, a near fatality while scuba diving in Mexico, nearly going off the side of a cliff in our four-wheel drive vehicle, and a very close call in a small, private plane when the wind suddenly and unexpectedly shifted. These and other lesser circumstances all occurred within about a nine-month period. I might add that there was an exact correlation between my elevated guilt level at the time my children were young and the occurrence of those frightening events. I now realize those incidents were directly related to my strong feeling of guilt. As an aside, it's very important that you hear that those types of attention-getting experiences never occurred before or after that episode of heightened guilt.

As any of us let go of guilt and shame, we let go of hurt and the events in our lives faithfully mirror that inner shift. The trouble stops!

At that time, I didn't know what to do about this situation other than to continue the personal investigation I had begun, and that felt insufficient. Despite my success with adults, I concluded I just didn't know how to be a good mother, based on having an unhappy child, or conflicts between the boys. Gradually, I became aware that my conclusions about doing them harm and taking unwarranted responsibility for their feelings were grossly inaccurate, and I kept on changing my mind and my perceptions, little by little by little. My children each have been through their own difficult situations, and both consider their subsequent learning priceless. They are now young adults and have a more accurate and loving perspective of their own processes. The encouragement I offer to you comes from a time when I thought nothing could be done about my constant feeling of guilt. I, too, was a fierce protector of my children. If I thought anything was threatening their welfare, I could almost feel my eyes narrow, the claws lengthen, and the mother panther move forward to take out the offender in one fell swoop. Over the years, happily, that has quietly faded away, and I offer that hope and possibility to you. I am living proof that relinquishing guilt is possible even after feeling deeply distressed about earlier interactions with my sons.

We must look at the seeming permanence of guilt, which is the fundamental building block in our layers of addiction, and what is required for its erosion. When we say, This guilt is just here and I can't seem to make it go away, we have identified the actual problem—the need to let it go.

Notice there's a part of you that regards guilt as a very uncomfortable feeling, resulting in unsatisfactory life conditions, and yet finds it attractive. To clarify, notice your response when someone says your actions and words don't really do much of anything, inferring they do not have power to alter other people, change the world, and make things different. We are now talking about *your* actions and words, the form of your expression, the things that emanate from your body. You might think, Well, I do want power over other things and people. I do want my actions, choices, and words, and the generally imposing nature of my ego to make a difference, and I most certainly do not like hearing that I'm not more powerful than you.

Whether you think you would have a positive or negative impact, the implication is, I'm special.

You've made an excellent point. If I have power over you in order to be helpful, I would also necessarily have power over to hurt, and in either case, it implies you and I are not created equal. It implies that I'm special and am created more powerful than you are because I get to decide your experience for good or ill.

So I can be clear, tell me how you impact me. I don't feel you have power over me, but I do look at you as someone who helps me, so say more about this.

I do not have more power than you. I do, however, have the choice to love you, to appreciate you, and to know perfectly well you are not in danger or jeopardy, you are perfectly fine, and you have not made yourselves unworthy. Whenever you choose to join me in that recognition, then it will all be over so far as your major pain and, therefore, addictions are concerned. My job is to keep the truth about you in my awareness. This is the greatest gift we can give one another.

Yet you show us ways to do that for ourselves.

Exactly. Because what I do not have are your answers. I don't have your power. I have my own answers that I'm certain will work.

I see you as someone who helps, but you help in the sense of leading us through our own confusion to our answers, to our own power.

What I can do is clarify how you're getting in your own way or how you're sabotaging yourself. I understand that my greatest gift to you is to know that behind the confusion, pain, distress, guilt, the drama of the moment, is a great Life you can choose at any time. When you decide to think well of yourself, your life is going to be marvelous. That I know for you, and I will never, ever move off that position.

> *That's very true. One of my favorite chestnuts is, "Technique won't save you. You can't learn strategies to make yourself or other people better." What Carol offers is her certainty of our innocence. What she does flows out of that and is appropriate and works. But the doing is just the box it comes in, just the package. Without the belief, you can do all the techniques, say all the words, and it will remain completely empty and meaningless. What she shares is the truth she knows about us.*

> *Carol looks past the appearances and recognizes our sinlessness.*

You have no idea how many times I think of all of you, this amazing group who has declared, "I'm going for it and I'm not going to stop until I am free of my baggage." If we had any idea of the value offered, not only to ourselves but to everyone, we would be astonished. My deep appreciation for the differences among us and yet the sameness in all of us, goes beyond words. It would be dreadful if the Life presence that we are always showed up exactly the same way, so we treasure the phenomenon of uniqueness, not separateness, and the great blessing we all are.

[Morning break at about 10:30.
There is much activity as everyone moves around and shifts internal gears in order to assimilate the material presented thus far.]

It's a great privilege to remind you that the pain you may now feel is guaranteed to be temporary and to keep focusing on how we most quickly and clearly can uncover the source of guilt, the real culprit, and the reason it seems so attractive and powerful. If we do that, we will move through this discomfort as quickly as possible. Guilt is the concept that must be addressed and healed if we are ever to be free of our addictions or compulsions. If we insist on feeling guilty—and please note it is an insistence on our part—what is required of others in our relationships? To continue to feel guilty, implying we are so dangerous to humankind with our errors making such an unfortunate impact on others, requires that they stay in a place of suffering. It requires them to remain in the one-down position, to seem to be hurt because, if they do not, we can't justify our guilt. We keep opting for guilt because we are deluded into thinking it offers something desirable or is virtuous, a sign of caring or remorse. As we think of those less fortunate, in many ways we truly do want to help. The unhelpful part is to intone, I'm so bad, so terrible, and I've done such a poor job. We have believed, for as long as we can remember, that self-condemnation is virtuous, as if saying, I'm so bad, I'm such a sinner, somehow reflects humility. This has exactly the opposite effect. It is not helpful or virtuous, and it serves no healing purpose to you or anyone else.

It seems to me, although I don't know about other countries or cultures, a major religious teaching of this country is that we are guilty and unworthy of God.

Not only in this country, it's everywhere. And notice that our educational, religious, and legal institutions follow our requests. Don't forget we authorize our institutions, which did not just drop out of the sky unbidden. They are an outgrowth of our collective belief, which is that we're guilty, we're bad, and we hurt each other. These beliefs show up in our households, churches, schools, TV programs, everywhere. Remember the three elements we listed earlier in this very simple equation: 1) the invisible essence or Life of us, which is missing in a dead body; 2) the form of us, including not only our physical form and the nature of our personality, but all the fantasies that accompany it about how life is supposed to be and how people around us should behave; and 3) choice—

what do we desire, what do we focus on and pay attention to? At any given moment we have only two choices, illustrated with a very simple diagram. We have two different possibilities as to where to place our attention. On the one hand, our attention and desire flow through our fantasies, our investment in form, and wanting it our way. They continue to manifest through our beliefs about how things are supposed to be, our expectations, the scripts we write for ourselves and everyone else, the "shoulds" and the "oughts"—all part of one package. Attention and desire either flow through that confusion of notions, beliefs, and contradictions, bringing inevitable pain or through the invisible, true, and precious Life of us. That Life recognizes us as the child of our Father that we all are collectively—unique and individual, but not separate. Our attention is focused through one of these fundamental ideas, or the other, all the time and there are no other options in between. The feelings of darkness—guilt, distress, upset, pain, terror, panic—all result from focusing on the world of form and ego, on what we want or lack, with very little interest in spirit, or Life, the "We, as we were created" side of the chart. You might protest that you know this in your head but still can't make the pain or upset go away. To make these statements relevant and real to you, reflect on how many minutes in any given day you focus on the body, what it seems to want or what you think you need to do with it or for it. Reflect on the actions and words of other bodies as we interact with one another. Notice how much time you focus on the actions and words of another person as compared to his or her Spiritual essence.

Maybe I spend one hour a day on the essence, around eight hours on sleeping, and the rest taking care of form.

Even in our sleeping state, we take our choices with us, so sleeping is no escape, as a lot of people understand who have unpleasant experiences at night. What does that mean to you?

We can choose how we feel.

We can choose how we feel because we can choose what we pay attention to, and the feelings will follow as inevitably as the tail follows the kite or the caboose follows the engine. Notice that neither kite tail nor caboose have any input into the final destination. They merely follow, crossing the same actual territory just a bit later than the kite itself or the engine. So it is with us. The feelings are going to follow what we select as important enough to warrant our attention and not one soul makes that choice about where to place our attention but us. Our distress comes from focusing on behavior, trying to protect ourselves from hurt, or trying to promote our cause in the world. We spend a great deal of time and effort trying to have our way or to protect ourselves from the various perceived threats that seem to surround us. This is the origin of the dark feelings of hurt or terror.

Now, think once again about a situation or person you don't like and want to resist or avoid. Remember that we avoid certain people because we don't like the feeling experience we associate with them. As you focus on that person, seeing him or her in your mind, what does the image reveal about why you think you don't like them? You may have come a step forward in realizing the reason you don't like them is because of what you feel within. The important question to ask yourself now is, What about them is triggering that feeling within me?— not an abstract thought but their behaviors and words you can image in your mind.

The guy I'm thinking about thinks he's better than everybody else.

Okay, you're watching this person think he is better than everyone else, conveyed through what he says or his body language. What else?

Arrogance.
Controlling, sarcastic.
Insincere, judgmental.

All these impressions are conveyed through their words,

through what they say or don't say, the way they move their bodies through space, and the way their bodies relate to you.

Especially their words.

Oh, those words will do it. Notice how consistently and with what dedication we focus on what they are saying, what their bodies are doing, and their body language. Would it be accurate to say upset is triggered and brought into awareness by what the body and personality are conveying?

If you concentrate on the reality of what they really are, their goodness and presence, all that upset disappears.

Yes, it does. And what if you decide that it is valuable, important, and your desire to see this adversary as the child of his Father, perhaps confused at the moment but forever the child of God? It's just as easy to travel down one branch of the diagram as the other, but with decidedly different results. It is not beyond our capability. We could focus on the purity of that person's Life essence just as easily as we invest in how they appear and what they are saying. Do you hear the implications of that? No one requires us to focus on the form and the words, and then despise them, which results in hateful, helpless feelings welling up within us. Nothing keeps us, at any instant, from saying and believing that both the other person and myself are the innocent children of our Father, now. However it's stated, we must realize that we may be insane or asleep, but our mutual purity is untouched. What do you suppose requires us selectively to focus on the wrongness of behavior and words, rather than focusing on the light we all possess and the help we are truly asking for?

My superiority is at risk if I focus on their goodness, or I just like feeling lousy.

Superiority is at risk; ah, your ego is at risk. Very good. And we have to acknowledge our preference for feeling lousy.

What would you do when you have acknowledged a person is a child of God and over time you have really thought that about them, but whenever that person appears, those feelings come back?

That tells you that you have not fully relinquished all self-condemnation, because hurt feelings can't continue when wanting to experience peace in the presence of, or even when thinking about that person really clicks into place. When you truly want peace and no longer want the conflict, things will change.

Well, what do you do when the situation of the two people meeting brings, by its nature, conflict?

There is no "by its nature" conflict. Any conflict in a situation is present because we have chosen to bring it along, even if unknowingly. Actually, that choice is often what brings us together. I'll give you an example, which also relates to all the mothers here who are feeling inadequate. When my children were preschoolers, "Joe," the boy next door, was "sent" by my own inner wisdom to help me with my feelings of inadequacy about mothering. Joe was six or seven years older than my older son and I didn't like him at all, even though I was fond of his parents and his sister was our chief babysitter. Joe, however, drove me crazy. This situation predated any significant awareness on my part of the ideas we are exploring here, so I struggled through it "on my own." I had some innate knowledge of the process of projection—the way we see our own fear or guilt in someone else—but did not yet fully appreciate all the ways it manifests. Nothing about Joe was okay with me. I believed he was too hard on my kids. He was too much older. When he played with them, he would wrestle around and inevitably one of them would cry and I just felt driven crazy. If I ran him out the front door, he would climb over the back fence in no time at all. Once, when I thought he had left, the children and I ran an errand, and when we returned, he was back in their room. He was still in my house, had not even left, which is very much a metaphor for what happens in our minds! Our guilt stays in our mind and does not go anyplace. I realized during this period, as I was involved in my self-discovery, that I felt guilty about being too hard on my kids. I felt that whatever was going wrong was because my expectations were too high or I was just inept at raising happy children. The belief in my inadequacy, embodied by the phrase, I'm too hard on my kids, I projected onto Joe. I looked for all the things he did wrong so I could be right. As my husband and I discussed this situation, I remember thinking, I wonder if we're going to have to move to get away from him? Certainly, that is an extreme but common example of how we respond when we feel we are being driven crazy. In time, I began to realize I was not a bad parent, and I trust you are realizing you are not, either. Even though they may be in small bodies, our children are the authors of their own experience, whatever that may be. When I really chose to stop focusing on guilt about hurting my kids, Joe vanished.

Did he move?

No, he simply vanished, although he and his family continued to live next door. He was never there anymore. Suddenly, with no overt action or discussion on my part, he had other places to go, other things to do, other children to play with. His departure was not the result of our having a heart-to-heart talk or a confrontation. When I let up on myself, what was there for him to mirror? Joe showed up to mirror my guilt, and when I chose to feel and, therefore, reflect something besides "being hard on my kids," then "being hard on my kids" did not and could not show up anymore. Again, it was not because we sat down, looked each other in the eye, and said, "This is how it's going to be." Changing one's mind is a unilateral arrangement. It's true that it takes two of us to decide to do the "dance," but one person can stop it. When a dance partner leaves, there is no more dance. You can find someone else with whom to continue the drama, but you cannot dance with a partner who isn't there. Whoever or whatever is mirroring your fear—

seeming to prove your kids are in danger and you are to blame—disappears when you change your mind. Joe grew up and occasionally babysat at our request when his sister moved away. It was a very happy and encouraging experience to know that when I changed my mind, the problem disappeared. And that will always be the case, no matter how insoluble the problem appears to be.

And we truly need do nothing to "make" the problem go away? The form changes?

Exactly. We call it miraculous.

I am reminded of a similar experience that I had when I lived in Maine, in a neighborhood of large, old, sea captains' mansions. The house next door to me came up for sale. A group who cared for retarded people wanted to buy it and turn it into a home for them, which the entire town found upsetting. I had the most to say on this matter because they were moving next door to me, and if I objected, they could not relocate there. Everyone said, "You're not going to have these people there, are you?" At the town meeting where everyone spoke against the plan, expounding "reasons" that made sense to him or her, I finally had to tell the truth. The decision to remove any inter-ference to their move involved a deep wrestling within my conscience, but it became a nonproblem when I recognized these were human beings and all they wanted was a place to live. If it was in their best interests to be there, then by all means go ahead. My concern had been about their "ruining my property values," but then I thought, This is not about the value of my property, it's about the value of human life; if they want a place to live, they can have it." That required a very deep soul searching for me, but when they moved in, it was fine. Although I don't live there anymore, I never saw anybody next door when I did.

And everybody lived happily ever after?

So far as I'm concerned, they did.

I want to go back to the conflict I spoke about earlier. For me, this conflict between the other person and myself is still an inner conflict between me and myself. I'm aware we all come from the same Father, but I still can't seem to escape from the conflict.

You can't escape your conflict? Who makes you be in conflict?

I do and I'm aware of that too, but whatever that core belief is, having awareness of it still isn't enough.

Intellectual awareness is an important step, and I understand what you are saying. That core belief or, shall we say, the inner conflict is constantly played out in our everyday relationships. The people and situations we object to, in fact, do become a barometer of our own inner conflict. Because most of us so often are unable to discover our beliefs by ourselves, the perfect people show up to help make us aware of the nature of that conflict. We pretend the other people are causing the conflict, but they are actually magnifying our own inner conflict so we can be aware of it. It is essential to ask yourself, What is this conflict about? Is there, within your mind, a little conversation or voice that endlessly tells you all that is wrong with you? Unless you don't want to disclose it publicly, would you share what that inner conversation tells you about yourself? What does it say that seems to be related to the conflict?

It basically tells me that the little part of me I hate and won't accept is more powerful than any other part. It tells me I am unacceptable and a bad person.

Does anyone else have a voice or inner chatter that says you have failed? It is often nonspecific, but it reminds you endlessly and consistently, You're not there yet, you're not good enough, you're bad. We all recognize, in one form or

another, the conversation going on in the back of our minds—
or maybe in the front! Why do you listen to it?

It's always been there.

Well, that's an excuse, not a reason. What else?

*The rest of the world shows me that the voice of condem-
nation is correct in its assessment of me.*

Everybody else thinks I'm not entirely okay.

Sometimes it serves you well.

That ego voice will try to convince you it serves you well.

*The inner self-talk produces a sense of danger or drama and
excitement.*

*I think most of us have never been told we do not have to listen
to it.*

That's a great observation, and today we must encourage and
support a new message in our minds if we are to feel happy
and safe. Nothing and no one makes us listen to that voice of
condemnation or failure. We simply have chosen to do so, or
are in the habit of doing so, or have been convinced it is the
truth. We have taken for granted the validity of this insulting
conversation but have never asked, Who granted this? Who
said this? Who makes this up? Why am I listening to this?

I need to keep it alive.

Some of us have accepted this negative inner chatter as
valuable, necessary, and true, and that yes, it must be kept
alive, but you now have a new option—one you *must* exercise,
sooner or later. When the chatter in your mind says you're not
good enough, you've failed, and you probably never are going

to make it, ask yourself *what* has failed. We carry a picture in our minds of what we are supposed to be like and to accomplish and how people are supposed to relate to us, ad nauseam. We have an image of how life is supposed to be, and this relentlessly critical voice says you've failed, you haven't lived up to your potential, you haven't carried it through, you haven't fleshed it out, you haven't made "us" ("us" being the ego and you or what you think of as you) the king of the world, the most important and influential being in your universe. In other words, without examination, we give credence to that idea of not being good enough, or of failing, or of not rigorously following the "shoulds" and "oughts." Nothing makes us listen to and agree with those criticisms. We have simply exercised our choice to listen to it. Now, let that sink in while you hear another message.

A new, comforting, and loving perspective reveals that our fear of failure and worthlessness is unfounded, is not helpful, and provides no reward down the line. We have believed that perseverance in denigrating ourselves will bring positive results, and instead, it keeps us limited, imprisoned, sad, deprived, and offers nothing we could really want. The critical, overbearing voice is present only with our permission and by our own election because we have never questioned it. Today is the day to question and to realize, once and for all, it's a fantasy. It's not true, and nothing makes us listen to it except our own choice.

The conflict we carry with us into all our relationships is this internal conflict between the ego, the critical voice of failure, and the glorious truth of us known and expressed in our creation. Such profound opposites cannot both be true. We must inquire about our basic nature, because within the confusion about that lies the root of our conflict. Now, what does that sound like?

I can't stop laughing at how silly we are.

Exactly! We are silly but not evil. There is a tremendous difference.

How does this relate to the fact that the conflict itself is hiding the magnet of guilt I need to feel and experience before I can let it go?

This is how. The chatter we listen to about our lack of value is consistent with and part of the seamless package of guilt. If we truly want guilt to subside—and notice that some of us do not yet want it to stop—we must become aware that guilt accompanies the "form" package. Remember: Life, form, and choice. If we want form, or the body/personality, to be the most important element, we will be attracted to guilt. We will not want to give it up. The muddled interior dialogue actually goes something like this: I want the form to be important, so I guess guilt will come along with it, but I want to be happy in spite of that and I don't want to feel the pain of guilt. This is forever impossible. If we want guilt and form, which we have invented, to be more important than our essence, which was created, then we must recognize that guilt, pain, and an unsatisfactory life are part of one inseparable package. We keep trying to combine what cannot be combined. We want our body/personality invention to be important, we want influence over other people, we want to be special and always right, *and* we want to be happy. Now stop. You have to make a choice. You must choose one or the other, rather than trying to combine them into a stew. What is more important to you? If you still experience guilt, it's because you still are attracted to it, believing it and the package of which it is a part offers something worthwhile. Today is the day to realize guilt is optional, never productive or in our best interests, and it can be relinquished.

I was thinking that sometimes we blame something on somebody, thinking our own guilt will go away but not realizing that when we blame anybody or anything, it comes back, so the guilt is maintained.

It doesn't come back—it never leaves. It just grows within us. You might tell yourself, Well, I'm a nice person, I don't attack people, and I'm not a problem to anyone, so why do I feel this way, regardless? The reason is because when your attention is on the form with indifference toward the Spirit, you are asking for trouble. When we have our awareness on the body and its script, the way life is "supposed to be," we are unaware of all that true Life really has to offer. For example: have you ever been completely immersed in a book? While you were reading it, you were almost in a hypnotized state. As you became involved in the subject matter, you were temporarily but totally unaware of what was going on around you, right? Then, when you stopped reading, you looked around and saw chairs, plants, windows, and your familiar surroundings. Everything was still in its place, but for the time you were focused on the book, you completely lost awareness of your surroundings, although the articles and the views didn't go anywhere. They were not altered or changed in any way by your lack of attention. The focus of our attention can be total and can successfully block out whatever else is in the environment. This is a simple example, but it makes a very strong point. If we are busy focusing on what's wrong with ourselves or others, or what we must do to protect ourselves, or analyzing who did what to whom and why everyone is failing, we are seeing only the form and what the forms are doing. It is like reading the book. We have put ourselves into a hypnotic state that blocks awareness of all the good available to us in this world.

In the same way, as we focus on form, our goodness, worth, and glory do not disappear either; they only slip into unawareness. We have merely neglected to focus on goodness in others or ourselves, and although those qualities seemed to disappear, leaving only the fiction about our defects or lack of value, the truth of us has never altered. Being unaware is 100 percent different from being altered, which would imply an irrevocable change. There is no need for penance or punishment for the former, which is temporary, merely a requirement to refocus our attention. This does not take skill, only willingness to see people and situations from a different perspective of what's right about all of us and to ask different questions. Instead of asking, How do I fix what's wrong with me or someone else? why not inquire, Why do I think I am defective in the first place? Using the book analogy, we can take heart as we notice, "Wow, when I take my nose out of the book and look around, it's a brand new ball game." When we lay aside the script entitled, "How come I'm not getting my way?" many new opportunities appear.

Do you ever feel you don't know what you want, but whatever it is, you're not getting it? When we shift from that self-centered mode to a focus on service and discovering everyone's good qualities and assets, our awareness changes and life becomes very different. Be very firm with yourself and realize no one makes us keep our noses in those old, upsetting books. It's our choice. No one makes us focus hypnotically on the world of time and space, on all the things we think we or someone else are supposed to be doing in it. Let's acknowledge we do this because we want to. It attracts us. We think our picture of how things ought to be offers something desirable, but we're beginning to find out it offers us pain and terror, without exception! Nevertheless, we keep focusing on the book, hoping it will become better and less terrifying. Our job is to put down this book of self-condemnation and look around to see what else is going on. What we find is the purity, goodness, and peace inherent in all of us here and in all Creation. We can put our attention on that as soon as we realize this book about our failure is no longer interesting or productive. However much the inner chatter urges us to hang onto the fiction, it's going to get better later on, we can skip to the last chapter and discover that the conclusion is equally as unrewarding as the rest of it. It's not going to suddenly get better. We finally realize that setting aside the old worn-out book frees us to focus on the present goodness and purity of whoever is in front of us. We live in a milieu of Love, as fish live in water. It is now time to raise our eyes, formerly devoted to our fantasy of worthlessness, and see instead the value of everything around us, all that calls for gratitude. When we do this, the recognition of what is right will become as all-consuming as the book we're currently reading. It is not up to us to *make* the purity, the love, or the flow, so that Life is wonderful and fun. It is, however, up to us to stop looking at the old images of failure and to start looking at something else. *When* you decide to change your mind, and with what degree of dedication, is entirely up to you. Some people will drag out this decision over a long period of time, and some will collapse that time. You will be motivated to do it faster only when you really begin to believe that this book about guilt and sin and "who did what to whom" and "what I am supposed to be" is not at all interesting or rewarding. We decide, with all our inherent power, that the old ideas are not fulfilling, and choose to change our minds. So what does this imply?

It sounds like we have a choice.

Always, we have a choice. The window of opportunity to choose again never closes and never exhibits impatience. No matter how long we have been reading the unsatisfactory novel, no matter the duration of our habits, we still have the power, at any time, to say, "I don't want to do this anymore." The book doesn't jump up in your face and say, "But, I insist! You have to read this, you have to finish me." Books don't do that. When you close a book, it has no power of its own to coerce your attention. When you choose to set it aside, it is set aside.

Does it make any difference if we don't know what we feel guilty about?

There's only one thing we pretend to be guilty about. I say "pretend" because guilt really doesn't have a firm foundation. We actually feel guilty when we are consumed with and focused on the form of things, including our own egos. You might say that this is what the world is about—everybody focusing on the form of things. And I would point out, that is why most peoples' lives are so unsatisfactory. The continuing and singular preoccupation with the form of things is what keeps us enmeshed in the world of form. It's as if we decide to keep rereading the book to see if it has a better ending.

So, I don't have to figure out what I feel guilty about? Do we just concentrate on the essence of love within others and wanting to wish them well?

Yes, because what you feel guilty about never occurred. Listen to this carefully. It might take years before this fact dawns on you, or you could get it this very second. What we want and are afraid we have accomplished by focusing on forms in time and space, is that somehow we altered or ruined the Truth of our goodness, leaving peace and joy, abundance and innocence somewhere else. As long as our heads are in that book, we are so hypnotized by it and our eyes are so focused on the three-dimensional world, we are not realizing any of these qualities. These are not abstractions. The good things of life are experiences built into us, they are right here. And if they are right here, we clearly did not separate ourselves from them. We didn't ruin anything. Guilt is not warranted because the eternal nature of others and ourselves has not been affected. We haven't permanently done anything to ourselves or to Love, oneness, or the universe. All we have done is to focus attention selectively resulting in the fear that we are destroyers.

Come on, get your nose out of that book and you will find all this weeping and wailing about being guilty is without foundation because we here, everyone else, and all of creation are totally unharmed by your mistakes, which you fear are permanent sins. For example, if we close the blinds across the front windows of this room, we don't remove or destroy the cars in the parking lot or the surrounding trees and grass. To worry over or bemoan our wrongdoing over destroying the cars and landscaping (which are, of course, still present) because we have covered the window would be ridiculous. You don't have the power to alter the landscape by drawing the blinds. Likewise, we don't have the ability to ruin ourselves or our truth, purity, or safety by drawing a veil of unawareness across our perception. Guilt stems from the belief that this is not a matter of unawareness, but that we have the power to ruin Love.

We don't ruin our safety and worthiness?

Safety and worthiness are always our present truth.

What if you're creating situations where you seem to be getting screwed all the time, even when you haven't done anything wrong? For example, twice this week I've been in financial situations where I have been unfairly treated. One was with an insurance company. My car was damaged in an accident and it was the other person's fault, but now I'm on the short end of the stick, not getting compensated like I should have.

You feel you are being betrayed and deprived?

Yes, and there are feelings of helplessness about being a victim. I'm having a lot of trouble today, and for some reason, I'm missing the boat. I don't know what to do now. I'm in two financial situations I need to straighten out, in which I obviously set myself up as the victim, feeling unworthy or deserving of punishment. I have no idea how I made myself a victim.

And that chatter in your head we were talking about, what has it been saying today or earlier this week about you?

Well, I guess this week I've been fighting against the desire to go to sleep because I know my ego is really fighting.

Something is getting really close to awareness if you desire to sleep more than is necessary or normal. It becomes an avoidance strategy. That often occurs as we start to seriously question all that we have taken for granted. We all want to tune out when upsetting feelings get too close. Tuning out pain is the purpose of addictions.

I've known for a long time I've had feelings of unworthiness and guilt and all that, but I don't know why.

You're wasting your time looking for "why." There is no reason. It's a choice, good news or bad news.

I sit here and say I'm not guilty, I haven't done anything and I'm whole. My intellectual mind knows I'm whole and God's innocent child, but the gut magnet doesn't. It says in the Bible that when the heart and the mind become as one you create your peace. I've never been able to get the mind to cooperate with the gut.

That's the state a lot of us are in, pretending to be operating independently of those gut magnets, and yet we are not. A question—do you want peace of mind now?

Yes.

Do you want it for everyone else now?

Yes, I have no qualms about everybody else.

Do you want it for your son-in-law now? I know from former conversations that he was a big problem to you.

Sure, ex-son-in-law.

You're saying, sure, you want that, but it's another process to actually desire it in a heartfelt way. Do you truly want for him to live in peace?

Yes, I don't hold anything against him.

Well, I don't believe that. I believe you've called a truce, so that perhaps you're not at this moment wanting to smack him, but that's not the same as really wanting peace for him. Scott, would you recount the dream you had the other day, because it makes this point in a wonderful way.

I had had some conflict with my employees earlier that evening, and I couldn't fall asleep until early in the morning. In the dream, in a meditative state, I saw this father figure above me. It was definitely a superior father figure who asked, "What is it that you want?" I replied, "Well, I want my employees to have inner peace, like I do myself." And this father figure looked back at me, right in my eyes, and said, "Are you sure?" In other words, he wanted me to look at whether I really felt that way deep down or if I was just paying lip service to the prospect. At that moment, I realized I had answered yes and believed the yes, and I did want this inner peace for my employees and myself. All of a sudden, the forms disappeared and there was this tremendous feeling of joy and harmony and awareness that everything was already perfect. I didn't have to worry—all events would take care of themselves and would be fine any way they worked out, because the goal of inner peace would provide everything. When I woke up, I felt as refreshed as if I had slept comfortably all night long.

There was neither pain nor guilt?

It was tremendously freeing and euphoric to have no pain or guilt. This is a seminar about how to let go of our addictions. There was no need for an addiction in that experience because this high was beyond drugs and alcohol.

That is absolutely the point. When we decide we want peace now for every one of us, the pain vanishes, and once it does, there is nothing to hide, nothing to cover up, nothing requiring layers and layers of "protection." The entire need for our addictions, which compensate for worthlessness or serve as distractions from pain, goes away. Until you reach an awareness of safety, pain comes and goes and addictions remain tempting. At any moment, we either feel safety or distress, with nothing in between—safe or unsafe, worthy or unworthy. Those moments of lack of safety or worth are so maddening and so uncomfortable, we will do whatever we have to do to distract ourselves from them. Distraction from pain, or madness, is what all addictions are for, what all busy-ness is for—what everything gets to be for.

I am fond of pointing out that we so believe being undistracted will result in a painful, fearful punishment, we attempt to provide just such an environment for our lawbreakers. We put them in jail, with the worst offenders isolated in solitary confinement, meaning they have the fewest distractions of all. In this book we are reading about the world, an unending supply of distractions is considered our paramount need because the pain we keep generating requires constant distraction. Now is the time to recognize this strategy will never work. The pain must be healed, rather than masked or banished to unawareness, leaving no feelings that must be hidden or that require distraction.

> *Part of me really wants peace for my ex son-in-law and for a lot of people I see in pain, but I don't pretend there would be no conflict, anger, or retaliation if they got in my face. Just as I don't want that pain, I don't want it for them either. I would like to see them in peace because everybody deserves to be peaceful and loved. One thing that strikes me very much is that when Jesus said on the cross, "Forgive them for they know not what they do," he meant all of us. We're all walking around not knowing what we do, so although we're responsible for our choices, we're not guilty. I haven't been able to let go of that piece that still ties me to guilt. I'm here because God created and sustains me, but the little part holding onto guilt won't allow me to be free to enjoy my life.*

We've been confused because we thought we were guilty. See if you can relate to this. We all often say we want inner peace— but not right now. A little bit later, but not this very second. Perhaps in five minutes or maybe now for some people, or maybe next year. Ask yourself if you can honestly say, "I really want complete peace in my mind and for everyone else this instant." Most of us, if the truth be known, would hesitate.

To say we want peace for everybody else equally is some-times hard to say.

We recognize we're not certain we want that for some of those "offenders."

It feels like it's almost a fear of the unknown. We want to hold onto what is familiar, what we have lived with our entire lives. The peace thing sounds good, but we're not entirely convinced.

Only a few months ago Scott was expressing that same concern, because peace is an unknown. We don't know what an alternative to our present state might be. It could be scary, awful. Yet he indicated a willingness to take a risk and really go for it anyway. He is living testimony to the safety of prefer-ring Life and Love to form and triviality, since he is still here and didn't get swept away or lose his identity, as many of us fear. He found it to be a fabulous experience, worth more than fifteen million workshops. He is living proof that the preference for peace of mind brings a wonderful experience, not one to be feared.

What do I do with the part of me that wants peace for myself and my family and friends, but not for that other person?

Thanks for being honest. Almost everyone feels that ambiva-lence. We can honestly want peace of mind for the great majority, but there is often one "villain" who, we believe, lost our money, hurt our children, or behaved in a dismissive manner. Is there one person who comes up when you think, I'd like most people to have inner peace, but not this one? As you consider the one you're having reservations about, what are you focusing on? What is it about that person that invites you to put him or her outside the circle of acceptability? You don't have to reveal who it is, but just say in a few words what you see that cries out for revenge or at least rejection?

I'm having trouble, although I am noticing a shift in my

perception, in the way I see things. My son-in-law is not even in my life anymore, but I see the shift in dealing with other people as I clear things up with him. Well, he may be in my life somewhat, but we don't interact in ways that cause me conflict anymore. When he does cross my path, it's a very pleasant experience, and I am finding I don't have as much trouble with people like him as I did in the past. I mean, there was always someone like him in my life, but now I find people are not so much a problem as are situations, such as my job. Currently, I'm not angry or resentful with a particular person, but I feel anger and lack of peace with the company I work for. The company is not a real person, even though I direct my anger to the guy who runs it. I don't even know him, so he's almost an inanimate object, more a symbol of the company, which is now the problem. Although I know it's stupid, and I know the company can do nothing to me and is not even the source of my supply, this is where I'm having trouble finding peace. Now that I have learned to handle most of my people problems, the conflict is coming out in other situations.

It doesn't matter if it's a situation or a person. Notice we think something should be condemned to lack of peace because of what is happening or how the form is showing up.

The form is unpleasant.

The form is merely neutral, but the inner experience being triggered is unpleasant for you. Realize within yourself this instant, with eyes closed if that helps, that the person or the company is the triggering mechanism. Heretofore, you have been focusing on the form of what they did in the past, what they said, or how they appear now. Switch your focus and tell yourself, I want to recognize that he is the child of my Father, pure, innocent, and limitless. I *want* to focus on the invisible, pure expression of Creation, which is true of this person. All I want to think about right now is the good that exists within him, recognizing that if I'm not seeing what is right about him, that is *my* problem. Focus on that as long as you need to, and when it really begins to dawn on you that this person is the child of our Father, note it's easier to want inner peace for him. How does that feel? Even though we spent only a few seconds on that exercise, when you switched your focus from the offensive actions or wrongs or betrayal to the awareness of this person as the pure child of God, did the behaviors begin to drop out of your awareness, suddenly becoming easier to wish him well?

I look at the company as the child of our Father.

To me, it helped get rid of the prickly edges. They began to soften and compassion began to come in.

Excellent! It's a very simple procedure and can be very fast. Did something shift when you refocused your attention on the goodness of that person, rather than on the form of his behavior? When you start reminding yourself that your difficult person is innocent and good, a very easy transition to peace occurs where formerly you were having trouble.

For me, the shift was instantaneous! I received the peace because at that moment I really offered it!

That's it! Now, we want to recap our three elements. We can focus on the Life essence or the presence of someone, we can focus on the form or the behavior, and it is always our choice. Three simple things. If you want a different life experience now, you change the focus of attention now.

[Lunch break: Instructions are given about where to eat and when to return. An assignment is given to be mindful during lunch of the two choices for focus—form or behavior, or essence or presence.]

[1:30pm Workshop resumes after lunch break and general visiting. The energy level is high despite being the after-lunch slump time, and the afternoon session continues with commentary directed toward a topic discussed before lunch.]

The reason the problem seems to move from the son-in-law to the insurance company to the employer is that all these places and people become storehouses for our own sense of personal guilt. Guilt is very compact and very transportable, like an alcoholic with that security bottle. You can move the guilt or the bottle from this one to that one or the next one forever, so long as you keep it available, and that's not giving it up. Letting guilt go once and for all is what we're interested in here, not just keeping it in a different closet.

I still have not really let go of the anger and guilt.

We must practice wanting to see whoever we are with as forever undefiled. If we do, we can have the most wonderful time, no matter what we are doing. Often, as we become willing to practice, we wonder if the other person will too, stating, "I'll do my part, but I don't know if the other guy is going to do his. Rest assured the "other guy" is going to do his part. Our doubt about the other person's appropriate participation can be a big excuse for not practicing ourselves—a sign we still choose to store our guilt, rather than relinquish it.

Now, I would like for someone who finds it difficult to be in front of a group to volunteer, someone who truly objects and would normally avoid this at all costs. Good, please come on up. To drive home a point stressed earlier this morning, tell us why you feel uncomfortable up here, why you usually would avoid standing alone in front of a group?

Most of the time, I'll be distracted from what I have to say because I'm nervous. I think about my sweaty palms, and sometimes I tremble, or my mouth quivers.

Rest assured you're not required to say anything brilliant, so see if you can follow my train of thought. So very many people hate to be in your shoes, up in front of a group with all eyes on them. You are speaking for millions when it seems all you can think about is possibly being judged or that people might be looking at you and thinking you look weird or you're not doing this right.

Yes, and they might pick out my flaws and tear me down by focusing on my physical body.

See if you can identify with this. We believe this little body/ personality package, which we have spent so much time getting together and perfecting, is our entry into the game of life, and we think, What if they just sit out there and take it apart, or don't appreciate my efforts, or compare me to someone else and decide I fall short of their expectations? Don't worry, you will not fall short, but notice how your fear is indicative of the focus on form we spoke about this morning. It helps to see the attention we place on the body/personality combination. Notice your discomfort with your immediate concern about what people are seeing in you and, worse yet, having no control over their perceptions.

Now, remember our goal today is to become aware that we can change our minds whenever we choose and refocus our attention; and our experience will shift accordingly. To prove this to yourself, look at everyone out here, set aside your concern about how they are seeing you, and decide how you want to see them. You can say it out loud or in your mind. Look at all the eyes out there and reflect on the fact that these are exquisite, incredible beings, many of them in their own pain and unaware of their possibilities. All of these children of our Father, all these gorgeous beings, deserve to find their own sense of peace. Now, even after only a few seconds, how does it feel when you want to see them as deserving?

I'm getting the same thing back, beautiful smiles.

In the deepest way, how does it feel when you focus on these really fabulous people with no particular concern about their actions or their thoughts about you?

When I look at their eyes, I see everything is fine. They are looking at my eyes and nothing else.

What happens to your sense of nervousness or upset? Does it diminish or disappear?

Yes.

This exercise is such an easy, simple reminder that if we are upset, whether feeling guilty, angry, dismissed, or rejected, it is our relentless focus on form that is the problem. We can stop complaining about what's wrong with us, what's wrong with others, what they have done we don't like. Stop questioning their lack of cooperation in our fantasies about life, and take your attention off the scripts we have unilaterally written for them. Then we can look into the eyes of whoever is before us and remind ourselves this is a truly loving, interesting person. Distress just disappears or, at least, certainly lessens. Now, do you feel better?

Yes, much better.

Did you have to know what happened in your childhood in order to benefit from this exercise? Did you have to have college degrees or read dozens of books? Did you have to worry about what you did yesterday that was less than loving? Not at all. The only requirement for a different experience, now, was that you change your mind, today, about how you wish to regard those present or those who come to mind. What a relief! We don't have to know what motivated us in the past or to examine reasons for feeling guilty. We have spoken previously about the origin of that sense of guilt about separation, but exploring it isn't necessary for our solution. All we need to remember are our three simple ideas: We can focus on Life, on the form—your own or anyone else's—and our choice. As we keep choosing correctly, moment after moment, all our hurtful past drops away as irrelevant.

Everyone seemed so supportive when I started looking at them from that aspect.

You could not possibly be in front of a more wonderful group, and remember, we keep a mirror with us all the time, whether we like it or not. Every group we interact with can be experienced as wonderful. That's up to us, because what brings peace of mind is not how they see you, which you cannot control, but how you choose to see them. We bought into the idea that to feel comfortable and happy and safe, everyone had to approve of us, and that it was our job to be in control of that. Now we are learning that someone else's approval is not the issue and never matters, because what you necessarily control is how you choose to see everyone else. That is the key. Is that an exciting realization to know you are in charge of how you see them, thereby assuring your contentment?

Yes, that's beautiful. Thank you.

As you began the exercise while she was standing there, her body was kind of drooping down, and as she went through this exercise, she opened up, her whole body just opened up.

The whole body does open up, and you will also hear your voice open up. This is true of everyone, including all of us here. Did you hear the tenor of her voice shift? It's fascinating to hear the changes in the way we sound when we allow ourselves to say what we need to say.

While you were conducting this exercise, talking about focusing on the form, I found myself in a kind of trap because sometimes, if you focus on form, you dwell on people not doing what they should. But, you can also focus on how people are doing what they should, on form that seems positive, rather than on what seems negative. The shock for me was to realize that focusing on the form, even though it looks good, is still not peaceful.

Exactly!

I used to kid myself sometimes that the right form of things is happiness, but no way. For so long, I didn't even know there were other states of consciousness until I had experiences like the dream Scott recounted, because I kept trying to look at what was good in the form, rather than getting away from the importance of form, period.

Precisely! The choice to focus on Life does not mean that, from now on, as in Scott's dream, the forms go away. Having them disappear is not the goal, as we are still going to see bodies, drive cars, raise families, go to work, and live in this world. Instead, ask this question: "Is my top priority to focus on the goodness and purity and deservedness of this person, without regard to my ego's opinion and judgment about his or her behavior?" You see, our egos define behavior as good or bad, depending on whether our pain rises or falls in that person's presence. Making decisions about whether someone is good or bad is a function of the level of comfort or discomfort.

Wait a minute! Say that again!

Our egos, our sense of separate personhood, check out the current feeling we are having and judge the person or event related to it as good or bad, depending on that feeling. We do this so automatically we are hardly aware of the process. If the current feeling is fine, we say the person or event is a good and desirable one. If the feeling is disturbing, we decide this is a bad person or situation. The point is we are letting madness itself determine what are good and bad forms. Just going for the good form will keep one stuck, because we remain in the service of the ego voice or conversation. We are still involved with our scripts and fantasies, whether they succeed or not. This self-talk, endlessly speaking of hurt, loss, deprivation, the need to make ourselves secure, and the badness of other people, is the result of believing we are separate and can be harmed. In other words, most of us are marching along as good little soldiers listening to the madman in our minds. If we want the hurt to be healed, we must stop following the madman and realize there is another awareness or perspective in our own minds that, when paid attention to, will bring us peace. It doesn't matter if the hurt we seem to experience is physical, emotional, or undefined—all are the result of the same incorrect focus. Although hurt comes in many different flavors, it all disappears by focusing on the true, invisible Spirit of everyone.

When we decide we want peace for ourselves and everyone else, right now, we simply start to practice. We don't take this interesting theory, set it up in the midst of our lives, and worship it. Wanting peace and seeing goodness has to be practiced in the trenches. When you feel distress rising within you, practice *wanting* to see the situation differently. Listening to that ancient ego voice keeps your nose in the book of drama rather than looking up and noticing all the goodness and warmth actually present.

We're a planet of "bookworms," aren't we?

Right! I want to reiterate a powerful fact, which is that the experience of this moment has its origin in this moment. Nothing in your past has the power to interfere with the choice you make now. What you decide is important at this moment will determine your current experience—pain and hurt or peace of mind and safety. And this can be changed hundreds of times per day. The window of opportunity to have a great life experience never closes.

What part of this process do our individual and specific addictions distract us from?

Our various addictions are able to distract us from our pain and keep us from becoming aware of the terrible price we pay for egocentricity and selfishness. They distract us from pain being generated on a moment-to-moment basis through our identification with form and ego. Self-hatred, hatred of others, attack, living defensively in the world, refusing to be authentic, refusing to get our noses out of the book that points out our defective nature are all constantly generating pain. The purpose of addictions is to keep us unaware of their consequences. This distraction plan never works because we continue to be engrossed in the book of worthlessness, which continuously generates the pain in the first place. We try desperately to read this book differently, perhaps upside down or sideways, to analyze or force a different outcome, but the result of believing the lie of our own worthlessness is terrible hurt, which produces the constant need for the distraction provided by addictions. The unexamined acceptance of our guilt keeps us in the pain. So we employ strategies and techniques, distractions and addictions to keep from being uncomfortable, even as we are generating the discomfort. What an impossible no-win situation!

Do we stay addicted to think that we're not in pain?

It's not about thinking we're not in pain, but to keep from *feeling* pain.

We medicate it to make it go away, to keep the feeling out.

My own experience in finding the difference between pain and pleasure was that whenever pleasure got too heightened, I would have to go to something else.

Addictions, whatever they may be, are distractions from feeling terror. An addiction is basically terror management. We have hundreds of ways to medicate or distract ourselves from terror or pain or hurt, which are all the same thing. That's why it's so important to understand that until we stop generating this pain, pain management will seem necessary. We need to be clear in the broadest, most overall sense that all pain, hurt, boredom, restlessness, and terror result from a refusal to love. They are the result of the choice to focus on questions like, Who did this to me? How can I get even? How am I going to defend myself? and How can I control other people and make them do what I want them to? We have believed pondering these issues would benefit us and keep us safe. When we decide to shift the focus to offering love and compassion to everyone, including ourselves, instead of anticipating all the ego complaints and rehearsing the responses, the pain begins to vanish, just as when the light is turned on, darkness disappears.

> *The problem will repeat itself over and over until it is completely solved.*

So very true. The way it's solved is for us, finally, to change our minds. If you can see all hurt and all pain as lack of love, what is the antidote for lack of love but to supply it? When you supply love, whether you call it wanting peace for yourself and everyone else, wanting to wish them well, or wanting to see their value, you provide the antidote. When people act crazy, which is most of us most of the time, the real reason for the insanity is a distorted attempt to try to reinstate lovableness and worth. Therefore, if we offer what the so-called lunatics are seeking—a remembrance of their worth—then we resolve the problem for all parties concerned.

> *So when I decide I want to "go home," I experience mass confusion because my world is reflecting to me what stops me from going there. That really means I may believe experiences I had earlier are in my way, but actually they aren't. My choice to remember them today is the problem.*

Yes, and this may be very disturbing to some of you. Today's distress has nothing to do with what happened when you were two or forty-two. We are in love with the idea that we will forever be defective because of what happened in the past.

> *But I keep experiencing pain associated with things of the past.*

> *You keep experiencing pain <u>and</u> associating it with things of the past.*

So, what I'm really doing is still refusing to let go of my own feelings of unworthiness, which would occur if I offer love right now?

Absolutely. If we could just have selective amnesia about everything from this morning backwards, there would be no need to try to associate what is happening today with anything from the past. If I am in pain today, it's because I have chosen to be unloving to myself or someone else today, period, end of story. What could be simpler?

Why do we keep saying we need to experience those disturbing feelings when they come up or, if I'm in pain right now, I have to let it out?

If you have a strong emotion and adrenaline is running through your body, you need to honor that and be with that feeling without judgment. To do so is cleansing, and the feeling is being transformed into a different quality of experience. Every moment is a new one and whatever we feel in this moment is being generated this moment. The idea that the same pain stays with us for a long time is a thesis that doesn't hold water. Actually, if today we are feeling or behaving in a hateful way, bad feelings or experiences will occur today. It is crucial to note that today's upset is because of today's hatred, not yesterday's.

How do you break the cycle of yesterday?

By realizing, if what we are experiencing today is not related to yesterday, we can drop yesterday out of the loop and become mindful of what actually is relevant. In other words, if we truly want to see things differently, we begin to de-emphasize the past, because we see it's not relevant to our process. For instance, on becoming an adult, one no longer plays with children's toys, seeing them as irrelevant and uninteresting. We realized at some point that we no longer enjoyed driving toy trucks around the carpet. In the same way, dwelling on the

mistakes of the past does not serve us and is actually imped-
ing progress. Cycling around in "who did what to whom" stops
because of your lack of interest. You don't have to force past
ideas and associations to go away as you move your attention
to something more relevant. They merely vanish like air escaping from a balloon.

*I can offer living proof of what you just said. I was in a car
wreck when I was eighteen, so I have no memories between
birth and eighteen. Even without those memories, I've still
been able to screw up my life!*

*You spoke earlier of peace as an ultimate feeling or event. Is
it a normal pattern to experience short times of peace and then
move forward in a stepping-stone way?*

Yes, because actually, in any given day or segment of our
experience, we cycle in and out of "I want my way, I hate this
person, I feel unworthy," and then in the next moment
selflessly being there for someone or allowing ourselves our
own self-expression. The self-expression, which is always an
expression of love, might be painting, gardening, doing your
job, being with a friend, or simply experiencing yourself. With
this mix of self-serving and genuinely altruistic thoughts, the
quality of any given day seems to be erratic. Up to this point,
you probably didn't know why. You thought that's how life is—
sometimes good, sometimes bad, sometimes painful. In truth,
it is not chaotic or random. Life experience can be graphed and
shown to follow, very faithfully, the focus of our attention.

Life may seem like a roller coaster, but it need not. As we
become more aware of the power of our influence, depending
on what we decide to pay attention to, things begin to smooth
out. Now our egos object, "Oh, how boring—I really like all this
roller coaster stuff," as if that rush of adrenaline on the one
hand, or the depths of despair we sink into, on the other, define
the limits of life's experience. But those are not the limits or
the opposite poles of life's experience. Both boredom and the
drama go on one side of the ledger, with an entirely different

experience possible on the other. Some people might have an extended period of peace of mind and others might have only a flash of it, but in all cases, its presence is still under our control, predicated always on our choice of how to think. When you leave here today, it will be impossible for you not to know what we have talked about, even if it takes a while to sink in and be assimilated.

I'm having a major brain wad, because I get hung up on that "who did what to whom?" You said what happened in the past is not related to today's pain, so I started thinking about getting laid off my job a couple of weeks ago. I discovered a letter written behind my back by my supposed partner, who had been fired a month earlier. At first, I was amused by her stupidity, but today I'm finally getting to some anger and I'd like to wring her neck. I understand I must go through that upset even though it's painful and it seems like I can't do anything about it. Even though the pain is today, the circumstances surrounding being laid off weeks ago feel very relevant to it, and I can't seem to get it.

As mentioned earlier, it's the choice to be unloving today, no matter how valid an excuse the ego thinks it has, that creates today's pain and anger. We must still recognize that if we, as sovereign beings, choose today to be unloving or insist we are being unfairly treated, today will be painful. Any desire to pretend the pain is about something that happened earlier doesn't nullify the fact that today it's my choice to be disturbed by this person or situation, regardless of when the events actually took place. In other words, your ego pretends the upset is all about what happened then, but in fact, you're choosing to be angry today.

In trying to get this wad loosened up, I keep being irritated with her or others, and then I come back to thinking, Well, if I create everything and I'm this all-powerful being, why do I create this crap? I'm angry with <u>me</u>.

You put your finger right on the button there. The thought that whispers, This is really all I deserve, keeps turning into a self-fulfilling prophecy. To get untangled, hear this loud and clear: TODAY'S PAIN STEMS FROM CHOOSING TO WITHHOLD LOVE TODAY. Your ego mind finds this totally objectionable and will try to shut down or wander off. It is today's choice about what we offer one another that counts, and we get all tangled up in trying to justify withholding love and acceptance right now. It doesn't matter why we think we are justified in condemning. If I choose not to love today, I get discomfort today. The culprit is your choice to keep in your mind that picture of people hurting and being hurt.

Well, even if I skip right over, blow all that off, and go right to Sharon hurting Sharon, why would I create this crap? That's where I really see the condemnation.

Did you say you aren't living your life correctly?

Yes, it feels like that.

Now, notice this conversation in your mind, Sharon, you're so stupid, you're not doing life right. That insulting voice back there talking to you has to be noticed and challenged. Does anyone else ever have one of those conversations? Today is the day you get to declare your emancipation from this voice and tell it, I'm not listening. I don't have to listen to anything that says I'm stupid and don't know how to do life. Someone mentioned earlier that we have listened to this voice for so long that we don't realize we're not required to do so. Without examining the hypothesis it put forth, we thought we had to listen, or that it was the truth or simply how life is. Today we come together to declare we are not listening to it. So, Sharon, what would happen if you said, "I'm not listening to this voice that counsels me to hate others?"

It replies, "Well, but see, you created this."

When it starts that, just tell it you're not listening.

Do you not listen even though what it says seems true, and when you look at this moment in your life, you see a mess? I don't like what I've created.

When that unkind ego voice keeps telling you to look at your life and that you've really made a mess, keep choosing to listen differently, not with resistance but with a firm, "I'm not listening." Choose instead to hear you are the child of a Father who loves us all and heed only this. We all certainly need to look straight at our mistakes and acknowledge them, but that doesn't require condemnation or punishment. Be very kind but firm with yourself, and refuse to indulge the voice that says you should be condemned. You do not have to cower before it.

To me, it's that deep belief I can be hurt. Only the ego can be hurt. Although you can kill the body, you cannot kill the Spirit. Is that right?

That's it. All that's called for here is a refocusing of attention.

Carol has been telling us where the answer is, which may be difficult to grasp or we may not want to grasp it, but it's very helpful to me to know where the answer is not. The answer is not in the past or in ruminating about grievances. Let's pretend for a moment that the world's beliefs are true and what happened when you were young is important and does remain effective. There is still no solution in that belief. We look for a solution where it doesn't exist. It doesn't matter whether the grievance is of the current moment, two days ago, or twenty years ago. There is still no answer and no peace in finding the so-called source of the grievance. You don't have to worry about the past because that's not where peace comes from. Ask yourself what the ego voice has ever gotten you, except more self-condemnation. Since it has never gotten us anywhere worthwhile, why do we keep listening? That question must be answered.

I can offer peace, and I can do the Father and child and all of that for everyone else, but not for myself.

Why not?

I don't know. Well, I do, sort of.

Tell me about this conversation that drones on endlessly in your head, saying how you cannot offer peace to yourself?

My self-talk says if I focus too much on myself, then I'm selfish, unworthy of whatever I'm trying to create out there, and that I should take care of everyone else first. I've gone through a lot of changes in the last few months, especially since I started working on seeing my relationships differently. My life is changing and seems to be getting worse rather than better, because I thought I'd gotten to a point of success and now I'm falling back—it's very, very confusing.

Whatever you may think, you are always going forward. How many here have a critical committee in your mind assuring you it's selfish to pay attention to yourself and you're not worthy of such loving attention? We all learned those lies.

I feel all these things and do want to offer peace to other people, but past events suddenly appear in my mind and convince me I'm unworthy for a while longer, despite what Carol says.

And each time that starts, what do you do?

I try to tell myself I will not listen to this voice, but all of a sudden, I seem to get overwhelmed by disgust or hatred.

Don't resist this voice—challenge it. That is very different. It's very important to recognize the presence of this constant conversation about how you are undeserving and must take care of everyone else first. That same programming teaches it's not humble but arrogant to focus on your own goodness or glory. Most of us grew up with some variation on that theme.

I do that so well. I know how to get rid of those conversations, but then it seems like I fall off the horse, or whatever you want to call it.

Keep practicing. What you can always know, for sure, is that whoever comes into your life is specifically chosen to assist with your unlearning. For our own peace of mind, it is imperative to want to see what's right about them, to really want their lives to succeed, to really want them to have peace now. You cannot truthfully want them to have peace and prosperity if you focus on all the wrongs they have committed. You can only want peace for them when you acknowledge he or she is a pure child of God. Then it's easy.

What if I want peace for them with just a little bit of something else?

Just a little bit of revenge?

One thing that has helped me a lot while working on any given issue was not having to know what the next step was going to be like. Because of the unknown factor, that was a tough decision. When I finally said, Fine, I'll just let the Holy Spirit handle the next thing, it was a lot easier to stay in the moment.

We all are undertaking a huge commitment. On the one hand, it is extremely simple to change our minds. On the other, it seems like a monumental task because we are flying right in the face of conditioned responses that point out our unworthiness, undeservedness, and guilt. It is imperative to stand up to this old conversation. Our great need is to be assertive, primarily, with the voice of our own ego, which undermines our basic sense of well-being with its constant assertion that a happy life is out of reach. Be very firm with this voice, speak with conviction, and declare your independence from it. This requires being proactive and practicing talking to yourself in a different way. Sit in a chair and say to yourself, I do not need to apologize or justify or explain myself. I have a right to be here just the way I am. My past mistakes are gone and I want to be my own best cheerleader! Think of all the things you've done right and list the things you're grateful for.

I got to the place where I wanted to send out love and gentleness to other people, but I didn't feel worthy myself. I worked with it and worked with it, then it occurred to me to do a very simple thing: Every day on the way to work I started praying for unconditional love for myself. After about ten days, there was a shift inside, which felt like a click, and it stayed there. There's been peace with that, with no idea that this is selfish. It was a complete shift in the way I see the universe and myself in it, and it came just by asking.

Wonderful! You see, because you sincerely wanted to hold yourself in high regard, it was yours for the asking. You demonstrated, through your prayerfulness and the focus of your attention, that you weren't kidding about wanting this experience. In the beginning, many of us feel ambivalent, so begin with a prayer of "I want to desire to" for as long as needed. Praying to be able to love yourself is a wonderful example of focus and determination. We will all come to this in our own way, realizing we most certainly can say what we need to in defiance of the voice in our minds that says otherwise.

If we could recognize we all share the same identity, it might be easy to realize that wanting peace for everybody would include ourselves, since we cannot disconnect. That shared identity makes it impossible to exclude anyone.

Exactly. Therefore, our task is to take that awareness from an intellectual level to a feeling level. We say we want peace, but we want it our way or with this particular person, so the fantasy will work out.

I didn't realize that until today! That's what I was doing. I thought I was giving this person all this peace and love without any agenda or expectations, but I'm discovering that was really incorrect.

If you've become aware of the strings attached, you have made a big leap. It's wonderful, finally, to realize how attached we are to getting our way, because only when we become thoroughly aware, are we motivated to admit we're absolutely stuck in needing to get our way and that we need some help. When we don't yet see how stuck we are in the tar pits, it's difficult to be motivated.

I get in trouble right at this point, wanting to condemn myself for being stuck.

This is where you become mindful of that condemning chatter back there in your mind and learn to stop listening.

Those of us with some experience of denial remember a statement in A Course in Miracles *reminding us that refusing to believe this poor opinion of ourselves is the proper use of denial.*

Yes, the proper use of denial is denying that pathetic self-talk. Denial is a neutral thing, just as memory or learning, or the world or the body is neutral. Thank you for reminding us of that.

This is a burning issue with me. Does the critical voice ever shut up?

Yes, it gets less and less insistent as you stop paying attention to it, like the air escaping from a balloon. When there is no more air in the balloon, it sinks quietly to the ground. Of course, the inner critic becomes much less dominant as we pay less attention to it and continually increase our ability to say no to it whenever it starts up. In other words, the relative sound level begins to shift. Like the volume on the radio, you turn it down again.

I find myself worrying about things today and their conse-
quences in the future.

Remember Scott's response to his dream, "I don't have to worry—all events will take care of themselves and will be fine any way they work out." For certain, this is where we must practice. Most of us learn to ignore the present moment by constant worry about the past and the future. This moment, in all its glory, passes by our awareness because we don't pay attention to it.

Is worry about the past or future the same as worrying I'll
cause someone pain if I say something wrong?

That's more of the arrogant guilt thing. If we can remember, at this moment, to offer peace and compassion to ourselves and everyone else, problems disappear, upset and tension drain away, physical pain, emptiness, and fear gradually diminish. All types of distress are merely signals reminding us we are holding back our own love. The solution to all our upset is so very simple, and yet we have made it incredibly complicated by convincing ourselves we must analyze and understand, undo, worry about, and anticipate. A new and better approach proclaims our experience *now* is a function of our focus *now*. That focus is entirely up to us, end of story. Not necessarily easy, but certainly simple. The lack of ease is only because we are very stubborn, very fixed in our own ways, and very undisciplined in becoming mindful and changing our minds. This is an ongoing cycle: becoming mindful, changing my mind, becoming mindful, changing my mind. If you object to this vigilance and mind changing on the grounds that it's too much work and you would prefer something else, what would that be—a silver bullet technique, perhaps? In actuality, what is your other option? Would you like to remain in your present circumstances? That's hardly a good option.

[3:00pm. Instructions are given for forming groups.
Everyone chooses a piece of paper from a basket handed around
and the numbers printed on them randomly divide the class into
many groups of four each. The chairs are rearranged all over the
room for the group exercise.]

Group exercise:

You will find yourself with the perfect group, as you will see
once we get under way. Your task is two-fold. First, spend a
bit of time revealing to your group the predominant message
your ego voice tells you about yourself and your place in the
world. Articulate the conversation in your head about how you
are not okay and why. If there are any particulars about your
imagined undeservedness or need for punishment, speak to
those issues. Reveal the inner conversation normally allowed
to hold forth in your mind unchecked.

Second, say out loud to the others in your group something
you have always wanted to express, which is closer to the truth
of your goodness and perfection than this tyrannical ego belief
has allowed. Say something you have always wanted to hear
yourself say but have not given yourself permission. This can
be on any subject whatsoever. You will notice how inhibited
you feel, how much you hold back, because this old, unchallenged voice says you must. It reminds you, as always, that
you are no good and have nothing important to say. Hiding
within the heart of everyone is something we long to speak or
express, perhaps to a parent, whether living or already passed
on, or to a child. Your expression may be directed to someone
who is not part of your group or not physically present, or you
may even want to sing. Take note, with the help and guidance
of your own loving, wise nature, how blocked you are from
speaking or asking for what you want. This exercise helps to
directly experience and become aware of the dominance of the
unquestioned ego voice that controls our internal airwaves,
perpetuating the myth about being wrong. Come to grips with
its seeming dominion over your life and realize you don't have
to listen to it at all. You can say what you want to instead.
There will very likely be a wide range of topics you'll want to
talk about or feelings to express. Proclaim something loving

about yourself or someone else, which you have not given yourself permission to do before. Acknowledge that disparaging voice and then declare your freedom from it right here on the spot, in the face of what it may be telling you. Assert something powerful or courageous, or true and loving. In these beginning stages of taking back power and focus, speaking the truth out loud is even more powerful than thinking it. You are actually making a commitment to proclaim the truth of your goodness for all to see.

[Exercise in progress lasts about forty minutes and then everyone is asked to conclude the conversation and remain where they are but facing the front of the room.]

Now that you're back, how does it feel to speak from your new confidence in your right to be here? Did you find the nature of your ego voice strikingly similar to everyone else's, speaking the same old boring lie to and about everyone? Virtually everyone who walks the earth has the same fearful conversation going on internally, and yet so many of us feel we are the only defective ones. We believe, laughably, that everyone else has it handled, and I am the only one out of place here. What was it like to stand up and assert your innocence or make that long overdue, loving remark to or about someone else?

Well, it felt very good. In our group two of us noticed that, as we began to speak, we got a very hot, tight feeling in the chest and throat. But once we were finished, it was released.

Was it very unfamiliar to allow yourself to speak something positive about yourself or someone else?

It was very freeing.

Strange and unusual.

It was nice to say what I really wanted to and to have the people in the group be so loving and supportive and to agree.

Wonderful! The idea is to be able to say lovingly, "I have the right to do this." Did you worry you would be misunderstood when you said something loving? From now on, will you be a bit less inclined to listen to inner arguments about your inferior nature or your lack of rights to express as you choose?

I got an insight just this minute! When we were talking about all the old ego stuff, it just came out. You open your mouth and it starts rolling out. Then we turned around and did the true-self part of the exercise. With that, the heat started increasing and you could feel the energy moving. There was an aliveness to speaking about what was good and right, while that other old chatter felt dead. It had no energy with it, and you almost don't have to move your lips. It just falls out of your face. But while we declared what's right about us, you could see every-one's faces become alive, and one woman even started giggling and wiggling.

It *is* being alive. It's a bit odd and, in the beginning, rouses some nervousness as we wonder when the "other shoe is going to drop." We look around to see if a critical parent or an author-ity figure or the thought police are coming to get us.

I didn't know the people in my group very well, and even while speaking my mind, my fear had nothing to do with them. Still, I found myself waiting for one of them either to laugh at me or say, "Aha, we know about you!" I have no intellectual reason to believe they would attack me or laugh at me.

Do you see how we expect criticism or assume we are going to be cut off at the knees? It takes practice saying, "I feel nervous about this, but I'm going to step out and realize I'm safe; no one is going to get me." Was that a new experience for you?

Yes.

You are realizing how uncommon it is, for the most part, to give yourself permission to be kind to yourself or others. You can be kind to your birds and animals, and now it's time to include you.

You are as deserving as they are. What happened with you in this group over here? Did this experience feel weird?

A little strange.

It does seem a bit strange to tell the truth, especially for those of us who are not usually in a setting where we're encouraged to set aside our false self-image. Remember our earlier talk about our love affair with form? That refers not only to the outer physical form but also to the internal image we hold of ourselves, and the tremendous defensiveness we feel about it. We pretend to hide behind the mask of self-image; it's the fortress in which we live. To be honest, to tell the truth about how we feel and what is occurring within, feels very strange because we are used to hiding out in our self-image. Telling the truth has not been held out as valuable or necessary. Quite the contrary.

Earlier, I was reflecting on people who keep getting into poor relationships, because of how they feel about themselves. Beating ourselves down applies to other areas of life, and I'm realizing I have gotten into various employment situations where I allowed myself to be put down. I acknowledge that and now want to undo it

You have taken a great big step in coming to realize that what you're encountering in your work life is not what you really deserve, but it is what you have declared and presumed you deserve. In unrecognized ways, you have declared this is what you deserve. There is a world of difference between what we actually deserve, which is everything, and what we have declared we deserve, which is very little.

I hear what you're saying about the past being gone, but sometimes, as I understand it, there is value in going back to when you were two or four, perhaps to find a single incident that may have resulted in being a turning point.

Would you be willing to hold that idea in a questioning place?

Sure.

Okay, let's pretend there are pivotal events that somehow shape our lives in an unfortunate way. Even if that were so, it is still *now* that I change my mind about how I choose to remember or to view them. Say I engage in endless self-examination about the past and do everything possible to seek out all those noteworthy events. Or, what if, like Marilyn, we had amnesia for many years? So, whether you have total amnesia or know in intricate detail everything that has ever happened in your life, you still do exactly the same thing today to correct the problem. Do you see, therefore, that having total information or no information at all about the past is not relevant to today's discomfort? If I am uncomfortable today, the cause is today and the release is today, so everything is about today. When we look at it that way, we find that the problem is today's preoccupation with the need to defend, to have the self-image honored by everyone, and to have our fantasies work out. Now, you might quickly respond that the reason you have adopted a defensive stance, realizing all of us have learned defenses of some kind, is because of this unhappy pivotal event. Let's pretend that (a) this is true and (b) we found the pivotal event, because that is the purpose of mining one's past. In any case, it is still a *current* change of mind that brings a sense of resolution. It's difficult to grasp the idea of having a new choice today, partly because it is so simple and the ego mind requires complexity. It's not at all complicated to realize, regardless of what we may have discovered about our past and its events, that what heals our hurt is choosing to be less involved with our egos. We need less focus on our specialness, defensiveness, and the way things have to be, and to be more involved with expressing what we truly are. This exercise is about realizing how infrequently we allow ourselves to express what we really want to say and how we really feel. Its purpose is to bring into sharp relief that we're dealing with more than an interesting theory. We really do defer to the form, our defenses, and that nagging voice insistently instructing us to defend, instead of to the loving presence within us that merely asks permission to be authentic and free. And when it does ask, the inner committee usually says, "Nope, no freedom for you."

This is so encouraging relative to conventional psychotherapy, which always looks back to other times, places, and people to locate blame. Now, today, we can let go of the entire concept that blame has to be placed anywhere. We merely are present and, at this very moment, choose to think differently.

That's it! I talk with a great number of people who have engaged in more traditional therapy and through it have come to very valuable realizations about the degree and scope of their denial. Therefore, a more traditional approach to self-awareness has tremendous value to it—*and* it only gets you so far. All of you here have come to realize that the more traditional approaches have served their purpose, and now we wonder, what's next? Taking full responsibility for today's choices is "what's next." We realize we've discovered many things and know a bit more about what makes us tick. Now we must begin to practice with new determination, realizing that if we want to feel comfortable, happy, and safe, we must step out and express our heartfelt feelings. We're asked to be less concerned about what people will say, their approval or lack thereof, and whether they will like us or not when we truthfully express what we feel. Sometimes, people won't like it when we express faithfully, and that's okay. It simply points out their need to relinquish judgment and projection. What if everyone who experimented with new inventions or broke new ground had worried about all the people who said, "This is nuts, you can't do this."? One of my favorite examples relates to the invention of the telephone. Alexander Graham Bell's associate said, "This is really crazy. Why would anyone want to talk to someone not in the same room? Who's ever going to use a telephone?" What if Mr. Bell had replied, "Oh, you're right. People might think I'm crazy. I guess I won't invent the telephone—it's a bad idea? Consider the thousands of pioneers, inventors, scientists, and countless others who have explored new ground. If we are ever to move forward in the physical world or in our spiritual development, someone must have the courage to declare, "You know what? It doesn't matter if nobody understands where I'm coming from or what's going on. I have to follow my own inner direction. I will not sell out to the possibility that people won't like me if I do this. Who cares?" Recognizing that we determine what is important to us and don't have to be driven by others' opinions is one of the greatest hurdles, and turning points, we ever encounter.

Within your group, when you truly expressed what was in your heart, you felt free. You will discover, for the most part, that people are not going to laugh at you or insult you or put you down. Occasionally in the beginning, someone might be less than generous and that's okay. That's part of your own unrecognized judgment on yourself being revealed to you.

What became very clear for me was a recognition my ego is a pansy rather than an ominous monster trying to ruin me. It is chaotic, fearful, and something of a loose cannon. Do you know what I mean?

I do indeed, and you're right about its fear. Rather like the *Wizard of Oz*. A lot of noise but not much substance. Did any others have some discoveries?

Yes, in our group we had a lot in common. We found it did feel good to say something good about ourselves and that, for the most part, we haven't allowed that.

She beamed when she started talking about this.

You can see the shift happen and the lights turn on when you finally give yourself permission to claim your own worth. How about you?

In retrospect, what really struck me was the instantaneous support and presence of the three people listening to the one speaking. That really got my attention! It wasn't that when the person concluded, the three sat there and thought of something nice to say, but they maintained complete support the entire time. It was a continuation of the thought process, like a melding of the minds, with no gap in time or understanding, just continuing to flow. It was really intriguing to experience what was actually a continuous conversation with no gap, even though it started off with one talking and then the other three following in turn.

Was that new for you?

Oh yeah! I didn't want to do it. I thought, Here Carol goes with one of her circles again!

Having to participate just pushed you right out there, so you reluctantly took another little step. Everyone is being pushed out of the nest. That's the desired result. What about you all?

I feel good and am getting better. It's ironic that all my life, everywhere I've participated, whether it's work meetings or places where people get together and discuss, I've always been criticized for opening my mouth. This is one of the few safe places people have regularly expressed to me they were glad I opened my mouth. That comes as such a shock to me, because sometimes I anticipate being criticized for doing that.

I am just delighted to be here. It has reinforced some of my ideas and opened my eyes to a lot of others.

Being invested in our images and concerned about what people will say, or having issues about doing something right, all require holding back and holding in. Remember the earlier comment about feeling heat or energy moving when you start to say what you want to say and do what you want to do? Well, that heat or energy flow is literally occurring. We have attempted to block the energy flow that we actually are, in both directions, so to speak. We decide we will not receive love because we aren't deserving, and we won't extend good will because the other person isn't either. So here we are with this stagnant, unmoving energy. Have you ever used the phrase, "I feel blocked?" Well, that is quite literally the problem.

Your own energy is not being allowed to flow. You might also have noted you really cannot feel anything, because we feel only the energy that flows and moves. As we deliberately choose to block awareness of that flow, then sure enough, it feels as if we are numb and without feeling. Our task is to open up the floodgates of our own souls and feel everything right now.

Let's do a quick exercise to make this point: Close your eyes and put your full attention on your throat and the entire heart area, feeling your shoulders and chest opening up. When you simply turn your attention to those two areas of your body, representing different areas of experience, what does that feel like?

It's as if my throat is the means to express my heart. All of a sudden, I was paying attention to my throat and it became a tunnel to love. Your throat is here to express your loving nature.

I'm having such an overwhelming experience of what we did just now in this exercise. The outcome, for me, was really to experience, right now, that I deserve to be loved. I'm sitting here with my mouth open, because this <u>feeling</u> is going through me that I really deserve to be loved.

And when you focus on your throat?

I deserve to be heard. That's real. What I was trying to say in the group didn't come to me until afterwards. My unworthiness, all of a sudden, disappeared.

Notice what has happened to the sound of your voice. You recall everyone has been asking you to speak up because we can't hear you. Your voice has sounded like it comes from way down inside somewhere. Notice how clear it sounds now and that it's rising in volume.

And it's interesting since, supposedly, I have one paralyzed vocal cord.

It most certainly is interesting and very much a non-coincidence that paralyzed vocal cords, sore throats, and other such diseases afflict this area. Having had a direct experience of the benefits of changing your mind, you can see you don't have to paralyze yourself from lack of self-expression again. Okay?

I was feeling rather tired from all this hard work of having to look at myself, and just then, my heart started opening up, and I got new energy, and I just wanted to speak out and share. Just as Lynn experienced, it was quite a warm, fuzzy feeling.

I know this is my perception, but in the group exercise, I thought I shared from both my ego and my heart. I thought I really let my ego be exposed, allowing my true self to express, but I don't think my fellow group members let their true selves out at all. That's judgmental of me, I know. One gentleman expressed himself, but he didn't really get to that point of being real, and I feel tightness because of that.

Did you have expectations about their telling the truth?

I was wanting the wonderful cleansing everyone else is having, and I felt this tightening instead.

It's not too late to have a different experience, so we are going to bring this issue right into the moment. Are you feeling a sense of disappointment now?

Yeah.

There is no such thing as wrong, and please recognize that someone else's participation, or lack thereof, doesn't get to impact your experience. Close your eyes, as will the rest of us. Direct your attention back to your own throat and heart, and say aloud what you want to experience.

I want to experience worthiness, truth, and being one with all of God's creation.

Okay, that is your request. Now in your own mind, speak to the three people in your group. Since your eyes are closed, you will not look at them physically. Now state in the most heart-felt way, what you truly want for them to experience and what you know is true about them. Speak out loud. Your eyes may be closed, but you are speaking to them directly. This is not theoretical.

You are truly worthy of everything. Everything that brings happiness is yours already. All you have to do is allow yourself to have it, allow yourself to experience and have that in your own heart, and know you are worthy.

As you speak to them in your most heartfelt way, what happens in your own throat and heart, as we sit here with closed eyes?

I'm starting to get that nice, warm, tingling feeling you were talking about.

Open your eyes. The nice, warm, tingly feeling is an inside job. If you are with people who do not choose, at this very moment, to honor themselves or to express freely or come into aware-ness of their own goodness, that's just fine. Know their goodness for them and for yourself. If it takes them a little while to decide to claim it for themselves, that's fine too. Have no expectations about when and how anyone else needs to claim their good, because it will never keep you from claiming yours.

 I am sure it has not gone unnoticed that the word "Addictions," included in the title of this program, has hardly been mentioned. That is purposeful, as plenty of energy and attention is already given to their study and prevention. We must ask ourselves if we are interested in the problem or in the solution. Our goal is not about acquiring coping strategies or techniques but about recognizing that, when we are feeling fulfilled, this contented state of mind automatically directs our actions appropriately, lovingly, and openly. Therefore, addictions and distractions, as we understand them, cease to be, not because we have effectively stamped them out but because they are no longer inviting or serve any purpose. There is no need for them when our feelings, being happy ones, do not call for covering up or distracting mechanisms. Addictions do not need to be addressed at all. The only thing we need to remember is if we are hurting ourselves today, we can stop today. We can make that choice five hundred times a day, which we probably do, in the beginning stages. If you notice lack of peace, upset, panic, or disappointment, you know you have opened the book about, This is how my life is supposed to be, this is what I'm supposed to do, this is how all the people are supposed to act, this is how they're supposed to respond to what I do. You have picked up the script of your fantasy life, and are disappointed because the fantasy is not working out. Fantasies never work out. In fact, the worst possibility is that your fantasy does work out, and you are left with the terrible realization that you have your way, but that the emptiness still exists, so now what? We stop focusing on the fantasy about how *my* life, *my* kids, *my* spouse, *my* house, *my* dog are supposed to be and set those expectations aside, as well as the accompanying voice that says you're still not doing it right or you still don't deserve it. We let go of the costume, the mask, the image, recognizing they have nothing to do with the truth of us, and begin to step out authentically, letting the chips fall where they may.

Thus, we grow in our ability to live without apology, excuses, justification, or having to explain where we are in our life process. We determine to live as lovingly as possible, honoring the goodness and value in other people and ourselves. We vacillate between only these two choices—love and fear—on a daily basis, and that's fine. As we become more committed to accepting our good and more vigilant about allowing and owning our upset, we notice more quickly when we have picked up the book of worthlessness, and choose to lay it back down. Hold your head up and notice what is happening around you. As you keep looking for the true goodness and deserving nature of everyone, you look right past the actions, behavior, and chaos, and say, "This is my Father's child, and I refuse to focus on anything but this." We are promised that, as thoughts of goodness become our choice instead of the more prevalent thoughts of being wrong, we will experience relief. Lift up your eyes from the book of worthlessness and notice all the caring and support here for us and suddenly you find life easy, with everyone the recipient of the good will that follows. Like any other skill, this takes practice. Upset, the barometer warning of the need to love rather than judge, occurs like clockwork when we have expectations of others that are not being met, or when we have decided life should be a certain way and it isn't. In other words, a *primary* focus on image will always result in pain. Then we will medicate the pain and find ourselves in a vicious cycle from which we seem unable to extricate ourselves. All we have to do is put down that book and declare we won't read it anymore. It is the simplest thing in the world and more fun than anything you have ever imagined. It does take practice, commitment, dedication, but look how committed and dedicated we have been to the voice that says we are no good—and how much we have practiced its rules. We already know about dedication to a goal, so now we switch allegiance to a new purpose, one that is very simple—stop condemning, start loving—and very deep—bringing all the rewards our hearts could ever dream of and more. Take seriously the goal of joining with others and we will never have to be concerned about addictions again!

[4:30pm End of workshop. Many look weary, but contented. As always, there is much conversation and hugging as friends, old and new, depart. Many helpful ones remain to straighten up the room or wait for tapes to be copied, and some have a few, private questions. Order is quickly restored and another day of offering a new perspective about how life works has taken place.]

Dear reader:

How are you doing? Take a deep breath. Particularly notice how you feel at the conclusion of this workshop. You may be very stirred up with the many new ideas presented. I hope you have gained your own insights as the workshop participants looked differently at their lives and the relationship of egocentricity, guilt, pain, and addictions. The ideas contained here are simple and uncomplicated. The way out of our seeming dilemma likewise is simple, easy, free, endless, and user-friendly. We are only required to realize that our usual approach to life has not been successful or adequate and to desire a new one. And it's ours! If the solution to our seeming problem is free, simple and ever available but we refuse it, then we must conclude that beneath the surface of substances and behaviors, we are addicted to guilt. We are addicted to closed-mindedness, having our way, and being certain we are right. The purpose of the workshop and the book is to strip away the confusion and lay out our dilemma as it really is. Now that you have a foundation for a different perspective, Part II, through an interview process, illustrates the steps necessary to change from tormented or disillusioned lives to greatly more contented ones. Many of the workshop participants have taken those steps. You can, too!

Part II

Interviews and Responses

Recently, friends from Denver were in town and we spoke of many things, including progress on this book. As an aside, our friend made a comment about people who are addicted and those who are not. My partner, Robert, interjected that a more accurate statement is that everyone is addicted, and we are in different stages of awareness about that. Her face lit up as she observed that life would be so much easier and simpler if we could realize and admit we are all in the same situation. No one would have to hide or pretend, and we could just get on with our lives. For those willing to take this perspective, it's a short trip to peace of mind. You are graciously invited to join in.

As mentioned in Part I of this book, after receiving phone calls from several people who were having great insights into their own addictions, it became crystal clear that personal examples would greatly augment the workshop dialogue. Little did I realize, as I outlined the questions included here, what a tremendously fulfilling and exciting adventure the interview process would be and what an honor and privilege to work with this group. One occasionally hears of "ordinary people doing extraordinary things." I would like to modify that to read, "ordinary people changing their minds in extraordinary ways," truly being lights unto the world.

With the decision to add a second section, the project unfolded with a life of its own. After drawing up a list of the major universal addictions or distractions, I intuitively chose candidates to interview. Some had attended the workshop presented in Part I and others were students, clients, friends, or all of the above. In all cases, these individuals were past their addictions or had significantly altered dysfunctional behavior and were now living lives of greater emotional maturity and fulfillment than is the norm in our society. They eagerly agreed to participate in our study in order to share their good fortune at finding a way out of distress. Moreover, when I assured them of anonymity, almost everyone responded, "I have no need to remain anonymous. I don't mind everyone knowing what my process has been." That openness and willingness to share with others coupled with a relaxed attitude about their paths, is a mighty tribute to their courage and determination to "get real."

Despite their willingness to reveal themselves, I have unilaterally decided to retain their anonymity in deference to friends and family who may not wish to be identified. The responses to the questions are listed but not given specific attribution. Also, as the content of the answers is the important issue, it may be distracting to try to keep track of who says what.

Without exception, being in the company of these men and women is truly an occasion worth noting. One rarely hears complaining, gossiping, or egoic self-promotion. Instead, there is a heightened energy, a sense of good will, lightheartedness, and good-natured humor. When distress occasionally arises, it is processed quickly and "owned" with a minimum of rancor or blame as part of the ongoing adventure of self-discovery. They are open and appropriate in their interactions with life and each other, clearly defining what is possible in a frightened and frightening world.

It is crucial to note that, before they changed their minds, whether driven to their knees by tragedy or plagued by a vague and undefinable dissatisfaction, all, in their own ways, acknowledged, "There must be a better way than this to live." They would be the first to acknowledge their short-comings, which included violence and abuse in some cases. They are just like the rest of us, with possibly one exception: They have been willing to answer their own inner call for transformation. Sometimes that willingness was very small, riddled with many objections and excuses. Yet, with determination they didn't know they possessed, they have yielded to mankind's most basic yearning—to love, to extend, and to be generous of spirit. They have been willing to face their fears and to challenge the inner ego voice that demands we be small and insignificant. They have been where most people are now but have chosen to go beyond that, and therefore, are in an ideal place to be helpful.

Let us be clear here. In truth, we are all far more alike than we are different, although in this world, the differences are given greater emphasis. No one in this study is inherently different from anyone else. They were not given special privileges, nor were they spared the difficult parts of self-discovery. They do not have something special that others lack. They were simply willing to ask for help and to recognize they weren't yet acquainted with some areas of themselves. Through that willingness, the unexplainable yet happy alteration of their lives for the better occurred. If enough people would make this same choice, sanity would be restored to our world in very short order.

Part of the fascination and relevance of this study is the great diversity of life experience among these who share this common purpose of changing their viewpoints. Within all the measurable categories we use to compare ourselves in this world, our participants represent an exceptionally wide range. At the time of the interviews in mid-1997 our group of twenty-eight participants ranged in age from nineteen to sixty-nine and were evenly divided between men and women. They came literally from the four corners of the United States and many places in between, as well as from Cuba and Canada. They have lived in more than half the states in this country, as well

as abroad. The most recent geographical common denominator is that, with few exceptions, all are now residents of Florida
and have arrived here through a great variety of circumstances. Most are Caucasian, but those of Latin ethnicity,
racial mix, and Caribbean black heritage are also participants.
Every possible familial combination is represented—single,
married, divorced, and committed partnerships of all variations. They have children, grandchildren, stepchildren, and no
experience with children. As for educational levels, the
nineteen-year-old had attended her freshman year of college,
while all others range from one and a half years of college to
multiple advanced degrees and postdoctoral work. Some
remained at one school, while others shopped around various
institutions looking for the right "fit." Some have seen military
service and others have not.

The group's religious upbringing is extremely varied,
ranging from no active religious affiliation through the
mainline Protestant denominations, Roman Catholicism,
and Judaism, to more fundamentalist Christian groups,
Christian Science, or so-called New Age philosophy. All found
that, whatever their earlier religious experience and training,
it left them essentially unfulfilled and failed to provide relief
from fear, meaningful answers, or access to a transcendent
experience.

Some moved often in their younger years, as children of
families connected with the military or government agencies.
Others had deep roots in one location with generations of
family history to support them. The nature of their childhoods
ranged from glaringly abusive through "garden-variety"
dysfunctional to as idyllic as loving parents can provide in this
world. Currently, some live simply with modest financial
resources, and others enjoy great affluence. Lifestyles, talents,
and levels of sophistication vary, and many of the group might
never have met if they had not held one crucial issue in
common: Life was not working out as planned. As an aside,
life not working out provided the opportunity for our paths to
cross. All of them, at one time or another, attended my classes
or workshops based on principles from *A Course In Miracles,*

a self-study course designed to aid in changing our minds to allow a return to peace of mind. You will hear occasional reference to that work throughout the answers.

Our participants' occupations and professions provide insight into their greatly varied inclinations and talents. Many have had more than one career, and several share an occupational background, although they are not in business together. Some have a national reputation in their field and others stay closer to home. Major career categories include: aviation, business—management, marketing, development, banking, insurance, advertising, consulting—education, law, medicine and allied fields, professional sports, real estate—architecture, construction, development, management—religion, technical and scientific fields, trades, and visual and performing arts. Whether involved with one or several careers, owning their companies or working for others, all found themselves on the perfect path to their own self-discovery, with their own individualized curriculum bringing them to that inevitable place of genuinely asking for help.

It is crucial to emphasize the great diversity within this group, because, in sharp contrast with the differences of form and outward appearance is the commonality of the journey we all share. The participants' answers to a series of questions reveal everyone's inner landscape and process. Their candor in answering these questions and their willingness to be positive examples to others is truly a gift of the highest order.

To restate, my purpose is to shed light on what appears to be an enormous, insoluble problem, one seen as overwhelming, complex, and deadly. "Shedding light" implies looking at addictive behavior in another, more helpful, way. There are solutions, different from those usually proposed and available to anyone who will listen. For those willing to challenge the ideas that 1) you already know everything relevant to addictions or 2) this does not involve you, here is the specific process by which all addictions are healed, given step by step. Each of the "heroes of the journey" interviewed here has found greater peace of mind and relief from the prison of addiction by using it.

At some point, everyone in this group allowed new seeds of awareness to be planted. Those seeds germinated and flourished as their willingness and commitment to adopt a new perspective about their addictions increased. Through excerpts from these interviews you can travel along with them from unawareness to an awakening about how to ask for a happy life. This exploration of their minds will lead into yours, as well. As each question is asked and answered, I have commented on them and specifically laid out each step of the healing process. If you are ready to significantly change the quality of your life, please join us and answer each question for yourself. When you find a response or comment with which you identify, underline or highlight it for future reference or to see if a pattern emerges as you proceed.

1. In your earlier, less informed days, what was your understanding or belief about addictions? What did that word mean to you?

It always meant drugs and alcohol. I never thought of addiction in any other way.

Addictions, to me, didn't involve behavioral things. I associated them with substance abuse.

Addictions involved substances—cigarettes, alcohol, drugs, that type thing.

I didn't have a clue, until 1988, that addictions could be anything other than ingested chemicals.

The usual stereotyped addictions—vices, basically.

I was very naive. Drugs, alcohol, and smoking would qualify, and that was about it.

I'm remembering thinking you could be addicted to a person, as in, Yeah, oh, you're addicted to that person; you don't really love him, you're addicted to him.

Almost without exception, the responses to this first question include the assumption that addictions involve only alcohol, drugs, or both, with occasional references to smoking, sex, food, or compulsive behaviors. In these representative quotes, the primary tone is one of distance from the problem or lack of awareness or interest.

I never thought about addictions, although in high school I worked with cocaine addicts for a semester. I knew people who drank and smoked a lot, but I never saw them as addicted, only that they liked it.

I didn't realize, until I was of high school age, that my mother was drinking a lot and definitely had alcohol problems.

My first awareness related to addictions was of my parents, whom I saw behaving differently after two or three drinks. I remember seeing other family members also, knowing their behavior wasn't quite right but not understanding that indicated an addiction.

Misunderstanding about addictions is not wrong or malicious, but it certainly keeps us from discovering meaningful insights about ourselves and those around us. This lack of focus on addiction is typical and the presumption that the problem lies elsewhere calls for a correction we all will inevitably make. Stay tuned for how to make that correction.

Actually, my first impressions of addictions were drugs. I was well aware of the term <u>alcoholism</u>, because I lived in a drinking culture. I don't know whether it was a form of denial or what, but I never related alcohol to addiction. I never heard anyone speak of it. In fact, the word <u>alcoholism</u> was never used in my house, even though my father was alcoholic and my mother *knew it. She referred to him as a "dipsomaniac," as if a little denial and a few euphemisms would fix things.*

I had a really strong opinion about addictions because I grew up in a household that displayed addictions along the alcoholic line, on both sides of my family. It was a military environment, and every occasion was an opportunity for drinking. Some were able to handle it, and some weren't. I witnessed a lot of the inability.

Oh, addictions were a scourge! It was a really fearful thing to contemplate what it would be like to have an addiction. I believed that wouldn't happen to me as long as I proceeded in the manner of my upbringing, which made it real clear I could overcome anything by sheer willpower and hard work. Therefore, an addiction was something that happened to somebody else, not to me, or mine, or anybody I thought I had some control over.

Here we have quite a spectrum—deliberate denial on one hand to outrage on the other—about the subject of addictions, permitting not one step toward the healing process. The avoidance or denial in these families guarantees that healing and resolution is continually postponed until a disaster occurs— one of sufficient proportions to make "looking the other way" impossible. As we shall see, those circumstances our public self considers disastrous, to be hidden or avoided at all costs, can precipitate the healing necessary for a truly happy and fulfilling life.

I don't know whether we had drug addicts back when I was in school, although there were very vague fears about drugs "getting" you, like polio "getting" you." I don't know that I ever really thought about it.

I thought the only way to become addicted was by repeated overindulgence, which eventually took hold of a person.

I believed addictions were physical. Basically, you made your body do it, and then your body got so accustomed to it that it made you do it. Then you couldn't live without it.

Addictions, to me, were a habit over which you had no power. I never thought of them in more depth than that.

These responses illustrate the common misconception that addictions "get you" whether you like it or not and that, basically, we have no choice in the matter. Nothing could be further from the truth. Our addictive behaviors stem from choices we constantly make, and our task is to unravel how and why we make them. Acknowledging our responsibility, not blame, for this behavior is the purpose of this book.

Basically, addiction meant you could not be filled up or satisfied by any substance, no matter how much of it you had, whether money, drugs, or alcohol. There was a constant requirement of more.

It's something you feel you have to have, and in the long run, it harms you.

It meant something you did over and over and over that was destructive to your life.

My first thought was drugs and the obsessive, compulsive behavior people use as a defense mechanism to keep from knowing themselves. It was apparent early on that it was an escape.

This group recognizes that addictive behaviors are not only harmful but also endlessly unrewarding. The goal of the behavior, whatever it may be, is never reached. No one in our group knew in their earlier years that self-destruction is a deliberate, though mostly unexamined, choice.

Thus far, the common element in the answers is hearsay, or "everybody knows" stereotypes fostered by lack of thoughtful, open-minded examination. Note the prevailing implication that whatever addictions are about, they aren't about me. We are inclined to allow vast areas of human experience, particularly our own, fall through the cracks of awareness. Early on, we specifically learn to deny and to make ourselves unaware of how we are feeling and what our natural inclinations might be. This is the price we pay to be considered acceptable, normal, and deserving of love and affection, or at least to avoid punishment. A heavy price indeed and, as we shall make abundantly clear, one that leaves us with nothing but despair.

The presumption that substances alone are addictive and are the only ways to hide our uncertainty, is the great misconception of our age; it must be challenged if ever we are to live with a sense of fulfillment and security. And so we commence our exploration with twenty-eight friends, truly representing everyone, each wanting to extend a hand to lead you through your own discoveries and promising triumph over all confusion if you are willing to take the first step.

Step 1:
Identify with some or all of the statements listed above, as you add your answer to this first question. Allow yourself to recognize you have had many of these same thoughts or beliefs, and that is perfectly fine. They are only temporary, no matter how long you have believed them to be true. Recognize yourself in the interviewees' stories, attitudes, and beliefs, and by so doing, allow yourself to be escorted by them to understanding and true peace of mind. In the beginning, you may feel challenged, even shocked, at the idea everyone is addicted to something, feeling you surely must be an exception. Allow that disturbance to be there, as it is part of a necessary and kindly process. The feelings that come up, even in these early stages, are crucially important signals, which must be correctly decoded rather than ignored and denied.

～ ❦ ～

2. What type of people did you think were involved with addictions?

I thought they were derelicts, really fall-down, stumbling drunks, with scraggly whiskers, basically living a useless life.

They were the "down-and-outs," the lowlifes who were weak and sick in their minds, insane, the unfortunates who fell in a hole and couldn't find their way out.

My picture of an alcoholic was a stumbling drunk in rumpled dirty clothes lying in his own vomit in the gutter, a bum. They were destitute people who couldn't take care of themselves, whose addiction had stripped them of anything and everything normal people had, like jobs and homes.

I would think weak people, lowlifes. I was very judgmental about their weakness and their sense of worthlessness. They weren't the kind of people I looked to as role models.

Well, addictions were bad, and people who had addictions didn't have their act together! They just didn't, and usually bad people had addictions and good ones didn't. It was very black and white, no gray areas. If you had an addiction, there was something seriously wrong with you, and the rest of us didn't have these addictions.

The people I worked with for a semester in high school were so-called white trash.

I put criminals in there somehow, since a lot of people in jail were addicted to a drug or alcohol. With eating, only big, obese people were addicted, not little people though. I thought small people couldn't be addicted to food.

Up to about twelve years ago, my impression was that addicts were junkies, street people, people who slept under bridges and participated in what are called "shooting galleries." They were lower-class people, weak characters, questionable characters, and just "characters," no one I would ever have related myself to. I never thought about them as having character flaws because I never got that far. They were of no character or just low character.

Repulsive! Despicable! Embarrassing! Shameful! Those were my very strong, very passionate, dramatic feelings and obser- vations about addicted people. I grew up with a mind-set that if you really didn't want to do something, you wouldn't, and I couldn't imagine it any other way. We were taught that no matter what we did, we were always in control to change our lives and be whatever we wanted, through willpower. [Carol: And if they didn't use willpower, were they defective?] Exactly. Or deficient in some fashion.

Nothing could be clearer here than the lightning-like speed and enthusiasm with which we rush to judgment of our fellow man. Without a trace of compassion or understanding, those "addicted people" who most certainly have nothing to do with "normal people," are dismissed as defective, undesirable, and generally "less than" the rest of us. This attitude of "us" and "them," this division of humankind into the acceptable and the unacceptable, which is fostered either overtly or subtly in all of us, makes a happy, secure life impossible. We have bought the idea, hook, line, and sinker, that seeing "them" as insane, weak, criminal, or generally undesirable keeps us safe. Ask yourself this question: How does focusing on the fear-driven behavior of other people add to my safety, happiness, or peace of mind? How are we safer and better off seeing the world as populated with those who cannot manage their lives? We are not better off—in fact, quite the contrary. Our focus on the helplessness and unworthiness in those "other addicted people" keeps us in distress, and the guilt-driven systems of the world alive, well, and uncorrected.

Well, those addicts just weren't exercising proper self-control! If they would make up their minds not to do whatever they were doing, they could stop. They were weak-minded, not strong-willed, nor did they live with conviction. It was all up to them, because they were choosing their addictions and could just stop! [Carol: Was this a matter of "Just say no?"]. *Right! Right!*

I thought two things: 1) they needed to go to therapy to stop whatever they were doing, and 2) everything I had heard about being addicted for life was true. I don't know that I thought very much about their character, although I didn't like being around people who were drunk. I was never around people who did "big" drugs, but I was around plenty who did pot, which to me was different. I thought addicts had to be dependent on something because they didn't have control over their own lives, and I didn't understand why they always wanted to be "out of it," so to speak.

Helpless, powerless, not being in control of their lives. [Carol: Did you see them as separate from yourself?] *Oh, I'm sure!*

They were people who couldn't get hold of themselves or control their emotions, could not act properly or be dignified. They were out of control.

The types of people who were addicted were those with lots of problems, not your everyday problems, but real problems. I stayed away from drugs and things I hadn't delved into that scared me, and I avoided habitual drinking, alcoholic-type people because they had no, what I considered, willpower.

This set of responses underlines our misunderstanding that behavior must be controlled to end addictions, and the evident difficulty in doing that. Behaviors cannot change through willpower alone because of a universal law—the immutable principle that what we believe about ourselves and our relationship to all others is the great driving force behind our actions. You cannot engage in behavior contrary to your belief any more than you can leave your shadow on the other side of the street. Your shadow goes with you wherever you go. No one in his or her right mind would accuse someone of lack of willpower because he couldn't dismantle his shadow in the bright sunshine and store it elsewhere. Nor would it be considered out of control to be unable to make the caboose of a train go in a direction different from the engine. We understand that bodies and their shadows and engines and cabooses are inextricably linked—they move as a unit. But it is important to note that although they necessarily operate as a unit, the elements are not of equal strength to one another. The movement of the body determines where the shadow goes, but the shadow cannot dictate the body's movements. The same is true with the train; the caboose doesn't drag the engine around. In just the same manner, our actions, thoughts, and feelings are all a unit with—and an inevitable outcome of—our beliefs about who and what we are, our value, and our right to be here. The beliefs, masked as truth, constitute the deciding element. Therefore, it is useless to try to control the secondary behavioral level without addressing the fundamental interior, invisible level of belief and attitude. Our ability to choose must be directed toward changing our minds about our value and basic nature, rather than struggling to change behavior—a change with only temporary, limited results. As we decide to see ourselves differently, behavior changes automatically and willpower is not involved.

I thought addicts had a weakness and needed the addictions or the substances as a crutch. I looked at it mostly as a weakness that, of course, I didn't have! We're so egocentric when we're young.

The word weakness comes to mind, people who were too weak to resist the urge, whatever the urge might be.

Let's see, people who weren't strong and couldn't control what was going on around them. They didn't have strength over these things and were driven to it.

My first reaction about addicted people was their dependency.

Later, codependency was a very interesting revelation—seeing how people reacted to each other and played off each other as addictions. [Carol: Did you have judgments about this?] *Absolutely! It was a great diversion from my own! I felt those with addictions were driven, stressed, strained, and needed crutches to help them survive or stabilize themselves.*

I couldn't understand why they couldn't get off it and why they would do that to themselves. What a waste! I wouldn't want to do it, as if I had control and they didn't. In a litter of pups, some are strong and a couple of them are weak, so maybe they were the "weak sisters." That's judging now, you know.

I thought addicts were people who really couldn't help it. I felt sorry for them, as if they were weak in some way.

Addicts were weak-minded, emotionally unstable, or weak in some other way, although in college I met a lot of very intelligent people who also had those vices, but seemed unaffected by them. I knew a medical student who was tops in his class and a heroin addict, but he had it under control, or so it was perceived.

Certainly with substance abuse, I thought they were weak and didn't have any self-control, and when you start associating addictions with behaviors, the same thing would apply. I certainly thought anybody with reasonable intelligence ought to be able to deal with it.

Just down and out, desperate, depressed. Desperate seems to be the key word.

The indictment of weakness is most prevalent here. Just as with the "out-of-control" responses, these comments indicate a lack of knowledge about the existence of universal laws that govern our experience. For instance, in our numbering system two plus three equals five. No one would be considered weak for not "making" two plus three equal seventeen. Laws are laws, and they have predictable results. What we consider weakness is actually a misdirection of energy. We are using the unique fundamental power inherent in us to energize the belief we are inadequate, hateful beings, separate from our good and from each other. What's more, we don't consider this a belief, but the truth. Until we are willing to examine such "truths" and question them, our packages of beliefs, feelings, thoughts, and behaviors will remain intact and be painful, not because of weakness but because of our own great power, misdirected.

As a young child, I feared being the derelict in the alley. Oddly enough, this wasn't a judgment, but a feeling of compassion and empathy for "those people," because I believed life had dealt them a bad hand; they were not in control, merely a product of circumstances. I saw them as victims of something outside themselves. On the other hand, I had an extremely wealthy aunt who had everything material life could give. She developed severe medical problems and became addicted to prescription drugs. I placed her in a different category and indeed judged her, thinking she should know better. She got the better hand and was abusing it, whereas others were simply dealt a bad hand.

If I knew someone was addicted to alcohol, I thought I needed to be more cautious around him because he could be harmful, go off on a temper tantrum, or hit you, or do something irrational. In movies you see that, also. As I got older, I learned my uncle was an alcoholic and, therefore, saw that my judgment wasn't always right, but at the same time, I was more leery of someone I knew was an alcoholic.

These responses address our incorrect belief in the random nature of life, where some are victimized despite their best efforts. Nothing is random, and the presence of danger or chaos in your environment reflects a self-destructive and confused state of mind, not a disorderly universe. Notice any upset that wells up within you on reading that statement. If you have a response, you are right where you need to be.

I knew everyone was involved with addictions, because my mother was. She took a lot of tranquilizers when I was growing up; later, I smoked pot in college, a lot of it. I was never around anybody addicted to stronger drugs such as cocaine or heroin, although I certainly knew there were people like that around, and I did judge them negatively, not really seeing that I, too, was addicted.

Since I was involved with addictions, those people were a lot like me. They were okay, a little crazy, a little off the wall. In fact, at that time, my perspective was that they probably had their act together.

These last comments indicate some small awareness, unrecognized by most, that addictions are omnipresent. Our refusal to acknowledge their presence does not alter this fact. We all experience pain and try to do something about it the best way we can. This book's purpose is to clarify the only process that will work permanently to bring us safety and contentment, which is to remove the internal source of pain.

Step 2:
List your own biases toward addicts and notice the nature of your judgments. Whether you label yourself or someone close to you addicted or not, be as honest as possible, because discovering and owning those long-stored opinions is a requirement for healing. If you are not experiencing contentment and certainty, be assured that judgments are alive and well, so now is a great time to acknowledge them. Having judgments does not make you bad or wrong; they do, however, make you confused and frightened. So remember, you are not asked to do anything about them at this point, other than to become aware of and acknowledge them. Don't try to justify them. This is the first step in relinquishing them.

3. When and how did you find that the traditional short list of addictions might be expanded to include almost anything—substance, activity, condition, or person?

After finishing college, working, rising up the corporate ladder, what really jolted me was attending a lecture where a doctor spoke about the way people function in the world and how they're not really "there," just going through the motions, seemingly successful on the outside but, on the inside, feeling very needy and lacking. Then he talked about black/white relationships and how it was the same coin with a different face, calling it the "human condition." He said all humans were suffering from the same thing, a spiritual lack, and were hiding behind all sorts of things, drugs, relationships, or whatever. That's when I first became aware of this concept of addictions beyond substances.

For me, that's been pretty recent, within the last four years. All of a sudden, I realized everything we do that we think isn't an addiction, usually is. We're very good at couching it in other terms. Now, all the behavior we use to distract ourselves, whether it's cleaning or shopping or anything else, to me is an addiction. If you keep busy, you don't have to look at any of your issues or at what's bothering you.

Two years ago, I attended a meditation class where the instructor talked about being addicted to things like work and TV, and I was stunned! My head was reeling because it had never crossed my mind those could be addictions. I didn't really understand the addictive nature until recently. Now I've realized the entire scope of sex could be addictive in different ways, and what first came to my attention was the need for variety among sexual partners, as opposed to a monogamous arrangement.

Not long ago, I broadened the list of addictions when Carol mentioned a whole string of potential addictions, ranging from relationship fantasies to golf or tennis or philanthropy. Wow! Having those words all hooked together was really revealing to me, knocking away the final idea I carried about addictions being separate from or unrelated to me. When I was going through my undoing process, attending workshops and classes and healing my own hurt, I realized it didn't matter how the addiction showed up. Whether it seemed, from the world's view, to be a good one or a bad one, it was still a distraction, a hiding out from looking at my own stuff.

After attending a training in 1988, I realized that anything in my life I used to deny my feelings or to avoid looking at myself could go on the addiction list. It became clear that addictions were like a ball, with the chemical addictions on the outside. As I moved toward the center, toward God, I recognized other things between God and me, layers and layers of denial, just like going to the core of the earth.

My ex and I spent over 50 percent of our marriage in individual and marriage counseling. Somewhere along the line, one of our counselors suggested I attend an Adult Children of Alcoholics meeting. When I did get involved, it was quite a surprise to realize my father was an alcoholic, having always thought of him as a nasty bastard who drank. Also through ACOA, I was introduced to the broader, more clinical definitions of alcoholism and addiction and found there was a whole universe of addictions, a vast realm of behaviors that could be and were addictive.

The above six responses represent those of us who are shocked or surprised upon discovering the possibility that virtually any aspect of our lives can be used to preoccupy ourselves, and who then have a sudden insight or new perspective about the addictive process. It's as if someone turned a bright light into their eyes, which could never again go unnoticed. We might ask, "Why didn't they have that insight before, if it's so obvious?" The ability to comprehend the obvious comes *when we want to see it!* That ability is activated in every one of us *when we choose it.* They did not suddenly become smarter; they became more honest in their questioning. It cannot be too strongly emphasized that our choice to deny our condition and how we regard ourselves makes it impossible for us to accurately assess our situation. As the saying goes, "You can't see the picture until you step out of the frame." Such is the power of our own minds.

I don't know exactly when I began to realize it, but I felt addictions were a form of escape, a substitution, to avoid honestly looking at what's behind them. It seemed necessary to be doing almost anything rather than just being. From being involved with A Course in Miracles *and other spiritual studies, I've realized that almost everything we find desirable or busy ourselves with, is really breaking the First Commandment, putting strange gods before God and putting our trust in something else to bring us peace and happiness.*

I had been in sobriety in Alcoholics Anonymous for perhaps three years before I grew into an awareness of how vast this area of addiction was. Interestingly enough, with each passing year, I see more and more things that can be addictive. The mind roves until it finds something it believes will make it feel good or more fulfilled, and it uses that as an addiction or a "worshipping of other gods. After thousands of meetings listening to people, it's my belief we are all at least dually addicted, and maybe have three or four addictions, and it's the last one that's hard. It seems there's a ladder or hierarchy, and it's important to find the primary addiction, because that's often disguised.

After getting divorced, I was raising my children and working in the hospital, and I started to get an inkling that people had certain behaviors or needs they never let go of, like being addicted to a certain kind of man, but that's about as far as it went. I could see patterns where we seemed to be stuck, calling it a rut or groove or a lesson we needed to learn that was repeated over and over and over again.

I can't pinpoint an actual age. My realization was gradual, but I started to become more aware upon noticing, for example, that even I always had to be so busy with swimming and field hockey and basketball. I always had to be busy!

Once I got involved with AA, my understanding of and perspective on addictions expanded considerably, and I recognized more and more addictive patterns and behaviors. This showed up most clearly through the several hundred twelve-step programs for different types of behavior or substance abuse, although the real expansion of awareness came as I got more and more into spiritual development.

That became clear through studying A Course in Miracles. *Prior to that time, I never associated the idea of addictions with the many, many things we're actually addicted to. Now I know that anything and everything can be a hiding place.*

When I was in my twenties, studying psychology in school, I realized almost anything could be a hiding place, and looked into it a little more then, because of my own addictions.

It came in small awarenesses, starting with my little list. I would notice other people, of course, and go, "Gee, I think they have an addiction problem with sugar." The list of addictions broadened slowly, but I remember the day so clearly, five or six years ago, when I actually got the universality of the problem at an ACIM meeting. They talked about how it was all the same problem that merely changed forms. I had fretted my whole life trying to pick between different forms of the same issue! It was this huge eye-opener, realizing the real problem was an addiction to a negative image of one's self, which we try to cover up with all these different things. Even before that realization, my categories of addictions had grown larger, starting with a few things like sugar and sex and expanding to a really, really long list, which I still, however, associated more with other people.

I would say it started to dawn on me less than five years ago when TV, particularly the news programs, began to explore the question of codependence in relationships as that idea started

*to become popular. I knew the list could expand when I started
to see the patterns.*

Awareness about addictions and distractions and their
purposes grows as we indicate, internally, our small willingness for a larger and more comprehensive perspective on our
lives, who we are, and our place in the world. In the beginning,
most of us don't really want answers but "magic bullets," to
make our pain go away. Anything that promises relief without
having to relinquish our treasured notions is greatly sought
after. Endless techniques and strategies are prescribed for
feeling great, or at least better, and we rush eagerly from one
to the next. We want the outer circumstances and our feelings
to be different without any substantive change on the inside.
To believe we can hang on to resentments, hatreds, and self-
doubts, the real engine that drives addictions, *and* live a great
life, is absurd.

Insights about addictions and the desperation that fuels
them come in accordance with our desire to see and interpret
things differently. They come through contemplating the
specific connection between how we think and what happens
in our lives, leading us eventually to adopt the viewpoint that
we are all precious beings, asking for help and reassurance,
rather than lesser ones deserving condemnation.

*The list of potential addictions expanded when I chose to exper-
iment myself, usually with hash or marijuana, and if I felt I
didn't have control with one experiment, I stopped. Early on I
left home, not having a clue as to what I was and scared to
death of the world. I recognized it was very easy to plug into
anything outside myself to try to get joy and happiness, through
marriages or dysfunctional relationships, anything that served
the ego or the body. I was always searching. Always, there was
the feeling something was missing in me.*

*The list expanded when I started experimenting with drugs,
partying, seeing other life-styles, thinking, Well, I'm not so
strange, you know; I'm not addicted. I realized that not only*

drugs or alcohol but anything could take my mind off my every-day life and whatever was bothering me at the time. I could stay busy twenty-four hours a day with many things, which could be an addiction. It's not that my problems were so big, it was more that life seemed mundane and I wanted to spice it up and make it exciting.

It became clear many things could become addictions when I realized my experience was my choice. Not only mood-altering substances, but anything could keep me unaware of Love's presence. Doing the lessons in A Course in Miracles *has been one of the greatest things to help me see that. I would go through the day with my lesson, meditating on it because it was signif-icant and spoke to me, and then at some point think, What is my lesson today? not remembering what it was. What interfered with my clarity of thinking? It used to be a drug. That was easy. Then it was business. Also easy. I used to think I had a memory problem. Now I realize it's just my choice not to remember. Anything that interferes with my clarity is an addiction.*

Acknowledging an addiction to alcohol led to an understanding that one could have multiple addictions, but I thought they were an outside force—work, sex, drugs, racing, or golf—to which one became addicted, either from hiding pain or a desire to create pleasure. I still viewed it as if the substance or activity "got you," and only recently have I come to an insightful understanding that it comes from inside. I remember concluding, erroneously, as I considered an item like cocaine, "You have no control over whether you want to be addicted to that or not. It has a power greater than yours." That was during my drinking years when I looked down on anybody who used cocaine. I thought alcohol was okay, because you could decide to quit drinking alcohol, but you couldn't make that decision with heroin or cocaine or some other illegal substance.

I could see people had what I called obsessions, like an obses-sion with fishing or skiing. I only started to perceive it that way or make those deductions recently, but I could tell when someone was obsessed with something, letting go of other things in their life, becoming a one-faceted person, with nothing more to them than that.

I don't know if this is part of addiction or obsession, but I knew I was superstitious and thought I had to do things a certain way or bad things would happen. I had to read my lesson everyday or something would happen. My knife always had to be in my left pocket and my keys in my right. In the military, when you go TDY (temporary duty) it's like taking a break from your regular duties; people used it for escape. A guy told me after he retired, "You never monkey around unless you're so many hours of air time from home." In the military a lot of men were involved with sexual misconduct or drinking heavily, all the stories you see in the paper now.

These comments about the choice to experiment and to quit various habits when we choose, or the seeming lack of choice that often appears as an obsession or lack of control, indicate the vast confusion that persists about "who has control over what," in terms of addictions. Regardless of what it seems, we always are in charge of our experience and can change our minds whenever we choose. Usually, we simply do not choose to change our minds because we don't yet see the relevance of doing so. To begin to see things differently, allow this to sink in. Every belief we energize with our attention springs forth as our external experience and internal feeling state. There is never a time or place when this process of translating thought into our worldly experience does not take place. It never goes on vacation, takes a day off, or stops operating. Out of enlightened self-interest, we must become aware of the universal laws by which we live. These laws are all encompassing and not of our making. For instance, we did not make the laws of gravity or of mathematics, but we certainly have discovered how they operate. A law might be stated as, "What you offer, you experience." If you offer anger, that is what you will experience; if you offer understanding, you will experience that, and if you offer awareness of another person's value, you too will feel valuable and deserving. And, when we feel worthwhile and necessary, our addictive behaviors cease.

I have had a pretty good sense of how many activities can be classified as addictions for a long time. When you see persons overwhelmed by golf, by affairs, by activities that keep them from focusing on the present now of their reality, that's addictive behavior.

And, finally, some have noted for a very long time that all of us are hiding out or running from something.

Step 3:
Our early steps in healing require that we fully notice how much we are driven and prepare to find out why. Our goal now is to facilitate recognition. Take some time to notice how you or those around you seem driven or haunted by something. Or perhaps they seem to be running after something. Notice the things you do, the places you go, the people whose company you keep, or the substances you ingest when you are less than comfortable and happy. Notice that virtually anything can be your hiding place. In fact, the entire world and all its activities can be a hiding place, if we so choose! Remember, no justifying or excuses, simply observations.

As the first part of an exercise, to be continued in a later question, close your eyes and recognize how long you have been running. Imagine yourself running through a forest, running into things, tripping over logs, and yet frantically running. You can almost feel the hot breath of "something" on the back of your neck. This "something" might occur to you as a fear, an idea, a thought, a person, or all of the above. At this point, simply notice what it is and write it down. Contrary to what you might have believed, there is nothing to fear in acknowledging its presence.

4. When or how (or both) did it dawn on you that you were included in the "army of the addicted," so to speak, and what was your response to that recognition?

The moment of truth came on March 26, 1983, at an EST seminar. That was my "Saul on the road to Damascus" experience, definitely a U-turn on the expressway of life. I discovered that no matter how hard one pitches an image, as I had done, people never hear the pitch, they always see the real you. And when you deny them the real you, that turns them off. The sincere essence of what we are is very attractive, and trying to paint it up to make it more attractive is like turning a fresh young neighborhood child into a hardened street whore.

We all have a tremendous attachment to our stories, and I wanted to be more worthy than anyone else because I believed my circumstances justified that conclusion. I had a successful marriage, a successful business, a new car, good sunglasses, clothes that fit, no weight problem, no drinking problem, sex problem, drug problem, money problem, no connection problem, or lack of pedigree problem—all to confirm I was less flawed than others. I denied I was addicted, believing I did things I liked but not to the degree of addiction. To me, addiction was a matter of degree.

Wow! I remember the day! I was nineteen years old, smoking pot, and I actually remember where I was and the thought process that went through my mind. I said to myself, If I don't stop smoking this pot now, this is going to go on for a long time, and I'm not going to be able to get back to where I was without a lot of trouble! With that, I lit up a big, fat joint, and continued smoking for almost twenty years.

I was in total denial about being addicted to pot, although deep down inside I knew I was using it to self-medicate and to keep away from I didn't know what. In 1992, I figured out the "what"—that negative self-image mirrored to me in my childhood—and it took me maybe three years to actually face that.

My awareness came through issues about food and overeating, which I fought against for many years and conquered many times, yet it continued to be a problem. I could hear myself say, Well, those other people have addictions, but my habits don't really qualify. Some denial there!

I owned my addiction when everything seemed not to work. All the props started falling, and I started having to look inward because I couldn't look anywhere else. My technique had been to look for candidates to be fixed or victims who needed my help, as a great diversion from working on myself. I tried to believe my own disguises, comparing myself with others and telling myself, They're addicted, I'm not. My habits are different and qualify under a different label. Obviously, I didn't want to accept that I could be addicted. I justified my behaviors as traits necessary to accommodate everybody, to operate in everybody's different arenas. I saw some behaviors as virtuous or responsible and didn't categorize them as addictions. For instance, drinking cocktails at business meetings or playing golf were necessary to get your job done.

Those occurrences of recognition were like light bulbs going off: "Oh, that's me. This is an addiction!" My response was mixed. On one hand, I felt liberated, but then in all honesty, denial would rise up within me, and I believed I wasn't in the category of desperate people. I went through a phase of thinking, All right, I don't need to do this anymore. But my ego would twist things, telling me, "Oh, no, you're not addicted." This was an intense period of major denial, the key word!

As my circle or list of possible addictions grew, I got more nervous and defensive because I was approaching the circle line! At first, when I presumed the activity was the issue, I thought the problem was smoking. However, as I stopped that, I noticed a craving or a requirement for another little thing popped up. I quit that and went to eating and, from eating, to Coca-Colas. Then, thinking the root problem was drinking Coca-Cola, I kept trying to fix that behavior, believing I was doing good because I went from cigarettes to Coca-Cola to ginger ale and then on to orange juice. I went through the process of changing the form of the addiction, but seeing it in any larger frame was harder and it depended on my mood. Sometimes I would think, Okay, I've got this small, little teeny problem, and if I can just fix the form, all will be well. And then, sometimes, I would get defensive and think, What's wrong with having this little teeny problem. It's only orange juice, for God's sake! It could be worse! Look at all the other people—they've got some serious mess going down! I did that for a while, but the day I realized what the problem actually was and that fixing the form wasn't it, I felt very free. It was a breakthrough to realize I didn't have to do that anymore.

Here we have the most common response of all when confronted with the obvious—denial! We cling to the notion that refusing to acknowledge our addictions is the safest position and that looking everywhere but directly at them will stave off disaster for a while longer. We further compound the situation by completely forgetting we made the choice to deny. "There is none so blind as he who will not see." Notice that if we were not terrified of the consequences of acknowledging our addictive patterns and the self-doubt that feeds them, we would face them much more casually and honestly. Although this may sound extreme, I have found that most people in this world would rather, quite literally, die than look squarely at what they now deny. And what terrifies us? That if we look inward, if we acknowledge our fear and belief in our unworthiness and feel the pain that belief engenders, it will be cast in concrete and remain forever. We completely overlook the fact that our refusal to look inward has cast our pain into concrete. Our avoidance and refusing to look has made our pain all encompassing because of another universal law: what we give attention to, increases. We give tremendous attention to whatever we avoid or resist. Our avoidance of a problem twenty-fours a day means we are focusing on it twenty-four hours a day. Therein lies the problem. Avoiding pain is a request for more pain, and the universe always says yes to any request we make. To resist anything is to throw gasoline on the fire. Simply put, we possess inconceivable power, although we are almost entirely blind to it, and focusing our attention, whether through loving or hating, is how we request and direct that power.

The doctor presenting the lecture (referred to in an earlier response) looked at me and, out of the blue, in front of the group, said, "Young man, you need to go on a sex fast. You're unstable and have a lot of things screwed up about you." I exclaimed, "What?" because I thought I was the cat's meow. I was offended at first, but I realized I was unhappy even though, on the outside I seemed very successful. Because what he said was ringing true, I made an appointment to see him later privately, since he obviously saw something I didn't. At that appointment, he talked with me to find out what was wrong with my life, my emotional state, my spiritual state, and he tried to get me to see that bodies reflect what goes on in our minds. He explained the body as a vehicle that is healed only because he works with the mind simultaneously. This was all new to me, as I had been raised in a very religious, strict, and puritanical manner, never making a connection between body and mind and believing they were totally separate things. This was a shocking conversation, extremely radical, since I was still rather arrogant, thinking somebody else had a problem, not me.

When the instructor in a meditation class started talking about work addictions and TV addictions, it hit me really hard. Physically, my head jerked back, as if I'd been hit from behind, and as he kept listing different things, I kept thinking, Oh, my! Oh me! I'd better become mindful of what I'm doing and what I'm choosing, and look at it to see if I can free myself. It was shocking!

I realized I was among the "army of the addicted" by the time I was in high school, perhaps my junior year, because at that point, I didn't have one half-hour to stay home and just sit. I complained about being really busy, but at the same time, when it was Sunday and I had nothing to do, I would go, "I've got to do something!" I was mad at myself for thinking I needed something to keep me going, but then I would tell myself, Oh, Megan, you just like to do sports a lot.

It came to me as one of those synchronicities when I attended a training that I thought was about women's issues, but ended up being about addictions and what we keep between ourselves and God. I realized I was numbing out, feeling neither good or bad, and restricting my emotional palate, so to speak. It pissed me off, basically, to realize I was addicted, and I internalized it, beating up on myself with, "Oh, well, look what I'm doing, I'm no good, I'm not doing it right." I was still totally unaware that everyone is addicted, believing I was unique in being the worst thing in the world, and self-abuse became an additional addiction.

There was a period when I felt a lot of guilt and shame upon recognizing my addiction, which at that time was primarily an alcohol problem. When I started dealing with it and becoming aware of other previous addictions, those guilt-ridden feelings left. I realized I had lots of company and that it was not strictly a control or willpower issue but, absolutely, a place to hide from yourself.

I probably didn't recognize my addiction until we started having marriage problems. I had been hiding all these years, as if I were two people. In high school a friend once said, "My mother says it would be okay to hang around with you, but she doesn't know you like I do." Way back when we were fifteen, he identified me as two different people, and that memory has remained my whole life. I had been in Vietnam five months when I was shot down. As I was hanging in that parachute, fearing I was being struck down because of the life I'd been leading, I thought, If I ever get out of here, I'll never live my secret double life again. But when I came home, it wasn't a year before I was right back in (the addictive pattern) worse than before; that should have been my key there was an addiction. I went to college with all the divorced women in the world and I hit on every woman I

4. When or how did you know you were addicted?   137

saw—ugly, pretty, anything. My sexual craving snowballed and got really bad. I never had the urge to leave my family and go with someone else in a committed relationship, so I had to realize it was an addiction. When I got serious about this, after some counseling in the eighties, I read some books on sexual addiction and was scared, because I realized men addicted to sex continued to crave it, and it got worse; it just magnified. I said, "Whoa! I'm not going to do that" because it builds, there is the constant need for more. I was living in shame inside, thinking I was really a bad person, not wanting anyone to know about this. I was particularly embarrassed because, on returning home, I was often invited to speak as a war hero, and those invitations went on for twenty years. Finally, several years ago I gave up speaking, not wanting to go in front of groups anymore and have them all praise me, thinking I was some kind of god. I knew that wasn't true, so I stopped the deception.

Being fed up with my lifestyle, I went to a Course in Miracles class and looked into spirituality and AA more seriously. Even though it was not with alcohol, I knew I had an addiction to fitness, health, and the way I looked. It was a negative, fearful feeling to acknowledge it, and my response was, "What's the solution? I'm admitting the addiction to myself, I don't like this, and I don't like me. Now, something needs to change here!"

Real early, somewhere inside, I knew there was a problem. I didn't realize the actual depth of that problem until I went to an AA rehab program, which my wife and I were required to attend because they were treating our son. I was "forced" into that situation because they told me they wouldn't treat him unless I came, as they rightly considered addiction a family problem, a family disease. They presented the disease aspect, which I did not initially accept, and indicated I would have to go through this ritual in order to have my son treated. I was willing to do that because I thought he needed attention, but I didn't. They requested we not drink or otherwise anesthetize ourselves for the duration of the class. I became aware that I had some affinity with what the instructors were saying. One drew a "ladder

of addiction" on the chalkboard, starting out with social drinking and going into blackouts, automobile wrecks, job losses, and
relationship problems. When I saw that ladder laid out, which
I was forced to sit and look at, and saw that I kept going up the
ladder until I was at the top, I said to myself, My God, I fit this
profile! That's when the light started to dawn. Initially, there
was only a partial admission. It was frightening because I had
seen where addiction carried people, my own father and uncles
and great uncles. I wondered if I was going to wind up the
same? There was no clear answer until I went into AA, where
they told me, with some authority, that that was not going to
happen to me providing I followed the rules. Then I was able to
freely and openly admit it.

No matter how I did whatever I thought was a good thing, it
always ended up that things never changed. I realized I was
addicted to approval, control, and being right when doing
something over and over didn't fix whatever I wanted fixed. Oh,
I didn't like this at all! I liked thinking of myself as different from
them (the addicted), but then I saw myself as the same, all of
us in this big pot.

I don't think there was any one situation that clarified my addiction to pleasing people, rather a gradual realization from
reading, attending classes, discussing with my wife, hearing
what other people had to say, and inward contemplation.
Realizing I was addicted to having to be the caretaker was not
a happy moment, and in the beginning, I fought that realization,
because I had always looked upon addictions as weaknesses.
It was disturbing because it seemed all the choices I had made
were disqualifications that invalidated me, rather than qualifi-
cations. I was addicted to patterns of behavior, rather than
being real, which was an upsetting, but necessary, revelation.

These responses of shock, anger, shame, and fear demonstrate
our tremendous and almost universal judgment on others and
ourselves for our perceived shortcomings. It is wrenching, at
best, to be backed into a corner, where we have to set aside

our fantasies, our carefully structured images, and look squarely at the obvious—the circumstances in which we find ourselves. As we progress through our questions, we see clearly how self-destructive and all-pervasive are our perceptions about addictions.

Many people in various groups I attended would talk about their personal history, what they had done, what life was like for them, and I was always very taken by the fact that the descriptions of their routes were similar to one another, but very few resembled mine. I eventually came to realize I had brought myself to exactly the same place as the rest, although I never saw myself as addicted or dealing with addictions, because I didn't use drugs or alcohol. Nevertheless, I knew that whatever I had or hadn't done with substances, the issues of those who had were my issues, their struggle was my struggle, and our insecurities and problems were the same. Initially, the discovery was disorienting but then freeing, because I felt much less isolated and could see there was some way out, a real sense of the possibility of becoming whole.

I went to a Zen community around 1978 because I wanted off the wheel. I realized I kept choosing the same man over and over—a different face, but the same person. I recognized I kept repeating the same patterns, always attracting either very deeply spiritual men or those with great potential for violence, and that was it. I didn't understand what I was trying to work out or work through, only that I kept getting into the same situations and was caught in something, not knowing how to escape. I saw the effect but not the cause.

I probably recognized my addiction when I was a teenager, but I didn't know the ramifications and broad spectrum of addictions. My viewpoint was myopic and focused on chemicals; I recognized I enjoyed the stuff, whether it was marijuana or black beauty. Not too much on the alcohol, however, because Mom was such a great example of what I didn't want to be like. I definitely never thought, of course, that my situation was very much like hers and her alcohol. However, what immediately occurred to me was that I had a choice about not doing this, and I needed to make one. Recognizing my ability to choose at a very young age, and realizing I had better be choosing differently, was very profound.

I realized the addiction early on and accepted it, although I didn't like the first principle of A Course in Miracles *that states, "There is no order of difficulty in miracles." I really believed there was no order of difficulty in miracles, except for quitting smoking.*

I saw we all are addicted to something, all of humankind, every-body. My response, four or five years ago, was, "Yeah, so? That's what the ego does."

This group's responses range from disorientation and lack of understanding to a keen awareness that addictions are universal. It is noteworthy that we have such a broad range of reactions to the same stimuli or awareness. The variety of responses certainly makes it clear that it is not any given situation itself, but our interpretation of it that determines our experience.

The realization I was addicted to "staying in my head" came much later than my recognition of an alcohol dependency, and I'm still dealing with being too analytical. My response to that realization is mixed. I've invested a lot of time trying to under-stand everything intellectually, but there's always that little bit of intuitive feeling that it really doesn't have anything to do with how smart you are. It's about something else. The process of discovery I've been in the last couple of years is about the "something else."

I'm still processing anger about the institutions that told me staying in my head and being smart was the way to be. Blaming isn't going to get me anywhere because the anger needs to be dealt with, turned over, released. That's been easier to deal with in the last year or two simply because of the infor-

mation made available in A Course in Miracles, *and from seeing people with an addiction or disability who have said, "I gave all that up and my life's gotten better." From time to time, I still wrestle with my ego telling me it'll work for them, but not for me. The whole notion of, "But you don't understand" is just an ego defense.*

I thought of my anger as an addiction because it was very much like a hallucinogenic drug or heroin that put you in a different state of mind. I remember feeling the adrenaline rush and thinking, Wow, this is really powerful! I can draw on this to make me different, and stronger! That was the first addiction I was aware of and I thought it served my purpose, keeping me a safe distance from people I shouldn't be with.

My first reaction, on recognizing the addiction, was that it didn't bother me in the least, as I thought anger was actually a good defense and a very powerful ally. I looked at relationships I'd broken up with it and thought, Well, that was good, because I really didn't want that anyway. I never considered whether I could turn it on or off because I liked turning it on.

Actually, it was never such a news brief, as I've always known I had addictive patterns. I started waking up after my horse fell on me and broke my neck; the accident shocked me into doing something about it. I felt relief that something could be done. For a long time, I'd been aware my mother may have been addicted to cigarettes and alcohol, and my father was addicted to work. In watching them, I recognized my pattern, although it manifested in a different way—being addicted to certain foods and hiding myself in my work.

I was going through a very difficult divorce and, being somewhat comatose, was not available to have a meaningful relationship. I was seeing an ex-boyfriend who watched my struggle and tried to be helpful in whatever way he could. Although he wanted more of a relationship than I could give, for several months he hung in there with me like a security blanket distraction, and we usually went out every Friday night.

Eventually, he met someone he found attractive and left. I vividly remember sitting on my porch the first night he stood me up for this new woman. I called a young widow, whom I barely knew, who had found someone to date through a singles group, essentially to see where I could find somebody. It was no different from being a drug addict—when one supplier is cut off, call another. She didn't have much information to offer and that was perfect, because as I hung up, I realized I was addicted. At that point, there was no more distraction, and I was there with those feelings. I probably saw thirteen movies that weekend, since going to movies was my "innocent" addiction; I had come face to face with my distress and was distracting myself yet again. Finally realizing my addiction probably had a little more impact, but it wasn't huge and hard to deal with.

About two years ago, after captaining a tennis team for a number of years, I quit playing. I went to bed one night liking tennis, and the next morning I heard myself say, You know, you don't have to do this anymore unless you really get a lot from it and want to do it for the pure joy of it. I didn't get a lot of joy from it, having used it as a marvelous distraction for a long time. I had been unhappy with it for a couple of years but hadn't really connected it with all the other changes going on.

Recognizing my addiction to sports was enlightening, with no judgment attached to it, only awareness I was right there with everybody else. Of course, we all find it easy to see addictions in others, never wanting to claim our own. With a sport, it may be more difficult to recognize because it doesn't have that addiction label attached to it. After all, we're so health conscious and are supposed to exercise because it's good for you; people never associate it with an addiction. And yet it can be. I thought its purpose was to keep me distracted, and it did that very well.

This group's responses were more positive. They interpreted their discovery about being addicted as being in their best interests, enlightening, easy, or a relief. Once again, perspective is everything. All our participants made the same discovery: They were addicted. Notice the wide range of experience related to that recognition. We all view our circumstances through our own particular filters, our own unique and distorted ways of interpreting the meaning of any given event or statement. And those filters determine our experience. Events are neutral but overladen with the meanings we give to them. The discovery about addiction is wrenching if we decide it means we are sinful or doomed forever. That same discovery can be liberating when we recognize we have made a mistake that calls for correction. The secret is now out in the open, and the next step can be taken.

Our final interviewee's response to question 4 is quoted below in greater detail because it so eloquently summarizes the journey we all go through in our self-discovery and the growth and grace that come from looking addictions squarely in the eye and moving forward.

Realization of addiction came in little waves, beginning with, "Well, yes, I am addicted to the drugs I'm taking, yet it's okay because it's socially acceptable." I could rationalize I was doing very high-class drugs with the highest quality people. Sometimes I would do it with the lowest quality as well, but I would forget about that. Then I moved on to recognizing I wanted to get high immediately and contemplating where to make my connection. Originally, I thought that if I didn't purchase the drugs and was very particular about the kinds I used, then I was free of any responsibility, in terms of becoming addicted. Another story I made up was that snorting cocaine would be okay, but injecting it would make me addicted. I rationalized marijuana or hashish was not really addictive because it had not been proven to be. In fact, many studies show it's technically not physically addictive, but of course, it's hugely mentally addictive. I continued making up stories about not being addicted because this particular marijuana was okay, and of course, alcohol, which is definitely a mainstream drug, was legal. Once I took my first two beers of the evening, then my first two joints of marijuana, I wanted to snort cocaine. Then I would look around for something else, such as 200 proof moonshine, because one thing wasn't going to be enough. It had to be a combination.

The moment the drugs were purchased, I would use what I had immediately, with no delay. It wasn't a matter of taking them home and using them when the time was right. "When will I run out?" and "Will it be as good as this?" became major issues. I rationed it out, almost to the point of not sharing with friends because I would be out tomorrow and then what would that be like? It would be hell, and I couldn't live! I recognized I was addicted but, of course, excused it with, "Oh well, what the hell, the world sucks anyway, so at least there's some enjoyment from the drugs. Besides, everyone else is addicted, and it's worth it because I'm going to die anyway, probably tomorrow, in a car accident." It became so very interesting, in terms of gradually recognizing my addictions, to see how I rationalized that it was still okay.

I knew I was addicted as I looked in my garage wondering what I could sell to get some ready cash without having it go through the normal channel of my bank account. I had already used every excuse about spending my money, wasting all I could come up with. We built a new house, so there were many things needed for it, many of which didn't get purchased with that money. Instead, drugs got purchased. I experienced a euphoria and comfort and safety, which didn't last. The minute I got to the downside, the withdrawal—not big ones like with heroin but nonetheless huge mental withdrawals—I was unhappy and aware the world didn't offer what I thought it should have, justifying my position with, Well, I might as well use because I'm going to get nailed anyway. I kept thinking the newest drug would surely not have any side effects and would deliver everything I wanted and make me happy, joyous, and free. Yet it never did. I got to such an extreme place of finding no place of comfort or happiness in this world, not through business or relationships, power or money, or alcohol or drugs. There just wasn't such a place, which brought me to the point of thinking, Well, do I kill myself now, or do I just do it on the installment plan with the drugs? Coming to that awareness and having to make that choice brought me to my greatest hour.

The following passage from A Course in Miracles *talks about the real alternative and states:*

"There is no choice where every end is sure. Perhaps you would prefer to try them all, before you really learn they are but one. The roads this world can offer seem to be quite large in number, but the time must come when everyone begins to see how like they are to one another. Men have died on seeing this, because they saw no way except the pathways offered by the world. And learning they led nowhere, lost their hope. And yet this was the time when they could have learned their greatest lesson. All must reach this point, and go beyond it. It is true indeed there is no choice at all within the world. But this is not the lesson in itself. The lesson has a purpose, and in this you come to understand what it is for.

Why would you seek to try another road, another person or [another drug] or another place, when you have learned the way the lesson starts, but do not yet perceive what it is for? It's purpose is the answer to the search that all must undertake who still believe there is another answer to be found. Learn now, without despair, there is no hope of answer in the world. But do not judge the lesson that is but begun with this. Seek not another signpost in the world that seems to point to still another road. No longer look for hope where there is none. Make fast your learning now, and understand you but waste time unless you go beyond what you have learned to what is yet to learn. For from this lowest point will learning lead to heights of happiness, in which you see the purpose of the lesson shining clear, and perfectly within your learning grasp" (*A Course in Miracles* text, page 608).

This speaks of the bottom, the bottom of addiction. I tried every road, every pathway in this world, including drugs and everything that goes with, and it led nowhere. Now that I have come through the addiction, I recognize that Course *statement is exactly right. There was no hope. That was the time I learned my greatest lesson, and reaching that experience was pretty traumatic. It was akin to death, with my options getting down to," Do I want to die now or am I going to have to live?" There was no more denial, and I really came to grips with that. That's where the grateful blessing comes because, at that moment, I said, "thank you" to cocaine. And that was the experience. It happened May 24, 1994.*

And so it must be that all of us, sooner or later, acknowledge that something is not right about our lives, that truly we do not feel certain and safe, and we make our first requests for help in releasing our denial. It is important to recognize that acknowledging and owning anything we have hidden from others or ourselves brings relief and clarity. What we are hiding is not nearly so important as the process of hiding. Hiding, keeping secrets, or refusing to own up to where we are, keeps us hypervigilant, with a sense of threat looming over us. As we chronically look away from the inner landscape, in a frantic attempt to escape what we fear is there, we buy into our own programming that a real threat is present and our defenses necessary. Looking at our unloving behaviors and attitudes about ourselves, rather than hiding them, removes the emotional charge and allows us to take the next step in our inquiry.

Step 4:
Stay with us by asking yourself the specific question, "Can I see myself in any of these stories or can they help me see my own?" If you can and are willing, breathe deeply and continue with us on a path of freedom. The only truly safe direction is one of acknowledging we all are addicted, all in the same boat together, and honoring your own emotional response, whatever that may be. Never forget help is always present, no matter how bleak any situation seems to be.

~ ❦ ~

5. What was your major addiction and what was its appeal?

The _need to be right_ would be the major addiction with "right" meaning that if I could analyze enough ahead of time, I could fix whatever might be in the future. If I had a large enough data bank and could figure it all out, everything would be all right. It was very disappointing to spend all that time figuring things out, over and over again, and still have no peace. "Figuring out" was supposed to remove turmoil and bring about a state of peace.

It would have to be _working out, sports, athletics, and food_. They go together in a way because I had to eat every day, and if I wanted to maintain a slender build, I had to exercise, or so I always thought. It would be very fair to say my focus was on the entire spectrum of body-related activities, every day. As with any addiction, it kept my attention off those big questions: What shape is my life really in? Where am I going? What am I doing here? What am I really all about, and who cares about me? What do I care about? Am I important? Do I have value?

Until very recently, my major addiction was a _particular form of caretaking_. It's sobering, very tasking, and at the same time, liberating to look back at my life and history. My father always spoke about the high level of his technical accomplishment at work and the great regard he held for people whose work was meticulously laid out and looked good. Somewhere in there I decided that knowing how to do things well was the path for me, never realizing its function was to compensate for unworthiness. I accepted that ever-present, gnawing sense of "not good enough" as a given and went on from there. In retrospect, as far back as I can remember, my approach to interactions was, "What do you need fixed and what can I do for you?" From my early teens, I was always doing and building for my relatives. It was the medium of exchange, the arena I tried to stay in, because edginess and a persistent sense of lack of well-being would come upon me when I moved too far from that field of endeavor. I hadn't realized, until you asked this question, how clear and evident that path has been, how transparent. I could *give endless examples, finding the weight of the evidence daunting. It's not so much what I've done as why, that seems almost overwhelming, and to see exactly what I was about is humbling.*

Shopping was the addictive adaptation of my mother's values. She was the shopper, knowing the price of everything. I've said, facetiously, she would devote equal stomach lining to worrying about the end of life on the planet and to paying fifteen cents too much for frozen peas. I saw her holding that out as the way to be or as the "path to salvation," to security. That sharing of information about where to get the "best one at the best price" is an extension of building the "best one." It's that same process of, What product can I bring into your environment so I'll be okay. What can I do for you? I got to be good by "knowing where to get it wholesale."

The addiction of family relationships was absolutely more necessary than anything else. Only in the last year have I stopped using relationships to stay away from my pain. Addictions to my children and husband, my relationship addiction, kept me so frantically busy trying to be the perfect wife, mother, homemaker, business partner, and boss to the employees, I had no time to know I felt anything.

Actually I used tennis as a wonderful addiction to avoid looking at things, never associating the two until recently. I played women's competitive tennis at a high level, three to five times a week for twenty years. I became obsessed with tennis, which I saw as my salvation and release, because I thought if I played well, I could feel good about myself. It was my outlet, one of the few things I could do really well, even though I wasn't always very nice when I was doing it. It saved me from having to look at stuff or feel those feelings, although I didn't recognize that process of hiding at the time. That was a real revelation! By that evening or the next day, feeling good about myself could be gone. It was very short-lived and didn't really work—like taking a shot of cocaine, you feel great for a few hours, but then it's gone and, unfortunately, your issues are still there.

Oh, wow, there was definitely more than one addiction! There were food items in there, as well as addiction to <u>drama, crisis, sabotage and uproar</u>. If drama was not happening, I would create it. Without uproar, nothing was going on inside of me, more like nothingness. The drama and all the victimhood issues were very distracting, and without them, a feeling of being out of control started to enter in, a very disturbing, peculiar, nerve-wracking feeling, definitely to be avoided. The uproar masked those feelings and avoided the pain, because I sure wasn't going for pleasure. Now I realize the common purpose for every-thing was to avoid pain.

A common theme was my doing certain things to prevent people knowing I might not always be okay. I always thought a lot about "walk your talk." I didn't want to be a hypocrite, and I feared if I didn't portray the <u>image of being perfect and having it all together</u>, nobody would ever listen to me when I wanted to be helpful. I couldn't sit still with myself, always having to be doing something. Otherwise, I would feel lacking, incomplete, agitated, or that I wasn't fulfilling something and be very angry with myself about this. Without distractions, I would have to face those feelings.

I would say I've had a habit of being dissatisfied with what is, always looking for something better, looking for things outside myself to make me happy. I look at <u>work and the drive for finan-cial security</u> as addictive behavior patterns because although we are financially secure, my innate insecurity drives me as if we weren't. The level of discomfort I carry about lack of success or lack of business isn't rational, though it's very acute. The key issue in the striving for financial success and recognition is my sense of worth. Human beings seem to be attached to evaluat-ing performance in some way, and I have a fear of letting go of being a professional person, of how I will feel about myself when I'm not busy. It's almost as if I'm kidding people into believing I'm competent, rather than knowing I'm competent. That underlying insecurity haunts me. I do carry a sense I haven't yet fulfilled my highest potential or that an innate gift has not yet flowered, so to speak. I know my life's work is no longer about making money, so I am having an inner tug of war right now.

That fantasy of <u>romantic love</u>, having the soul mate or partner, riding off into the sunset with Prince Charming, was my addiction of choice, and it has prevailed throughout most of my life, from teenage years to recently. I was addicted to that <u>false special love</u> because if Prince Charming were with me, everything would be okay. With those fantasies always in my mind, I was not thinking about not being okay now.

I remember exactly, at thirteen or fourteen, when I started pining away for a man. A next-door neighbor and I seemed to like each other, but the day he gave me my first kiss, he left to go to military school—gone, out of the picture. As soon as I started to make a commitment to care about somebody or to be with him, he was gone. I kept that pattern intact for many years. It showed up as many long-distance relationships and involvement with men who were emotionally unavailable or they were married or still involved with an ex. On coming to the realization I was unavailable in my heart, instead of blaming those guys for being terrible, I had to face being the common denominator in all those relationships. I decided not to enter into another one—knowing exactly how it was going to end, with unhappiness and hell—and determined not to do that anymore. I had to change and heal my thought system, and then my relationships could reflect my current happier state of mind just as they had reflected my miserable state of mind. Now I know the longing for somebody was really a longing for my Self, from whom I was so distanced.

My major addiction was a <u>highly effusive sense of humor</u>, if not refined, at least energetic. Instead of being real, I would attempt to provide amusement for others, in the hopes it was attractive to be around people who were laughing and having fun. Its appeal was to make me feel attractive to other people. [Carol: May we presume a lingering suspicion of not being attractive otherwise?] *Right.*

<u>Food</u> *was one of them. I was preoccupied with what I ate. I went to Weight Watchers, learned a lot about foods, and lost a lot of weight, and that was great for a while. Several years ago, I did the same thing with a similar eating regimen. Not long ago, I recognized it was nervousness that made me want to put something in my mouth. Food's appeal was to focus my thinking on something else, away from feelings of discomfort that I didn't even realize I had.*

I always needed the <u>sexual and romantic love</u> thing and, for a long time, didn't see this as an addiction. I often spent long periods by myself, so my first reaction was, "No, this couldn't be an addiction because I haven't always had an on-going relationship." However, I came to realize I always had the fantasy of one. Several addictions were interchangeable, so when I wasn't in a romance, I could easily and successfully switch to food, putting more time into planning meals, cooking, or drinking. For a long time, I have to interject, writing and performing my music was my main crutch, providing a sense of safety, companionship, or being occupied and full and busy. Anger and defensiveness are no longer major addictions, although they certainly were in my early days. Another crutch or dependency was to exhibit flippancy, nervous laughter, or kidding around; sometimes, before going to a party, I would actually think about what I was going to say to be funny.

I spent a lot of time manipulating women to get their acceptance and make the scenario work the way I wanted, because the way they treated me represented either power or loss of power. When I could get them to do as I wanted, I was powerful, and when they got me to do what they wanted, I was powerless, resulting in a constant struggle.

<u>Victimization</u> *was the addiction, where I could hide out behind the screen of "all that's happening to me." It was also a convenient excuse when I failed, because I could say "Well, I'm a victim of this or that, and that's why I didn't do it properly or wasn't functioning effectively." Also, it was a red badge of courage during the time I was swashbuckling my way through*

corporate America, where being a victim opened some doors. We're talking back in the late seventies when this country was coming to grips with racism at the corporate level, and some people were feeling guilty. They were looking for qualified minorities and women who could fill certain positions, actually competing with one another in saying, "We're not a racist company. We have one of them!" If you could do the work, it was so much the better, and some people pushed me along because they honestly wanted me to succeed. Not having to look at myself was the overall appeal of this entire victimhood syndrome.

Through my addiction to <u>being in control and acquiring various credentials</u>, I thought I could determine what people got to see. Nobody really got to know me unless I decided, and only as far as I chose. I had no clue what would happen if someone were allowed to "discover" me, on their own. I simply recognized that common fear of "if you really knew me, you wouldn't like me, and I wouldn't be accepted.

I think I'm addicted to the <u>past</u>, such as habits of having a drink at 5:30 or a cigarette when I want to. It's almost as if stopping those things would be giving up something I really enjoyed in the past that were pleasurable and part of my identity. I don't feel like I'm really fearful of any inner self-discoveries. In fact, I'm really quite anxious to have them.

With my addiction, I avoided having to be with "just me." I'm certain that had to do with the way I saw myself as inadequate, a failure in many ways, coming face to face with all I'd tried to paint over or bury. I painted a picture of myself I liked to look at and show to the world, hiding feelings of insecurity, fear about the future, regrets of what might have been, questioning my decisions, or doubt.

Well, the appeal of <u>drugs</u> was pretty significant, offering a feeling of completeness, wholeness. It was the illusion of happiness but, nonetheless, a pretty darn good illusion. The drugs took my fears away and were very good at placating, eliminating, *or masking a feeling of being alone, unsafe, and unworthy. I used them to the fullest because I didn't feel whole, as if something were missing from me, inviting something fatal, such as lightning striking me down any minute or a slow, painful disease to deal with for the rest of my life. It was all fear, and when you take a powerful substance, relief is almost instantaneous. I would relax, thinking help was on the way.*

Also, when I was younger, drugs took away my fears about relationships with women. I could perform, being happy and funny, the life of the party, like everyone else, or so I thought. I had patterns, going to the same bars where everybody knew me. Some were aware of my problems with addictions, and others were not. I clearly remember, not too far from the end, when my loving wife said, "Do you think everybody in this bar is totally unaware of your condition?" And thinking they were, I said, "There are some people here who know and understand, but this whole crowd doesn't have a clue!" I thought I was invisible, doing an excellent job of hiding. I could consume a lot of substances and not show the effects, having social graces that allowed me to do that. Also, I traveled with crowds that permitted this indulgence and stayed hidden from people who would not, and held back, tons. Holding back hurt, so I took even more drugs to make that hurt go away.

Behaviors or pastimes, such as <u>reading</u>, I never considered an addiction earlier on. I really got into books in my twenties, and that was it! They were my escape from everything and I knew it. I read two kinds of books, self-help or the latest best-seller. Then I progressed into murder mysteries, with gruesome aspects or an element of surprise. Just as a drug addict needs more, I had to "up the dosage," going from mere murder novels to serial murders, standing in a bookstore saying, "Why doesn't somebody write another serial murder novel that's better than Silence of the Lambs?"

Until recently, I had several books anywhere I went, not leaving the house without a security-blanket book. They did wonders for keeping things out of awareness. I could sit in a room, open that book, put my head in, and not look up, completely escaping in my reading, cutting out any person I didn't want to talk to. That was especially true with my family and relatives, all talking, mostly arguing and fighting, not wanting to hear what they were saying or wanting to participate. Otherwise, I felt trapped and wanted to stand up and scream, "Stop, why can't everybody get along and be happy?"

I wanted to stay an island unto myself where I thought I was in control and safe. I feared discomfort would pull me into a participation I didn't want, talking of the trivial, stupid, and meaningless. I felt upset by being trapped in trivia, which, of course, was my own stuff, but nonetheless, I didn't know how to get out. The world might have seen all this reading as a good thing—"Isn't that great, she reads. What a very mature response to upset"—except for my family. They said just the opposite.

Even though I wasn't always feeling excellent and successful, I thought I had to prove I was, or at least appear that way, and I adopted certain traits to do so. Guilt drove me to be <u>perfect, successful, and the best in the business</u>, so to speak. I was completely armored at all times! Another ongoing habit was trying, out of guilt and need to be successful, to help other people and then wonder why I always got hurt or wasn't appreciated. I felt I was doing a good thing, when in reality, before looking at my own short suits, I would look at theirs. Understanding I was interrupting their growth pattern, hindering rather than helping them, was a revelation for me.

Distress made me feel "less than" or inadequate, and I felt a compulsion to find a way around it. If I couldn't do something, I'd BS my way through it or create a diversion. I could get someone else to do it or to believe I had done it, whether that was through a lie, an exaggeration, or some other technique. There seemed to be no other option but to do everything just as expected, which was better than anybody else. That's where the pressure came in, and all because I would not accept the fact I couldn't meet all those expectations, and it was okay that I couldn't. Instead of simply saying, "No, I don't know what you're expecting of me" or "I don't know how to do that," my *famous quote for life was, "No problem," for anything or anybody. That put the pressure on, but it also was an avoidance. I just didn't have enough time for me.*

My addiction to being the best hid inadequacy, where I didn't have to deal with it, identify with it, or accept it. I always felt I had to earn love and respect, rather than its coming naturally, because I believed being who I was wasn't good enough. I had to climb the highest mountain or do the best deed to get approval, or people would never recognize me as anybody but a common, ordinary little guy out there. It was very stressful or frustrating not to be able to relax with the idea of imperfection. I always had to be on cue or on stage, which also had an effect on my sleeping patterns, because I couldn't ever let go. It was like being trapped, as the need for perfection and approval built up, but I didn't know any other way.

Becoming aware that <u>risk taking</u> was a huge addiction has been relatively recent. Interestingly enough, I couldn't have any intense feeling, happy or sad, so I reduced or narrowed them through any of the addictions. Any large or intense feeling brought aliveness, which was scary, so I'd have to deaden it through preoccupying myself with the thrill of an adrenaline rush. I'm not sure I had any clear view of it, but aliveness was a big, bad, very dangerous thing, as if it were going to kill me. I didn't know how, but I thought I was going to blow up or disappear. As I changed the forms of addictions to more socially acceptable ones, I dealt more with anxiety or boredom than with the need to deaden all feeling.

Gambling, risktaking, or doing something dangerous was okay because people thought I was a fun gal. So, not only did I get reinforcement for heroism, it also fit into my family system, where my role was to distract everyone from whatever else was going on by being somewhat rowdy and fun, in an exciting but not rebellious, way. They would say, "Oh geez, what are you coming up with now?" Or my Mom would say, "Oh, my God, she's sky-diving!" But that would keep her from drinking, so it was a whole, huge family system.

Back in my twenties, <u>work</u> was a major addiction tied in with perfectionism, trying to be perfect in anything and everything I did. Also, <u>food</u>, which allowed escape from the turmoil, as well as the feelings of hurt or anguish or pain.

I have many addictions, but my major one was <u>getting people to like me by taking care of and pleasing them</u>. I thought that if I cared for them enough and was kind to them, they would like me in return. I was the caretaker, the reactor-type person, and being addicted to a low self-esteem, I had to do things for people. I was very afraid of abandonment, with which I was so familiar, and thought my addictions would prevent that.

The appeal of the priesthood was that I wanted to rescue people. I was very, very much into wanting to help people who were suffering, wanting to go to bat for the underdog, the disadvantaged. I didn't realize, for a long time, that was a great place to hide out. I grew up always feeling unworthy, the only stepchild of a woman with ten children of her own. She said she felt sorry for me and told me, "Your grandfather abused women and alcohol and so did your great-grandfather. It's in your blood—you're just like your grandfather." My father was an alcoholic and had abused women, including her, and she explained how my mother died when I was born, while he was out drinking. When I was about twelve, she would constantly send me out to rescue him. He would fight with her and I would jump in, physically taking him on from the time I was in the seventh grade. When I was in the eleventh grade, I was sent to the state juvenile reform school because I was always fighting, always taking on someone and never losing. It was the only thing I was good at, and although I'd get beat bloody, people would admire me. I was the bodyguard, the savior of everyone, especially the underdog. I never acted out or did really bad things, but the guys I hung around with would always set me up to get into fights. All battles would be worked out between me and whoever else. I was a gladiator and felt very good about that. Since it made me feel loved and admired, I'd let them get me into fights.

My addiction to <u>intellectualism</u> occurred because of my inability to read, due to dyslexia. As a child, I knew I couldn't read and was fearful of bringing that to anyone's attention, as that was before dyslexia became well known. In fact, I was thirty-one when dyslexia was suggested as my problem. I remember huge feelings of relief, the most memorable I had ever had, on being told I wasn't defective. From late teenage years through current times, I've been on a continual quest to learn. Naturally, if one couldn't read well, the opportunities for learning had to come about differently, so conversation always interested me and, in retrospect, that's how I learned in school. I would cause disturbances in class and challenge the teachers to induce conversation, to get the information in a different way. I wasn't conscious of that at the time, but looking back, I recognize that's what I was doing. An unsuccessful quest to attend medical school, thwarted by my inability to read, encouraged the obsession with intellectual information. I do believe it's as much a compulsive behavior as anything. I still have behavioral characteristics that show me it's an addiction.

I feared not knowing, and recently I've wanted to say to hell with it, I already know and it isn't important if I do or don't. I always thought that if I didn't know something I was "less than." Only recently have I come to the realization that this is not different at all. There's no question this compulsion for intellectual information and understanding is just as debilitating as alcohol. It's rather a scary place to realize the alternative for that is to trust and know everything's okay, and when the moment of truth comes, what information you need is there.

Two weeks out of high school I left home, and the military became my home where I did well, felt comfortable, and was able to compete. When I think of it, maybe it was a hiding place since I didn't want to go out in the world and have anybody find me out. Although many hate the <u>military, its structure</u> and purpose kept me safely in my comfort zone, because I knew my family would always be provided for, and I'd always have a paycheck. I thought that as long as I didn't cross the line and never got caught, it was much better than having to work as a civilian.

While being detained in a POW camp during the Vietnam War, I lived a lot in solitary, which I found easier than living with others. I felt condemned because I couldn't communicate like they did, and I may not have resisted physical abuse to the extent they did, but I thought it was stupid to get hit in the head everyday. A lot of men were scared, embarrassed, felt they'd done the wrong thing, and as I look back, each of us had our own way of resisting. For about a year, there were three foreign interrogators who selected twenty of us for "special treatment." The result was a psychological nightmare that so frayed my nerves I had diarrhea constantly. Day and night I tried to outguess what they were going to interrogate me about, and I brought a lot of that mind-racing and second-guessing home with me. I fantasized so much it drove me crazy sometimes, but I learned to survive through it, living in another world. I stayed preoccupied constantly with memory work and prayers I would say for hours while walking back and forth. Near the end, when we lived in a large group, we had all kinds of education classes, which weren't allowed but we had them anyway, putting a guard at the door and having little groups here and there. We stayed so busy you could hardly get everything done. I was in Toastmasters, studied French, German, Spanish, meat cutting, photography, eighteenth-century English literature, religion—all being taught from memory, often by guys who were instructors at the Air Force Academy. Early on, after coming home, it was so hard to sit and talk to my wife, and after a while, I'd have to say I couldn't take it. It was like my gut was open. In the military I had a shield. It was my shield.

When I returned from Vietnam, after seven years away, I thought I could reward myself, as if being there gave me more of a license, and after about a year, the ball started rolling on the <u>sexual obsession</u>. I thought I could indulge myself all the more because I had suffered, even though I had sworn to God that if I ever got out, chasing women would never happen again. Just as some get a high from heroin or other drugs, I must have gotten a high from this game of conquest, but when an encounter was over, I couldn't wait to leave. I've recognized my inability to love anybody else because I was so much in love with myself, *always putting myself first, although I never thought of it that way then.*

Alcohol was my first major, recognizable addiction, as a way to escape from "reality," from problems and issues I didn't want to face, a way for me to cope with situations too difficult to deal with in a sober state. It was absolutely clear I was escaping from a feeling and from myself, because I wasn't real happy with me.

I also used a lot of different things to avoid recognizing those feelings, some very socially acceptable such as *work, sports, golf, Little League baseball, tennis, bridge*, almost anything to keep me busy. Booze was lurking in the background, but when engaging in the other activities, I didn't have to use it, and that seemed more appealing because the others were acceptable. Who's going to say playing golf is a rotten thing to do? It ceased to be a good escape route when it stopped appearing to be a hobby. Then I found playing bridge three or four nights a week was a good way not to think about the troubling things. About the time our son got active in Little League baseball, I no longer enjoyed endlessly sitting at a bridge table, so I gave it up and began coaching. During the five or six months of the season, I was at the ball-field five nights a week; when our son outgrew baseball, we were there every night keeping score and running statistics for 120 other kids, without benefit of computers, until 1:00 or 2:00 in the morning. Recognizing that obsession, I went back to school full-time after a long layoff, spending as much time there as I could. The next thing you know, they opened the horse track here in central Florida, and we were out there five nights a week, not for the gambling but just as another distraction so I wouldn't have to deal with uncomfortable things.

My major addiction was *relationships, particularly abusive ones*, and, for a period of time, food. The way I played around, behaved, and acted to make the other person react was always a form of control. I knew exactly how to manipulate the other person to react the way I wanted, to get the attention and love I needed and because it temporarily relieved the pain. I can tell *you right now, in my younger days I brought on the physical abuse consciously and then, in the next breath, forgot it, denied it. I knew how the other person would respond at the moment I consciously said something or acted in a certain manner, knowing it would provoke an attack. I'm very good at reading people and always have been, so I knew how to manipulate. You might call it the "Jewish mother" syndrome, and we're all "Jewish mothers," although my heritage is Spanish and French. Deliberately escalating a situation into an abusive one was my way of punishing myself. Since I felt I wasn't worthy, not good enough, or had done something wrong, I brought on punishment. I was very fearful, very introverted and quiet, and even though I had a strong personality, my extroverted, normal self only came out later.*

I used <u>marijuana</u> *to cover up that negative self-image, and it was certainly true that when I was stoned, I definitely felt that feeling described as cosmic consciousness. Of course, as soon as I came down from that, I was back where I was, with the additional problem of coming down. Other major addictions could be some* <u>promiscuity</u>, *stemming from a desire to be liked by others or to be sexually attractive to guys, and I used to* <u>sleep</u> *a lot more before I started recovery. Sleep was my mom's major escape. I would come home from school, and she would be in bed asleep. If I made one little sound, she'd come out of the room screaming, "Shut up!" slam the door, get back in bed, and sleep the rest of the day away.*

<u>*Smoking*</u> *was my major addiction. I loved cigarettes and thought they loved me back and were my friends because they made me feel good. I had to find out that idea was an illusion. When I wasn't involved with cigarettes, I felt bad, so they did a good job of hiding the discomfort. I would always resort to a cigarette to deal with any type of distress, rather than any mental factors. Sure, if there was some heavy-duty emotional stuff, I'd have to go through and process it like everybody else, but the typical response to life's bumps, day in and day out, would be to light a cigarette.*

Alcohol was my major addiction. There were others, now partially healed. My body is not able to use alcohol, and experience has shown it would be a form of insanity to challenge it, although my thoughts and attitude about it are healed. To speak about its appeal is easy. I had my initial experience with alcohol and tobacco, which, by the way, is a very wonderful drug too, because my peers suggested it was manly and in vogue. I used it and actually had, as I now realize, a spiritual experience. I became the person I wanted to be, one I knew and admired but thought I could not be without help. I was witty, very, very relaxed around girls and in the company of other men. I was okay, an experience I had not previously had. It was a refuge from a chronic feeling of inadequacy. I likened it to Dr. Jekyll and Mr. Hyde. I drank the potion, just as he did, and the same thing, change of personality, happened to me.

I trust you are able to sense the ease, the kindness, and with some, the amusement with which all our friends here discuss their major addictions, their mistaken beliefs, both about the nature of addictions and about their feared lack of value. You can see that in the beginning they were just as unaware, as outraged, as confused, or uninterested in the topics of addictions and the hurt they conceal as any others on the planet. Like everyone else, they had engaged in intentional, deliberate refusal to see the very obvious patterns of thought and behavior in which they were engaged. They didn't dare to admit their private hurt, either to themselves or to others. I'm certain they would be the first to assure you that if they can change their minds and look straight at what they so desperately fought against, so can anyone.

At this point, we hope it is impossible that anyone could state, "Well, I just can't see myself in any of these people." The range of our addictions is testimony to our individuality, our creativity misapplied, and the lengths to which we will go to run from the demons that haunt us. It is also evident, from their answers, that the appeal of their many and varied addictions was all the same. Regardless of our societal beliefs about acceptable vs. unacceptable addictions, all these behaviors were acknowledged to be distractions from fear, pain, and feelings of unworthiness, not being good enough. There were no exceptions. Until we ask to be made aware of our own inner experience, we cannot commence our own healing process.

Step 5:

You are invited to survey the representative list of addictions mentioned in this section to see if they fit for you. If you do not recognize yourself in any of these answers, kindly but firmly reread them with this question in mind: "What if acknowledging addictions is okay, and their presence does not mean I am a flawed or worthless person?" You are asking yourself this question in the privacy of your own heart and mind. What can be the danger? Once you are willing to acknowledge there might be an addiction, look squarely at what that offers you. Recognize that some part of you seems to benefit from the excessive self-destructive behavior or substance. The operative word is "seems," and in the deepest recesses of your heart, you know something about this behavior is not bringing you contentment, despite your persistent attempts to try harder. Are you willing to see that the demons you listed in the earlier section and many of your own repetitive behaviors are intimately linked? Recognize you engage in such behaviors when the upset breaks into awareness. And remember, be kind to yourself!

6. What did you need to keep out of awareness with your addictions? What was your belief about discomfort?

Question 6 addresses a pivotal idea in our exploration, so please take some time to be with it. Be assured it is safe to explore these issues and that only good can come of it. Also, note that parts of the answers to this question were given previously. However, since it is so important to look directly at what we believe must be kept out of awareness and why, it is dealt with here in more detail. Specifically note the ideas and beliefs that are indicated about feelings in general, and upset or discomfort in particular. The word *discomfort* is used to represent the myriad descriptors that denote lack of peace and contentment. Reread the question, if necessary.

Feelings, first of all, were not something I experienced. I had rules and life experiences given to me secondhand by my parents, such as the way to dress, the way to speak, and the things to do. One of the clear lessons was not to be emotional, not to feel, and the only safe place to be was, "Never let them see you sweat," as the old expression goes. Certainly, never let them see you cry. My God, that was totally out of the question!

Discomfort just wasn't discussed at all. We pretended it didn't exist and was to be totally and completely avoided. We believed those who held in their feelings were the strong ones, and people who revealed their distress and were authentic in their feeling nature were weak characters, easy to run over and be used. I don't recall having a structured idea about any of this until looking back on it later in life.

When I was little, if I felt physical pain or if someone hurt my feelings, I would never cry. Always, if I were close to my bathroom, I would run in and lock the door. Sometimes, I would be up there crying when Mom called me to dinner and, if they asked why my eyes looked they way they did, I would say, "Oh, I was hot and splashed water on my face," not wanting anybody to know I was ever upset. I thought only weak girls cried and tough girls didn't, and feeling upset was terrible.

I had very low self-esteem, but when I found I could do music and be loved and accepted by audiences, distress was pushed below the surface so I was safe from the upset feelings and from being "found out." My involvement with women hid the sense of powerlessness, the worst feeling in the world that needed to be eliminated at all costs. Even when I was engulfed in my addictions, there was always the subtle sense the upset wasn't gone, just lurking. A man simply wasn't supposed to show distress, as upsetting feelings were a sign to the whole world of your weakness. I'm reminded of the story attributed to the Spartans of ancient Greece of a person being basically eaten to death, without showing any emotion, by a fox hidden in his coat. It was considered better to die than to show your emotions.

I definitely believed all feelings of upset were wrong and that if I felt them, I was broken, bad, or "not good enough," rather than something merely being amiss, which could be discovered and fixed. I thought other people didn't have these upset feelings but were happy, except for a few alcoholics or drug addicts, and I wondered why I wasn't like other people. Now, it's clear that help was trying to be given me, like having a guardian angel saying, "Excuse me, excuse me, your upset could teach you something." And I'm like, "Get the hell out of here. I need some orange juice; I've got to go skiing. Geez, I need a trip, that's what's bothering me!" I was constantly getting a message or guidance but saying, "Go away, I can't deal."

I had some kind of fantasy about what a good, spiritual person was like, and she definitely wouldn't be uncomfortable. She would be at peace. Therefore, being uncomfortable, with all those fantasies going on, meant I was neither good nor spiritual. It meant I was damaged goods. This belief about distress was around as far back as I can remember, and I wondered about that many times. It didn't make sense at all to hide those feelings, but I kept trying.

Nothing was kept out of awareness. I was aware of my chronic pain, but thinking I could fix it, I denied it a lot. I remember Mom saying one day, "Carmen, I haven't seen you smile in ages." That hit me, and I realized that at some level I was really choosing this masochism. I always said my first marriage wasn't basically a bad relationship, but I was deliberately antagonistic. For instance, knowing my ex-husband hated hospitals and couldn't deal with them, I fell ill with pneumonia and was admitted to the hospital. While there, I had a heart attack and stayed for three more weeks. It was deliberate, so that son of a gun would have to go to the hospital! As I began to become aware of how insane this was getting, I shut down, and then it really got bad. For me, it was like a pheromone, where I just exuded anger and the response came back.

As for feelings, Mom taught me not to open up. She traveled a lot, and I spent a lot of time in boarding schools, which made me more shut down but also gave me a sense of independence. Even though my dad wasn't around much, I was very afraid of him because of his temper. I also feared revealing distress because it meant I wasn't happy, and Mom might have more guilt than she already had for leaving me alone. I was very much protecting my mom.

When I first started smoking, it always seemed to add to my stature and I felt like I was "more than" what I normally would have been, so I must have realized I felt "less than" when not smoking. Only since I quit have I been able to feel what had to be kept out of awareness— abstract feelings of uneasiness and agitation for no seeming reason whatsoever. I thought if I felt them I would suffer, so I never allowed them into awareness.

Feeling "less" was kept out of awareness. There was a certain aspect of "whistling past the graveyard," not so much because of knowledge of what was there but from the fear that something to cause concern was there. I suppose I was like Scarlett O'Hara at the end of Gone with the Wind, "I'll think of it all tomorrow."

Absolutely, there was a fear of discomfort. I came from a family that needed the excitement of upset. It was so distasteful to me because I could never depend on being in their company without tremendous risk of embarrassment by their inappropriate and overly emotional behavior. Therefore, I had a real aversion to being caught up in the emotions of other people and instead of wanting to be present and real with a legitimate range of feelings, I wanted to keep them absolutely under control. If we weren't laughing, I felt, This ain't right. I was also uncomfortable with distress because of the unfamiliarity of it. I had been so very skillful at avoiding it, that when it came *around, my best response was to shut down, disengage the sensors, believing it a fairly manly way to react! I thought experiencing pain meant I would go from being in control to being out of control, like the other family members who were living such muddy lives, while I was having such an orderly one. Another corollary, of great concern for me, was the fear that when it came time for emotions to be appropriate, I wouldn't have them, being this cold fish human being. Because they were so in check, I wondered if I might be permanently flawed, an unfeeling, insensitive beast of a person.*

I chose the most classically codependent profession, nursing, for an adult child of an alcoholic. It's a given for anyone with that background always to nurture, support, be needed, or create an invaluable space for yourself to get the sense of worthiness you don't know how to give yourself. We are the altruistic, "give until you drop" group, and the whole world thinks we're so awesome and wonderful, but our feelings are not even in the equation.

If I allowed myself to acknowledge fear, I thought I would find myself to be someone I didn't like or had no control over, or I might find myself face to face with God. Because of my upbringing, I still had guilt around religious issues. The way God was portrayed didn't seem real, yet I was afraid if He were that way, I was going to hell.

I learned two things about upset feelings as I was growing up: Either I was being persecuted for God's sake, or I had done something wrong and God was punishing me. It was all about God, and "damned if you do, damned if you don't." In our family, discomfort or feeling "less than" was caused by the devil that was always lurking around to make you feel miserable. I was not doing God's will. It was so confusing to me that God was allowing the devil to persecute me, but I was told it was to test my loyalty. So I never knew why it was happening, only that it was happening.

I believed in the ostrich attitude of hiding your head in the sand. If upset didn't go away, then you hid again and hoped it would or that you would be better able to cope in another few years. I felt like other people managed to deal with their upset, or they didn't have the same levels of discomfort I had, and I didn't know what was wrong with me. Sure, I had judgments about feeling upset. It was interesting to realize most people think they're the only ones going through those discomforts or situations and wonder why the universe has selected them, when, in truth, everyone is going through the same things.

I was very sensitive to feelings of inadequacy, as they meant criticism and embarrassment. It was shameful, and God forbid someone should see me this way! I think it all started from taking on the molds of my parents. My father demanded perfection and I learned from him that whatever comes your way, whether it be financial distress, relationships, or anything else, be tough and handle it, although don't necessarily resolve it. I never realized he was a workaholic and those were disguises and facades for him, so I adopted those traits and felt abnormal if I didn't conform to them. When his way didn't feel comfortable, I would try to be more giving, more open, and more concerned about other people. Not that my father wasn't, but he didn't show it. I moved between the sensitive and hard parts of myself and wrestled with adopting my mother's softness and tenderness and my father's toughness. It was very confusing, not knowing which mask to wear. Even as an adult, part of me often thought, I can't handle this any more. If I could only go home and have my mother hold me, everything would be okay.

I grew up in an environment with endless attack and derision, with the premise of "the best defense is a strong offense." We seemed to be very aware we were upset and that life was unsatisfactory, but it was always someone else's fault. Being humiliated, being the butt of the joke or the subject of scorn and derision had to be avoided at all costs. Upset was definitely not to happen, and if you couldn't avoid it, it meant you'd failed, you were wrong.

The whole object, almost like a card game, was to leave somebody else holding the guilt. By our "no holds barred" rules, if you wound up holding it or if they got the better of you, you lost and you were lost.

It was absolutely necessary to keep distress or disturbing feelings out of awareness, primarily associated with memories of my childhood. My father would come in and beat any one of the three of us unexpectedly, so I kept on my toes and walked on eggshells. I remember being ten years old, lying in bed, scared to death. I'd finally get to sleep at three or four in the morning and wake up with Mom pulling my hair putting it in a ponytail and sending me off to school, where I'd sleep during class. At least I felt safe there, but coming home was upsetting. So the whole day, except for the safety of school, was a constant adrenaline pump.

I constantly defended against my upset because I thought acknowledging it would confirm I was what they said—Bad! When I was growing up, if we said something not allowed, my dad would use this old saying about "spit out the words." With a screaming, neurotic, obsessive-compulsive mother and an abusive, violent father, I was never allowed to express myself, and I felt so oppressed most of my life. Also, I learned to believe that I wasn't fit or healthy, or right or good, or certainly, my body wasn't beautiful or wonderful. There was always something about a threat to my body—it was going to suffer or die—and there was a lot of fear associated with that.

I needed to fix the upset because it felt terrible! And for another reason, it interfered with my need to analyze and control everything. I couldn't analyze well when it was there! Upset meant I was not okay, or guilty, with feelings of worthlessness and shame, which words cannot describe. They were dangerous, destructive, and needed to be gotten rid of. I couldn't stand to see anyone cry; I wanted to rescue, and of course, that's my profession.

I thought responsible people didn't have all this distress—it meant I just didn't have my act together! I knew what people expected of me, and perceiving myself as a very stubborn little *cookie, I would dig in my heels, grit my teeth, and by Jiminy, get through anything. And by God, I wasn't going to let people know how I felt, putting on my little happy face and saving upset for when I got home, where later I might rant and rave. With a horrendous, terrible feeling, I would often tap it back down, or put it in a little box with the lid on, telling myself this wasn't a convenient time; maybe I would deal with it later when I wasn't so busy.*

Twenty years ago, if asked, I would have said, "Sure, I'm a deserving person, a good person. I'm just fine and there's nothing wrong with me. I'm pretty okay with myself." We may say that, but I've found that we no more believe we're okay and fine than the man in the moon, and until we address that, we stay with the addictions and the distractions.

What jumps into my mind was a fear I really wasn't very nice. In fact, I was bad or a bitch or not good enough. Of course, if that were true, the appeal of the Prince Charming who was going to make me feel good would make sense. In my family, one didn't show feelings of upset. Early on, my mother learned not to cry. She used to be a crier, but not getting comfort from my dad or anybody else, she learned to stuff it. She didn't say that, but that's how she acted. On marrying my dad, she inherited his two teenaged children and then, ten months later, had twins. She was thirty, had never been a mother before, and now, with four kids, had a challenge that could make anyone cry! My dad had a bad temper, even though he didn't show it much, and if I showed any bit of angry feeling, I was labeled and told I was just like my dad, the bad one. Whereas my twin sister was always said to be like my mom, the good one. So having feelings or expressing yourself was not appreciated. I had a very strong belief that if I looked at and gave myself freely to feeling upset, I would be consumed, never returning to sanity, or I would die.

I kept upset feelings out of awareness because they were so intense they seemed all-consuming and unbearable. If I did let them come up, what would happen to me? I feared I would just give up, and what did that mean? Maybe never leave the house again? Maybe die? Of course, I judged myself because I thought if you had these feelings, it meant you were a failure and not the same as everybody else.

I recall feelings from my earliest memories. It's very difficult to put a handle on, but it was beyond fear. It was a sense of terror, and I've always been curious about where that started. Certain events would trigger it, and I recall being allowed to have that feeling by my parents who comforted me. My siblings, however, ridiculed me and as I grew older they reminded of the event sufficiently to put me in that state of terror. As I grew older and busier with other activities, the upset slid into unawareness, although it didn't go away because certain things continued to resurrect the identical feelings. I've come to realize that early on I formed a network of unawareness that ran the show underground. Reflecting on my early recovery period, I recognized the anger, frustration, hurt, or upset were all the same as when I was a very small child.

One therapist, with whom I had a wonderful relationship, had a box of tissues right on the coffee table, and I commented, "Well, I guess we're going to cry or something." She responded, "I hope so." There was no way I was going to let go and cry about how I felt or to get in touch with those feelings that would totally consume me, annihilate me because I was taught crying was definitely not a manly thing. It was derided, as in, "If you want to cry, I'll give you something to cry about."

Owning up to anxiety meant I had totally failed, was absolutely zero, and had lost myself as this structured person in control. It meant I was not whole, or I was defective, and I worked real hard trying to overcome it, keeping it unknown to anyone but me. I saw everybody else as perfect, or at least as having the capability of being perfect, but I believed I wasn't perfect and needed to hide.

Feelings of anxiety were very stressful and reinforced my constant awareness I was very bad. I always called the bad part of me the devil. I had to do absolutely everything I could to keep that devil inside, thinking my anxiety was part of my craziness and its presence was proof of badness. Becoming a priest was the first opportunity ever offered to me where I could escape from those devils; if I became a priest, I'd never get married and would be able to help rather than hurt women. Also, this would prevent anyone getting close to me or getting to know me. My plan was to escape my fear through deliberate, excessive work, knowing I wouldn't have to deal with it because I was so distracted.

My father was a very angry man and hit us, and my husband was an alcoholic, though not a daily drinker. When he did drink, he became violent against me. I wondered why I had such an angry, violent father and how I wound up with a violent husband, thinking I certainly would never choose that! I later recognized I came to this earth to heal my own very deep-seated anger, since I could get equally violent; I was always afraid that monster was inside of me and the addictive behavior was absolutely keeping my demons out of awareness.

Here we discover the true heart of the drive behind our addictions. Every single person interviewed held strong, unquestioned beliefs about the loss, terror, the demons—and, ultimately, death—that would "get them" if ever they permitted themselves the simple experience of becoming aware of feelings. We have taken our need to conceal ourselves very seriously and truly believe we are in a life and death struggle against something that would harm us. It takes great courage to enter into this dialogue because of our solid conviction of the danger that feelings might lead us into. The promise of your twenty-eight friends is that your safety is guaranteed as you continue to delve into this topic. They're still around and doing just fine!

I have worked with thousands of people, in addition to the participants in this study, and have found that virtually no one grows up with a healthy or accurate understanding of feelings, where they come from or what to do with them. Feelings are not stepchildren to be looked down upon with disdain. They are as inevitable as having a brain or a liver. The problem is not with the feelings, but with the interpretation we make of those feelings and how we address them. We have learned to be so afraid of them, from our very earliest days, that even to approach the subject rationally seems a threat. We have bought into the "everybody knows that upset must be avoided" syndrome and have not asked ourselves the most basic questions: "What part of us finds these feelings so disturbing, so wrong, so threatening that a great part of our lives must be devoted to their avoidance or eradication? What part decrees feelings to be the great centerpiece around which we do our dance of resistance or which drives us to self-destructive choices and decisions? The feeling, non-verbal part of ourselves, that faculty within, which ultimately allows us to experience great joy and contentment, is systematically cast aside as evil, unreliable, and serving only to bring us to a tortured end. How in the world did our feeling nature get such bad press? And is there any true basis for it? Happily, the answer is no.

At a very early age, we become aware of discontent. For most of us, expressing our discontent was met with displeasure or had negative consequences. At this point, virtually everyone erroneously assumes there is something the matter with us or our feelings to invite lack of support and love. Even when we do have supportive, emotionally mature role models, we are still prone to strengthen the notion there is something wrong with us. The process of projection—seeing the things we fear in ourselves mirrored in the behavior of others—is unknown to us as children. We do not realize that our upset triggers suppressed feelings in the adults around us who want us to "shape up" so their own distress will disappear back under the rug. Many parents, without realizing what they are doing, use their children as distractions from their own pain; therefore, unhappy children are not welcome for they bring the parents' buried angst and guilt into awareness. We systematically learn to be as afraid of feeling upset as our parents, and the cycle of denial is endlessly repeated.

It is beyond the scope of this book to explore the ultimate "beginnings" of our upset. However, it is completely our point to elucidate what must be done today. The short-range need is to know how to effectively handle the strong and disturbing feelings we may currently have. The long-range goal is to understand how we, from the inside, are generating our upset in the first place, so we can stop. Take some time to reflect on the idea that we create our own upset through our choices. Yes, that's right—we create our own pain and we do so through hatred, resentment, and endless judgment. The people, places, or situations in our lives merely trigger and bring into awareness that omnipresent feeling of anxiousness that judgment engenders and our addictions would conceal. Once again, there is no X-factor; our upset is related to our choices, no matter how cleverly disguised.

As we continue to explore the origin of our upset as simply as possible, it is imperative to realize that in this culture and many others, most of us take the prevailing ideas and beliefs for granted without ever examining whether they make sense. Most of them do not. The reason they do not is that, with almost no exception, our rules, mores, traditions, politics, religions, and social structures serve the ego mind, the self-serving, personal part, and not the authentic spirit or essence of us. We do not need an academic definition of the word ego. We have all heard the expressions such as, "He sure has a big ego!" or "She is such a phony. Why does she put on airs like that?" or "What a superficial, egotistical bunch of people." We know perfectly well what those phrases mean, and they are not complimentary. We recognize something contrived and lacking authenticity, something artificial—designed to have a specific effect.

The ego mind, hereafter referred to as simply ego, might variously be known as the self-image, the invented self we thrust into the arena of life, the mask we wear, that part of us that is always insulted or must "save face." The ego takes things personally and is entirely self-absorbed, although it may have learned how to look good. In its eyes there is only one purpose for this world; it is the place where it strives to be recognized as good, important, real, valuable, or special, and everything is seen as a potential avenue to get its way. All our institutions, which we have not thoughtfully examined, serve a common goal of perpetuating our ego's goal of getting its way, through manipulation, negotiation, control of all kinds, force, contrivance, selling out, or outright attack. A pathetic little thing, this ego of ours, this invention that we did not realize we invented. Yet we adore this image of ourselves and will do absolutely anything it seems to ask of us. It is as if a madman has taken up residence in our minds and has attempted to take over our entire existence. And it is very single-minded in its goal. It wants to be supreme, it wants to be the center of the universe and will use any and everything around for that purpose, including you, your talents, your energy, all your resources, if you cooperate. And that is the key element, your cooperation. The ego gets the cooperation it needs to exist because we buy into its program that we are in a severely compromised and dangerous position because of our weakness and that, without its protection and defenses, we are doomed.

We have all marched to the orders of our own internal "madman." We have never questioned it, as it spelled out the should's, ought's, can'ts, won'ts, and admonitions to try harder, or when it urged us to sell out, hold back, and hide our legitimate feelings, thoughts, inclinations, and intuitions. Hear this well, this allegiance to the ego and the unquestioned assumptions it fosters that we are ruined or defiled, that we dare not let anyone see who we really are, and therefore, that we truly need this ego, is the cause of all our upset. In our confusion, we bought into the notion that the ego was our friend, our comrade in arms, our ally to save us in life's many dangerous situations. With its "help," we have systematically learned to put ourselves down, to dishonor ourselves, to put ourselves in second place. Listen! We are creatures of outpour-ing, and when we choose to block the full, unedited expression of our basic, unique, and loving nature, as our ego commands, pain results. We verbally express those feelings of madness and anxiety by saying we feel trapped, blocked, imprisoned, angry, frustrated, empty, or lonely. And we make that power-ful, far-reaching choice to hide on a daily basis.

Remember our earlier statement—what you pay attention to, you have more of; paying attention results in a request always granted. When all your attention is on your ego, your defender, that mask perceived as necessary to hide your defects, you create pain for yourself. The ego retains our allegiance because it also forbids our questioning whether these commands or the tales of danger are in our best inter-ests or not, forever shutting off any possibility of real inquiry or relief and imprisoning us in an endless, closed loop.

Now, if we are ever to be free, we must challenge these ideas by looking straight at them and questioning this ego, which is experienced as that self-critical voice in your mind, a commit-tee that endlessly chides you, exhorts you to be better or different, and holds up your shortcomings and flaws for evalu-ation and judgment. To make a point, silently ask your ego this question, as if you are speaking to another person or thing because, indeed, this ego-voice is alien to the truth of you: "Are you interested in my welfare?" Listen carefully. Be as open as you can in discerning the response in your mind. If you are truthful, you will perceive some version of, "Absolutely not." I have directed many people to ask themselves this question as part of their self-discovery and every single one "heard" the same lack of support of interest from the "inner critic." Here we find ourselves in a most insane situation. We are following the directives and guidance of a thought form in our minds that has no interest whatsoever with us, the real authentic us, though it pretends to. It intends only to use us, and directs us from morning 'til night to behave only in ways that uphold and maintain it—this image or concept of ourselves. Be very clear, this unquestioning allegiance to this insane ego voice that proclaims our guilt, smallness, and worthlessness and our need for it, is the true source of our distress, terror, pain, and suffering. And no one makes us listen to it.

All the beautiful, precious people in the world, including you, have been hoodwinked, seduced, and enslaved by this ego mind, which has quite literally gotten away with murder. And all because we have been frightened into believing we dare not question or look squarely at this idea in our minds and than choose differently. We must look, we must challenge what we hear in our own minds, and we must choose again to liberate our essence, the spirit of us, which has been so long imprisoned. Do you feel imprisoned? Or trapped or blocked, stuck or squeezed? We all use these adjectives to describe our state of mind. And have you not thought the culprit was the job, the kids, the wife, the century, the color of your skin, or a host of others? In fact, it is none of those, but only the relentless adherence to a crazy idea in our minds that says, "You are not okay, and never will be, and don't let anyone find out what you are really like! And so, we lie, we evade the truth about how we feel, we hold back and hold in and the anxiety builds, all for no legitimate reason. And as our distress increases from repressing our energy and feeling, we hold in and hold back even more, until we die or cry out, "There must be a better way!" And indeed, there is!

We sealed this prison of our own making by asking the ego to find us a solution for our unhappiness. Several years ago a movie was produced entitled, *Sleeping With the Enemy*. I didn't see it, but the title is very apropos of our situation. We are sleeping, eating, living, and generally in partnership with the "enemy," that fearful idea that we have ruined ourselves. To ask that which causes our pain to remove our pain is truly madness. And we wonder why things are not working out.

For the first five questions, you have been asked to become acquainted with your own ideas on the subject of addictions and how they relate to your life. The process of transformation, which means to change the form of something, begins with the willingness to look at what is actually going on in your life, without denial, and to be the observer as well as participant in your own personal drama. Much is accomplished through acknowledging your feelings and ideas and owning your allegiance to your own ego. Perhaps you already feel a sense of relief from identifying with so many of the statements and candid revelations thus far.

As we progress toward healing, we must ask a different

part of our minds and hearts for another interpretation of our circumstances. The wise, all-knowing, authentic part reminds us that the ego always feels attacked and hurt, but our real presence is not involved with the battle. We are safe and beloved. Identify with that. As the next step to getting free, we face the fear or the feelings and allow them to be transformed, because fear does not reflect anything true about us but is only the natural consequence of holding back our feelings.

Step 6:

What do you believe will happen to you if you tell the truth, primarily to yourself, about how you feel, what you secretly believe about yourself, what you secretly wish would happen to those who are not serving you as your ego thinks they should? And what do you believe will happen if you should choose not to listen to that ego voice? I challenge you to risk addressing those questions and write down your answers, which are for your eyes only. After all, it is your mind, and you are responsible for what is happening in there.

7. What was the turning point that required you to find a better way to live and what was your process of change? What happened to the addictive behavior?

There is some overlap between this question and question four, which asked how our group discovered that the label "addicted" applied to them. Therefore, some of the "turning points" were included in previous answers. Together, these answers make heartbreakingly clear that we have bound ourselves over in slavery to our own ego minds with its harsh directives about what is and is not acceptable. Our partici-pants, like the rest of us, tried every way they knew to satisfy the ego's impossible request, which is to be phony, constantly hiding and keeping secrets, and to put ourselves down while, at the same time, attempting to get whatever is required to be happy. The impossibility and pointlessness of this mission finally breaks through for all of us if we are even partly honest with ourselves, driving us to try to find a better way to live.

Below are the synopses of some of the turning points of our group. On finding they were addicted, some embarked on a search for help at once, and others held out a little longer, or a great deal longer, before adopting a willingness to approach life in a different way. For some, the turning point was a specific event, while others gradually became aware that something was not working out. Their answers illustrate a key point—the turning point events and circumstances are extremely varied, but the conclusion they all reached and the process they all embraced was identical. Therefore, you will hear many statements of the same process in different words. Perhaps reading these stories will hasten your turning point so that you might, at last, cooperate in your own healing. Please note: as mentioned in the first part of Part II, most of these men and women are students of *A Course In Miracles*, among other things, and several of them refer to it as part of their turning point. It is a self-study course designed to help people see where they interfere with their own good and how to make healthier, more loving choices. This book does not infer that the *Course* is the only way or the best way to become more self-aware. It is simply one way.

My turning point goes back to when Mom and Dad got divorced. I had just come from eighth grade graduation and was supposed to be picked up from school, and Mom didn't show up. That was the day she left. I remember being numb like a brick wall. I don't even remember most of that whole year. After about a month, I exhibited symptoms similar to arthritis, then my fingers began to go white, and I was diagnosed with Raynaud's disease. I didn't question the disease and was, more or less, getting used to it.

The divorce made me rearrange the way I looked at things and somewhere in my freshman or sophomore year, I started wanting to figure out where this upset was coming from. I knew I was holding in, but at the same time, I was mad at myself for allowing hurt to come to the surface. I kept a smooth exterior but turned the anger inward on my body. As I became more aware, whenever I felt a certain way, I would tell myself, No need to sit here and try to analyze it; it's just there, so own it. That resulted in upset feelings going all through me but also out, rather than staying inside. I sometimes notice I still pull myself back and say, No, this isn't the right time. Later, I let it out and try not to wonder why it's there, because if I start trying to figure out, I decide I don't have a good enough reason and then get mad at myself.

My turning point is very clear in my mind. My girlfriend and I were splitting up, as I thought she was seeing someone else. The most incredible, blinding rage imaginable used to come up about women making me feel powerless, where I was actually capable of anything. It came up over this incident, and I felt so vile and sick of it, I thought, I can't and I won't feel this anymore! This rage wasn't about anybody but about my own feelings triggered by loss of control. For years, I thought my anger was under control, but when it came up, it controlled me and felt sickening and putrid. I can even feel it in my stomach as I'm talking about it. My life began to change when I recognized I couldn't do this anymore.

Letting go of anger was a very slow and sometimes frustrating process, and occasionally, I would still try to use it as a tool. For instance, if I needed to get away for a day, rather than saying, "I need to get away," I would start an argument because my anger justified going away. I became aware I didn't like being angry, even on the smallest scale, and from that, letting go was a natural progression.

The process of transforming upset feelings was letting myself feel them without judgment. When I kept them hidden in the closet or battled to justify them, they had all the power. I learned to look at them and ask myself, What does this actually feel like? For example, about a week ago I had a little feeling of jealousy come up. Rather than accepting it as something that had to be there, I became aware of how that didn't feel good, as if I'd eaten something rotten. I was willing to ask if I liked this feeling and the answer was always no. Many things aren't gone completely, but they've faded quite a bit with much less need for the addictive behavior. When you're comfortable, there's no need for it at all.

I know the exact time a turning point happened—December 24, 1996. I had run an ad for my business, and one person called to complain about the way it was worded. I magnified that call into, "Oh, this is going to ruin my business!" and "Oh, I've dissatisfied somebody!" I was so uncomfortable, experiencing and noticing it at the same time. I called a friend who runs a counseling program and told her I had to come right over. I was almost having a breakdown as it all came together in a crisis. I told her I couldn't even rest because my mind was so active and hassled and that I was self-destructing. I went through four or five weeks of intensive psychotherapy, and am now reaping the benefit. All the study and introspection over the last decade is now starting to come together and gel.

Now, two simultaneous events happen when I become uncomfortable. I am conscious, mindful about what I'm experiencing and I choose consciously what to do about it, not necessarily acting compulsively on it. This applies to watching television, food, alcohol, friends, my relationship with my husband, or my business. Watching upset come, experiencing it, and watching it go. That's the way it works. It's bringing valuable information, not always feeling pleasant, but it doesn't put me in the grip of something unhealthy because it does go away. This morning I woke up very happy, and I've been happy all day. I don't even know why. Being purely happy for no apparent reason makes up the minority of my days but it's happening more often, and today is one of those days. Addictions were all about not feeling as if I really fit in someplace.

After Boston, I moved to Philadelphia, continuing to look outside myself for answers. I was in turmoil after losing my job, discovering my wife was having an affair, and having to sell, at a great loss, the house I was building for us. I was very hurt and in such a fog and so numb I couldn't feel or see, as if my senses were cut off. In the midst of this crisis, I was almost hit by a car and thought, "What would happen if I died right now?" It wasn't a suicidal thought, but it did jolt me.

Almost immediately after that close call, I saw a storefront sign, "Flotations—Relaxation." Recognizing something was really wrong, I went in to ask what this was about. The owner described the process and I decided, "What the hell, I'll try anything." I entered the flotation tank, and a sense of peace came over me for the first time in three years. There I was, lying naked in this egg in total darkness, when I had a flash of insight regarding the connection between what had occurred previously in my life and where I was at that particular moment. I began to question everything I had experienced and all I had been taught. When I came out of the tank, I felt relief but, from long habit, returned to my "videotape" of painful memories: Oh, I'm divorced, I've lost my job, woe is me!

As the day unfolded, I began to have emotional feelings again after being numb for so long. With a real sense of relief, I began the gradual process of letting go of my armoring, which took perhaps twenty years, because I was pretty stubborn. For example, whenever I reached a certain level of peace or content-ment with a girlfriend, boss, or client, my "happy meter" would go off with, This can't be right, you're too peaceful; this can't be real because it's never lasted before. I would fall back into the victim role, believing I was undeserving and happiness was out of reach.

In 1992, my second wife insisted we go to a Course in Miracles group since we had tried therapy and everything else. I grudgingly agreed. The instructor emphasized we were all responsible for our own experience and were not victims. Not understanding this concept, I challenged her with examples of innocent victims. She repeated, "No, you're not a victim of the world you see, because everything you see is of your own creation." It disturbed me, but at the same time, it was comfort-ing because it seemed here was an answer, a way out, and the old patterns of victimhood began to fade on their own, without fighting against them.

In 1989, I was a newlywed, in a second marriage that initially had a lot of appeal, but I was already starting to feel impatient and critical of my husband. One evening I was returning home and basically said to the invisible universe, I've made a mistake again, and I don't know how to save face; I don't know how to get out of this marriage or what to do. I was giving myself an extremely hard time when I was hit by a huge dump truck. After making that statement, I had no further memories until I woke up the following day, having undergone surgery throughout the night. I knew if I lived through this accident and learned to walk again, there had to be some major changes in my life. Several months later, I ended the relationship, knowing my whole life was changing and I was going to have to start looking inside.

I still don't enjoy pain but it's allowed, and I end up sitting with it, always feeling free to express my emotions by crying and verbalizing. When I'm able to do that and let it out, I get over it. When I'm feeling something, I stir it up, wondering if I really feel a sense of loss or if I'm just making up a drama. I've learned I must ask whether that victim/victimizer role is still being embraced, as that's really what our lives are about before we truly wake up. Most of the time, I can allow the feeling of disturbance to lead me to a belief about myself. Not that I stop it immediately, but I don't sit in my little parlor having a pity moment. As I've cleaned up my beliefs, I notice in an upsetting situation I can say, I'm sorry I came off that way. I'm working at changing, and thank you for letting me practice.

Now, the thing that caused the light to come on was interesting. In one of the meetings at the treatment center for my son, the facilitator helped put a woman at ease with a kind act, clearly an act of unconditional love. Because I had not been using alcohol, which blocks the light of the spirit, I was able, for the first time, to recognize an expression of love. After the meeting, I started to tell the instructor that it was the most beautiful thing I had ever seen. The words didn't quite get out before I broke down in a state of total emotional collapse and began crying uncontrollably. Unable to stop crying, I locked myself in a bathroom for a number of minutes, because this was not a manly thing to do. After I got "control" of myself, I went back to apologize to the instructor. She smiled and said, "That's good for you and I'm glad you were able to do that." The point is I saw love for the first time. It hadn't seemed to exist around me before, but that moment of awareness, just that tiny light enabled me to start an entirely new life.

About the fifth year of AA, I was at the lowest ebb of my life, spiritually, financially, and physically and in an utterly, completely desperate search. I had been sober five years, and all that really enabled me to do was to feel pain very intensely. I was looking for a way to get out of pain without using alcohol and hadn't found it. I had some interesting experiences, but the most profound was my introduction to A Course in Miracles, wherein I found both the logical and spiritual explanations that made sense to me, and I began to study it as the second phase of my recovery.

As the pain decreased, the addictive behavior just fell away. There was no battle. As a matter of fact, that doesn't work at all. One of the primary tenants of the AA program is to cease fighting, which was very difficult because, based on my previous beliefs, it was nearly impossible to envision winning without fighting. However, I came to realize nonresistance requires much more courage. Martin Luther King and Jesus were a lot more courageous than I was! There are millions of stories where people say they suddenly lost the desire to drink. I actually had the experience of surrendering to a Higher Power, at the same time admitting I had a problem. Miraculously, the desire to drink disappeared. In fact, the day after it disappeared, I realized I had not thought about having a drink. All it takes is an awareness and admission of the problem, which we refer to as the first step, and then admitting a need for a Higher Power, which is the second prayer step. In other words, we have to depend upon a Higher Power. That's the difficult part, I think.

There are still moments of free-floating anxiety, and my evolution hasn't reached the point where my first reflex is to call on a Higher Power. I have to get really quiet and be conscious to do that. When I don't, I'm into my upset. You may not remember, Carol, but you gave me a little booklet several years *ago that talked about the vortex. It was very helpful, describing that when you're in the vortex, you're not able to make discerning judgments and decisions; therefore, the secret is simply to be aware you will come out, and when you do, you will pop out into the light. You must keep that in mind until you get through the upset.*

Three weeks after attending a powerful workshop on how to change your life, my husband had a heart attack. That was a catalyst for me, because I had believed that if I fed him the right nutrition, did everything right, and was a good girl, so to speak, no calamities would befall us. That crisis was one of the most wonderful things that ever happened, because of what it taught me about me! I became very aware of my own need to control, feeling so very out of control at that time. Thankfully, it was such a lesson in letting go, trusting and being with the feelings, because formerly, so much of me would have been trying to control this moment to have an outcome. Now, I didn't need an outcome. I didn't attach a meaning to life or death, or being alone or with someone. I truly didn't, not from numbing out but rather from allowing myself to experience where I was and not needing to control. I was in a phenomenal state of peace during that whole period. It was such a wonderful, wonderful lesson!

As I saw this, I was able to accept the experience of feelings as a friend, rather than as an opponent. I actually looked forward to upsets because they were going to help me identify where I saw myself as separate, shining a huge flashlight on that place. I remember hearing in class, "Why do we have to go searching around, wondering what to forgive? Whatever the upset is, that's where it is!" That was the greatest news I'd ever heard. I didn't need another workshop or book, because all my upset was enough; I had everything right there in the form of my upset feelings to help me learn who I really am.

First in my own therapy and then working with patients, I recognized that simply owning feelings, not fearing or trying to get rid of them, actually achieved the result of more peace. That was a surprise! The major problem I see with those who come into therapy is running from feelings, which absolutely causes more upset. My addictive behavior began to go away when I no longer saw the problem as something external I needed to change or fix. That's what all my previous analyzing had been for.

I remember the day my attitude shifted. A friend noticed I was very stressed and suggested I needed a massage. I recognized she was right, so I followed her suggestion, which eventually led to my introduction to A Course in Miracles. I read it, understood what it was saying, and the games I had been playing started to dawn on me. For three days I was in a haze but I began to put two and two together. That's when all hell broke loose!

In the beginning, I didn't realize upset was only a signal. That came gradually, as I stopped fighting and judging, because more than anything, I was a controller. As I continued to change my mind, I was not inclined to get into the old abusive behaviors, and even when I tried, people didn't respond in the same old way. When there was no response, I stopped trying to control.

It was a huge thing to realize that feeling upset didn't mean I was bad or wrong or damaged, but that I believed something that wasn't true. The biggest shift is to see it as guidance, a warning signal. It's the yellow light at the intersection that warns us to stop what we're doing, because if we go through it, we're going to get hurt.

On a good day, when my peace is disturbed, several things happen. I become aware of it, stop, breathe, relax, and have a little conversation with myself. Other times, when upset comes, I distract myself from it and am unwilling to change my mind, which is amazing because I'm conscious of what I'm doing! After it's over, I get the opportunity to practice the forgiveness process. Or, sometimes I'll whip myself a little and then practice. And sometimes I'll miss the pre-feeling up front, depending on how hectic I create things, and catch myself promoting some exciting behavior, for instance, "You know, I'm going dog sledding. We'll stay on the ice for seven days and I'm sure we can do this." So, *off we go, and after three days of hiking up the side of the cliff, staying in the snow, and dog sledding on the ice, I think, Damn, I did it again! This isn't fun, it's crazy, and you'll never catch me out here again! Then I reflect on the whole process and remind myself, with greater clarity than ever, that this isn't fun. It used to work and now it doesn't. So those are some ways in which I still operate.*

Now I realize it's not the activity but its purpose that matters, and to put that in my language, I get into "intention" to guide myself. The old ways are still familiar, but I consciously ask, What's my intention? especially when I feel upset coming. Now I'm more likely to catch the behavior and to exercise choice. Compulsive behaviors have become nonexistent. Once I get to the point where any feeling is all right, I'm left with wondering what I would like. It's simple, very eloquent, and saves time— you just choose. Intuition opens up, freeing me to decide what I want in a more direct way, as opposed to lying on the ice thinking, This is the dumbest thing I've ever done.

No battling against feelings. That's unworkable. The neatest thing for me, because I work with children and am now teaching adults with very disturbed children, is to witness the process happen in front of me repeatedly, keeping it really fresh. Just yesterday, working with six pairs of adults and children, I was trying to get the adults not to fight the children but to accept, join, and then redirect them. One little girl covered herself in a blanket, and you could see the adult thinking, Oh, damn, she shouldn't be covered up. She got real tight although, of course, the training had been, "Relax, it doesn't make any difference if that child's covered her head." I watched the adult practice. She took a big breath, let it go, and as soon as she relaxed and nonverbally indicated it was okay that the little girl was under the blanket, the child uncovered her head and sat right up. Thinking, feeling, and watching reinforce my awareness because I get to see results that quickly.

During the Olympic selection trials in 1988 my horse fell on me and I was paralyzed. For the longest time afterwards, I had so much pain that I thought I had to hide, but since I couldn't use the work addiction anymore, I was a bit lost. I got incredibly caught up in getting better, striving to be the best—the world's best "super-quad"—so instead of doing the horse competitions, I turned rehab into a competition. I totally lost myself in the challenge of getting back to a normal life, which took about two years, and anytime I felt pain I would work harder in rehab. Finally, I realized more clearly than ever that upset wasn't going away and things weren't changing.

The turning point was when I simply had had enough and didn't know what to do. A couple of years ago my self-hatred was getting too intense for me to handle. All this self-denial and trying to fool myself and others was so very uncomfortable. Feeling good about myself was totally foreign. How could I feel good about rolling around in a wheelchair? I felt so ugly, inside and out, but now it's a whole new ballgame.

Throughout my rehab I was always in the future, believing that "living in the now" meant pain. For instance, in the hospital I would think, Well, I'll get back to the horses. Then, when I got back to the horses and realized I couldn't do it, it was, Well, I'll go back to Florida. When I got to Florida and found it was going to be tough there, too, I went to graduate school. It was always something in the future.

Now, I'm practicing living in the present. Finally, I'm realizing it's okay to feel the feelings instead of running away from them. I had definitely forgotten that! Then they disappear and I've usually learned something. They're a teaching tool, not a punishment or deliberate challenge. I can know a ton of stuff in my head and that doesn't do any good. Getting comfortable with myself is the only way to make addictions go away. Even a few moments of feeling the truth about myself brings peace or good feeling, like a ray of sunshine on a cloudy day. It's more than peace, more like a good old, really warm hug. When I start to feel good about myself, I want to create that feeling more and I'm gradually learning how. Neither I nor anyone else I know has ever been successful in battling addictive behavior.

I moved to Orlando from California, because the 1989 earthquake scared me so badly. I didn't know anyone and didn't *want to look around for pot, so I pretty much quit cold turkey. That was exactly when the panic attacks and colitis started, and if somebody had given me some pot, I would have smoked it. My recovery started when my mom sent me a book called Toxic Parents because she recognized she and my dad had been abusive and wanted me to get help. Reading that book and accepting the ideas in it as true about me was very hard. My physical symptoms continued, and three years later when my grandmother died, I went through the second phase of colitis and feeling at my absolute bottom. I wasn't using pot to escape anymore, so I had no place to go but to the truth. It was so hard. I couldn't eat for three months.*

Looking back, it was when I was having panic attacks that I did the most growing. Not only do I have the right to have feelings, with the panic attack, all I could do was feel. Adrenaline was pumping, I couldn't eat, and it felt like I was going to die. I was able to get through them, survive, and do the personal growing I had always known someday I would have to do, the exact work I was trying not to do when I smoked that big joint so many years before. At that point I came to you, Carol. The day I met with you was the first time I ever realized I was okay and that it was okay to feel. No one had ever told me I was really okay, just as I was. That was the turning point in my life. Right there.

When I came home from Vietnam, nothing was working out. I got a job but was always getting in fights with other officers, almost going over the desk after someone. After that, I taught flying for ten or eleven years, which is another place you're almost always on the edge of your seat. During this time, I had severe sleep apnea and had trouble doing everything—job, driving—with things seeming to get worse. Driving down the road, I would imagine I was killing people—that's how I could stay awake. I finally came to the end of my rope and I remember wishing I'd stayed in the military! Then I started getting help.

I had been in an aggressive mode my whole life, always fighting, but not anymore, thank God! The various addictions were an escape from all this upset, the demons, and I didn't know it. With the idea that it's okay to feel bad, I feel free for the first time in my life and not having to hide feels good. I'm working on getting over the shame, and I feel I've come a long way, especially with judging. Judgment is holding up a mirror for me to see myself. That mirror idea is the best thing in the world! Now, when I stop running from the demons and allow feelings to be there, they disappear and are replaced by peace.

Addictive behavior is gone. No battle, and this is what I prayed for. For years I thought if I prayed hard enough my obsessions would go away and they didn't. I couldn't figure out why. Now, it's as if a mist arose. I can still see a woman walking by, but that's it. The aggressive desire for sexual conquest doesn't come up. What a difference to look at a woman as a person instead of an object! I've come to have more compassion as I've gotten older, something I didn't know the definition of before.

Only very recently has it occurred to me that keeping upset away through resistance is impossible. It's been a very gradual process, like digging a tunnel and always having the end of the tunnel in front of your nose. This awareness has evolved through exhausting the recourse to intellectual understanding, starting with religion, then psychology, metaphysics, and A Course in Miracles. I call it the studying, analyzing, thinking, or "looking for a way out" approach. I tried everything I could think of for as long as I could and gradually realized this was never going to work.

Since my whole rationale for safety and salvation had been to make other people wrong, I came to see I was never going to get out of my upset by continuing to make others wrong. I began to accept and believe that the primary condition of healing was that we are not healed alone. To the extent I tried to exclude anyone from being worthy of peace, I excluded myself from being worthy, so the only way out was to make other people right. Sometimes I preoccupy myself trying to figure out where upset came from, not so much to analyze it or make it go away, but to be aware of my own issues. However, that has nothing to do with what makes it go away. When I find myself in the grip of the addictive behavior, I literally use that word, "Help!" and nothing else. A sense of surrender is where it starts, stopping the judgment, surrendering to a power greater than myself, to that unnamable source of good.

My entire life had been an addiction, a defense against the indictment of unworthiness, a pointless strategy of defense. I now approach feelings with my guard down, and the help I ask for comes. My motivation is long experience with the fact that fighting does no good. The feeling of upset is replaced by reassurance, though I'm not aware of the exact process. As people who recover from hangovers express it, all of a sudden you realize it didn't hurt when you moved your head. Doubt, uncertainty, and a sense of pointlessness just go away, by some process other than "making it happen," and are replaced by well-being. When I'm not judging, I'm automatically comfortable and the arsenal of addictions becomes nonexistent. In a state of peace, fighting is irrelevant and unnecessary; addictive behavior has no appeal, no meaning. It's judgment or peace, and there's no third category, no middle ground, no place else to be.

The turning point for me was triggered by my divorce and several difficult business situations all arriving at the same time and smacking me between the eyes. It was like being in a pressure cooker. It occurred by the process of elimination when none of my strategies worked anymore, a progression of running out of room, time, and talent. I could still pull many tricks out of the bag, but something was still missing inside. It might be working "out there," but it wasn't working "in here."

During an exercise in one of Carol's classes I pierced through to a feeling, which I had always avoided, and realized it was not as threatening or fearful as I thought. I realized all the masks I had cleverly created were really the same mask, not a whole wall of masks. I don't think there's any other way but to continue feeling and trust that. If any circumstance appears to be negative or upsetting, I recognize it as a call for me to pay attention to determine its positive aspects. Tying back to the classroom exercises, discomfort is not only welcome, I'm in pursuit of it.

For example, when I was at the beach a couple of weeks ago, some friends were supposed to come over, and they didn't show. That was fine. Just my dog and I were there, and I recognized how peaceful I was with being alone, formerly a very miserable situation because of memories, wishes, and desires that hadn't worked out. On this day I was truly comfortable and enjoying where I was, when a motorcyclist came down the beach. I was annoyed and thought, "Hey, this is my beach." I had gotten to a point of serenity and now I was being disturbed. I stared at the motorcyclist as he came back down the beach because I assumed he wasn't supposed to be there. He waved and went on by so I thought, "Okay, no problem." Well, that wasn't good enough to get my attention. Next, I noticed a couple walk over my neighbor's steps and down onto the beach with their blanket, dog, suitcase, radio, and everything else, making themselves at home. Knowing the neighbors weren't home, I thought, "Well, wait a minute, they're trespassing." The boy had dreadlocks, a big tattoo on his back, earrings all over him, and I was sure they didn't belong there, bringing up this sensation of upset that intruded into my space again. I stared at them and they went on with their sunbathing. My neighbors had had a break-in a few weeks before and, therefore, it would be appropriate to call the police, so I did. Although I felt justified in what I had done, they turned out to be friends of the son of the owner and were allowed to be there. I thought, "Whoa, what's the lesson here?" I apologized; the guy was very cordial and didn't attack. I thought that was a very interesting little exercise, having given myself credit for achieving some peace of mind, but realized I needed to go further. It's hard to explain, but those types of insightful events are occurring. I realized other disturbing people were the "same person" and I had to reflect on why I was creating this, what they were bringing back to me. I'm now internalizing more than I ever did before, instead of pointing out errors and blaming everybody else. If I focus on more positive things, the addictions merely slip away. I turn around and realize I don't do them any more. What's been sticking with me is the idea of looking forward to searching out how we get in our own way, almost like an Easter egg hunt.

My strategies weren't working. I was searching because I knew that obsessing about working out to look good and about what I was eating were not going to be enough anymore. I recognized a need for change and became more introspective than ever before. I found spirituality, becoming more involved with church or God. I learned to depend on Him more, calling on Him for strength to overcome those fears.

My process with upset depends upon the circumstance. If I'm in the middle of something, I can't be quiet and shut my eyes, but when I do have the opportunity, I get internal, asking the Holy Spirit to show me the truth about this situation, or correct my thinking on this matter. I'm willing and asking from my heart to connect with whatever I'm having discomfort with and then let the Holy Spirit take over and show me the way. All of a sudden, or within a short time, the whole form truly changes. It's happened so many times. Upset reminds me I have some agenda other than joining, and it's such a gentle lesson. I don't fight addictions anymore, which is really great. When I shifted my focus, they all fell by the wayside.

I was in a great deal of pain, which this time I knew I wasn't going to walk away from. I felt a strong intuition to reconnect with the gentleness and kindness I knew was within me, but I didn't know how. With everything I had done in my life, all the books I had read, all the philosophies I had gone through, I didn't understand why pain was still there, stronger than ever, and I needed to find someone who had more wisdom than I. I was ready to listen. That's when I went to a psychotherapist, which was the beginning of the big change in my life. Early on, I also recall sitting in one of your classes, Carol, thinking, "If somebody in here says the word God one more time, I'm getting out of here!" because, at that point, if there was anything I was angry with, it was God. I thought, I'm a human being and I wouldn't do to people what he's done to me! I was turning my back on Him if it was the last thing I did. I didn't recognize that my pain and upset was caused by me and that I, not God, had turned my back on myself. My own self-hatred was extremely profound, and my rage still has not completely dissipated. Most of the time, yes, but there are moments when I could grab onto that again.

The pain is a feeling attached to a belief, and neither can disappear so long as I keep them held in. The feeling is what's generating my life. So as long as I feel not good enough, I will find myself in situations that reflect "not good enough" to me, thinking I've chosen the wrong person or the wrong profession. I never try to sugarcoat things, and I don't try to bypass my feelings. When my mind starts to wander or choose something else, I say, Nope, that isn't true and you know that. You are part of the Universe. You have a place.

Looking back, it's clear the old ideas were falling away one by one. I could choose to be violent or not. I want to recognize that the choices I make every minute make a difference. Now I've made the decision to follow my heart, my instincts, or my inner intuition and I naturally go to more joyous things. And addictions just fall away.

So many of my addictive behaviors really eluded me. I kept going from one thing to another to finally get to a point of asking for help. I was not what most people would consider a "low-bottom drunk." I didn't have to lose my house, car, or job, and I still had creature comforts many people seem to have to lose before seeking help. However, I hit bottom when I felt I couldn't rely on myself anymore. Of course, I'd been doing a terrible job of relying on myself, but I thought it was very weak not to be able to handle these problems on my own. When I decided I needed help, there was a lot of relief in that, and my life quickly started to turn around. Early on, however, I couldn't recognize some of the other addictive behaviors because, when the lights are off, nothing is obvious.

I was, to some extent, constantly feeling victimized by other people or events, and I've found today, when those feelings and discomfort start to come up, I don't have to try to fix things or get people to correct their behavior. It's time to stop running, sit down, and work with it. It's always about taking a hard look at yourself, because the solutions aren't out there with somebody else. What's going on is happening inside of me, and if I can get *to the root of that, then the rest corrects itself.*

˙ Discomfort as part of the healing process dawned on me as I dealt with it; then I recognized other past addictions, other ways I used to hide. When I'm in a good space, I don't have to battle against addictions at all. I would like to say all old behaviors have disappeared, but occasionally some of them resurface. However, the time it takes to become aware of them and to deal with the discomfort gets shorter and shorter.

I tried, unsuccessfully, to quit smoking five or six times. I believed the withdrawal would be a form of suffering to be avoided at all costs so I pushed it out of my sight. All my techniques—acupuncture, self-hypnosis, hypnosis by hypnotherapists, the patch, you name it—were an attempt to separate even further from the withdrawal symptoms, which actually increased the pain. Recognizing that was the wrong approach all the way, I had to do a complete 180-degree turn. I had to try exactly the opposite of those five or six failures, which I didn't want to face in the beginning. But I said, "God Almighty, I'm going to try quitting for at least one day to see if it works." I did, and it didn't kill me, so I tried it again for another day. I had to face the withdrawals square on. I pressed into the feeling to see if I could feel it, and as I did, I remembered how much I wanted the peace of God. It was that simple. I would feel the withdrawal symptoms and make a categorical, unequivocal decision truly to want the peace of God instead of a cigarette until the craving subsided or went away. The suffering disappeared, and the habitual response got weaker and weaker. In fact, I was amazed that about four days after quitting, the attraction to smoking disappeared. Then it came back with a vengeance—I mean, the craving came back like a freight train on about the sixth or seventh day. Those two days were the battleground for me, but once past, the craving subsided and was gone. No more battle. Smoking lost its attraction, and I would say that my real sense of freedom came about a month after I quit.

The whole process of getting this level of freedom was exactly the opposite of what I thought it would be. My other attempts always failed, and I couldn't recognize why. I had smoked for forty-three years, and you can image that daily pattern. The thought of smoking a cigarette and then actually doing it as a physical activity, anywhere from twenty to forty times a day for forty-three years, ingrains itself. It was amazing that my symptoms, including a typical smoker's cough, were gone within three days when I quit smoking. Just gone. I used to have bronchitis like hell during the wintertime, but this winter there was no bronchitis at all. I can remember smoking, but I have no craving. There is a huge difference.

Distracting myself from my pain literally involved running to hide. I did a kind of isolation thing where I would hide out at home, shut the door, make the room dark, curl up in a ball and numb out, shut off and shut down. Also, I hid out in television or movies, trying to escape. The motivation for everything was to avoid acknowledging how I felt It was about control and trying to be good enough, thinking, Well, when this happens, or if I get this, or when I accomplish this goal, then, then - - -. I've recently discovered that's not true and "then" is never going to happen. With that discovery, I went into a period where there was no motivation to do anything after realizing the old fantasy wasn't going to work, nothing, thinking I was going to die. Now I recognize I was experiencing a major transformation.

   Only recently, have I begun to realize experientially that feeling uncomfortable is okay and that it doesn't mean anything about me. There was no encouragement to ask questions about the meaning of distress when I was younger, not to the deep extent where addictions were uncovered. Wow! I'm noticing how uncomfortable I was with everything! I need to be disciplined in making my choices, even with the smallest one. I must specifically look every day at my intention and motivation for doing this or wanting that because everything in the past was about avoiding pain. When I can let everything be, the discomfort dissolves, disappears. It's astonishing! I'm so very thankful I have this realization now!

My better way came through finding that God, Divine Life, didn't exist outside but inside of me. As I opened myself to new ideas, *my true nature dawned on me from the inside, although I fought that for a long time. I was already on antidepressants when I discovered these new ideas about the connection between upset and addictions. I hadn't dared be without them because everybody would know and might disapprove, since anxiety is impossible to keep secret. I began to share my situation with all my clients, wanting them to know that feeling anxious was okay, perhaps requiring medication, and that was okay too. That would give them permission to tell the truth. Honesty was essential; I liked seeing that other people didn't have it all together, and that we are all alike.*

The anxiety or depression occasionally reappeared, but I began to accept it, discussing it with my wife instead of hiding, and said to myself, John, thou art the Christ, the son of the living God and you have divine life. That's who you really are. You are not the anxiety or the depression or whatever the world might think. That's how I would reassure myself. It took a long time to realize I had made my stepmother's words about "having demons inside" into a self-fulfilling prophecy. However, I've come to know beyond any shadow of a doubt that she was wrong. They are not there. That's not who I am! Now when discomfort comes upon me, I'm not afraid of it because there's no power in it. I'm having much, much more peace of mind. I'm not experiencing shame or blame or fear about the future. I'm more into the here and now, feeling it's wonderful to be me, no matter what I'm experiencing. I don't have to lie about who I am, or pretend, or create stories. So far as what happened to addictive behaviors, they don't exist now.

It didn't occur to me, Carol made it occur to me. Her addictions' workshop tapes opened up a lot of things for me. I've learned I need to feel what I feel, not push it away. When I do that, it's not so bad, but fighting against it wears me out. I become aware I'm feeling something and that recognition leads to wanting to feel it, at least sometimes. Although I may say I'm going to deal with this, the immediate situation may prevent it and I acknowledge I'm the one who sets up those obstacles.

When I stop fighting upset, I forget to eat as a distraction. I go to get a snack and forget I wanted something to eat. My mind isn't focused on it anymore. There isn't a need to distract myself from the feeling, because the feeling isn't there.

The first six months after the drinking stopped, it was a process of the fog lifting. I know what science says and what my experience was, and they don't agree. I didn't have any withdrawal or the shakes, although I had severe mood swings for days on end that were probably borderline manic-depressive. In my first year of sobriety I began experiencing anger I wasn't aware was there. I didn't realize the two were related for two or three years. In fact, I would ask in the various AA groups if anyone else was experiencing anger, and inevitably one or two would say they were. When I inquired about a solution for the anger, they said, "Don't drink, and go to meetings." That was wonderful advice, but didn't solve the problem. Even though I faithfully went to meetings, participated fully, and stopped drinking, there came a point when I knew deep down there had to be more than what they were presenting. About three years ago, this compulsion or notion that something was missing pushed me—where, I didn't know. I had felt frustrated and unfulfilled for a long time, becoming re-acquainted with the feeling shortly after getting sober.

I'm coming to realize that physical pain was perhaps another avenue of distraction. From early childhood until well into my twenties, I had some type of physical pain. At sixteen, I was diagnosed with possible stomach cancer, because it was continually in a knot. I went through a comprehensive series of tests with a leading gastroenterologist, who finally concluded the attacks occurred only when I was not in some mode of sports training. Years later, a second physician pointed out I was living too stressful a life. I listened to his suggestion to take some time for myself and thought, I can't spend time alone, because I'm liable to find out the truth, that I'm phony and defective. I simply could not consider the consequences of exploring my defectiveness.

There was a sense both of relief and disbelief, however, on considering that the same thing drives everyone. The understanding that almost everyone operates from that same point of "better not show who I really am, or I'll be found out" has been a real breakthrough, a real growth in coming to know that no matter the circumstances, we all shared the same internal feeling about ourselves. The reason I had not believed this, to be honest, was fear of admitting I was like everybody else. I didn't get to be special, even with these neat physical challenges nobody else had. No question about it, my special-ness was about being "worse than" rather than "better than."

What "getting found out" means to me would be seeing myself equal with everyone else, and I'm not quite at that point, still feeling subordinate to a lot of people and still unwilling to accept my own divinity. I talk about it, tell others about it, and have no problem understanding divinity about everybody walking the face of this earth—except myself, which is nuts, clearly insane. I do try consistently to remind myself I am a creation of a power greater than myself, but it's almost like He made six billion good ones, and one defective one. I know that's crazy, but I still hang on to that specialness block.

The first bold steps of being authentic resulted in more positive feedback than ever from people who wanted to be around me to have fun. A great freedom comes in finding that showing the real you actually produces better results than using humor as a mask. As I became more real, the humor, which is one of my skills, became more appropriate. Now, it can become a way of joining. Without a sense of good will, it can be very distracting. You cannot deal with people abstractly and have fun, say like a joke teller. There's absolutely no sense of humor involved in repeating a joke. It's a way to fill airtime without being personal and, ultimately, is a pretty offensive pastime. When you really do put yourself into a present state with people, you find out what they find amusing about themselves. People love certain things, like the sound of their own names, the things that play on their "okay" vulnerabilities. You can't talk about blondes or women in general. You have to be specific, and in order to be specific, you have to know about them, what's different about them, what's okay about them, what they value. It's the differ-ence between focusing on things to embarrass people or on things that create their signature. For instance, you could not embarrass Jack Benny by criticizing his violin playing; however, you certainly could embarrass a professional violinist with such criticism.

We all have learned a bias against feeling discomfort, but in my own untutored way, I invite it. All our systems are telling us to find a comfortable place and stay there, yet to be perfectly comfortable is a great way to have no life. Generally, when I feel there's a hot spot in me, I'm willing to let it boil because it's wonderfully freeing. I know if I don't deal with issues, they keep recurring, showing up in all different ways. I keep telling friends, "Your life happens when you're uncomfortable. Don't turn your back on it. When you're having all this upset and misery, it's because you're being given instruction. Listen and ask what must be learned to prevent this happening again.."

When I finally left my marriage, I was smoking only two cigarettes a day and my behavior was great, but I was a sick puppy. I was so sick from anxiety and worry, I had no idea that my addiction to being in control of the kids was the problem. I thought it was their behavior making me sick, rather than my trying to make my picture real about how things were supposed to be. After all, in my picture my children were soccer players, swimmers, and healthy, outgoing, loving people, not drug addicts sitting in the closet smoking dope all day. Those terribly upsetting feelings led me to believe I was shit, had obviously missed the boat somewhere, and had never done anything right, because if I had, the horrible things occurring in our lives wouldn't be happening.

I absolutely battled against behavior in the old days and I had a treatment plan for everything. I understood intellectually that feeling the distress was the fast way to healing; however, what I didn't know until recently was that I didn't have to figure out where it came from, or why. Even though I had been told that, there was such a block, such an addiction to learning, intellectualizing, and staying in my head, that no matter how many times people said it to me, I never heard, "You don't have to figure it out." Plus, I was in school studying social work, which is all about problem solving. My ego was providing me with problem-solving strategies, so my heart wasn't hearing that I didn't have to figure it out or blame anybody. No one getting blamed was the key for me. Now when I feel upset, it doesn't last as long, and pain is replaced with peace, a grin, hopefulness, giggles, and acceptance of myself.

Now I can see my kids provided a tremendous service by doing drugs and not fitting my picture—it made me wake up. With gratitude already about my younger son and his situation, I've now started to have it about the older one. And as I am grateful, I notice they get better. It's really incredible! Great learning has come through them, but not the kind I was counting on. I planned my children down to the hour of their conception. When my first child was conceived, I was nineteen years old, reading a book on how many sperm are emitted, what time ovulation happens, and what's the best opportunity for the healthiest kid. We're talking control freak here!

The need for control and to have perfect kids was to keep me safe from myself, from self-discovery. It would also keep me satisfied, I thought, keep me a good little mommy-girl, make me sit still and do everything right, with no opportunity for that wild-child spirit in me to get loose. That part was under lock and key because I was terrified of it, afraid my family would reject me. If I had known that feeling rejected wasn't a problem, boy, would my life have been different! I remember, at my first son's birth, holding him and thinking, Oh, this is a gift to myself, one I can have anytime. At twenty, I didn't have a clue how true that was—the tremendous learning that my children would precipitate.

When distress appears, I recognize it's something I need to look at. That sure took the pressure off. It's our doorway to peace, but we have judged it very harshly, looking down on it as something that's not supposed to be there. We may recognize our upset on a time and space level, but we never recognize how truly distressed we are, going way past being upset because your husband came home late or your mother-in-law chapped you off. It goes much, much deeper than that and drives us horrendously.

If I judge someone, I'm judging myself, and I'm really out of judging myself! Realizing that is my biggest gift. I find judgment still creeps up in the most ridiculous places, but I recognize it, know there's nothing bad about it, and don't beat myself up, noting, Well, that was an interesting little judgment. It temporarily interferes with peace of mind, but it doesn't mean I'm bad. Judgment is just what we do. Finding peace is absolutely an unlearning process, and the greater the willingness to give up judgment, the quicker it happens. I can honestly say I wanted peace more than anything else, and that's exactly what I got. It was a wonderful gift, the easiest thing in the world, and certainly not difficult or painful.

Changing behavior was not difficult; once I changed my mind, it was very easy. It simply lost its appeal. There was no battle at all against obsessive behavior. It just wasn't there. If someone had told me that several years ago, I would have replied, "You're crazy, I'll play tennis till the day I die. You know I love this game!" Now, you couldn't drag me onto a tennis court.

My process was the willingness to let go of control of my life and to realize it's not my place to judge everyone walking around in this physical form. As long as I keep my goal of wanting peace above anything else, nothing else is required and everything falls into place. The last four years have been phenomenal. If someone had told me back then that this is where I'd be, I would have said, "You're nuts. There's no way. Other people get to have all these great things happen, but not me." Peace has been my purpose and wanting that more than anything else has been the ticket out of all the anguish, taking no effort on my part.

My turning point was studying A Course in Miracles *with experiential classes week after week where everyone would share what was going on with them. We were guided and supported to walk through the upset and the main thing was knowing we weren't going to die and were not alone. During that time, a friend and I decided not to date for several months until we finished going through the class. Even though it started out as a joke, it became obvious that this was exactly what my healing called for. Formerly, there had been a series of very brief affairs or interludes that quickly burned out. Uninterrupted fantasy, one way or the other, was always occupying my mind. If there wasn't a relationship in process, I was in mourning over the last love and anticipating the next.*

As the first step with any addiction, I had to stop indulging my relationship fantasies to let all that discomfort come up. Otherwise, I would have gone back into the dating situation with the same type relationship I'd had with everyone else, and I knew I didn't want to repeat that endlessly. For the first time in my life, I began learning about and practicing having whole, healthy relationships with lots of people where no romance was involved at all. The biggest blessing of that period is that I practiced relating without conditions, demands, and expectations about wanting to change and shape people. With friends, male or female, there was simply a casual accepting without concern about where they went, or if they called or not.

If I'm willing to let the discomfort come up and not stuff it, I can listen to it and ask if it makes sense. Sometimes I get a clearer message of what I need to let go of than others. With opposition gone, I can allow peace to return and the need for addiction leaves.

The business I'm in, the whole healing field is to help people look beneath their masks, so I'm trying to be very honest and discover what's underneath when something causes me anxiety, anger, or an unpleasant feeling. I go into my shell and am very quiet and things are revealed through introspection or meditation; then my intellectual mind makes some logical structure out of that and I can talk about it. I have made some real self-discoveries about my fears and parts of my personality that are controlling. I feel like every feeling I have comes from some deeply ingrained belief I have about myself, one that was put into my computer brain a long time ago. I see so many examples of people who have frequent eruptions of anger, and much of the psychological advice is about releasing that anger, appropriately. My feeling is that the anger and the incident that triggered it blow a hole in our mask, so to speak, and letting it out is good.

It decreases the tension. Before, I tried to go down in that hole introspectively, with an intellectual flashlight, so to speak, and find out what's at the bottom of that gloomy pit, bubbling up as anger, and now I see I don't have to do that. I can just let the anger go, feel it, and be with it; then all of a sudden, it will tell me what it's about. The most helpful thought is that God created me perfect, and thank goodness, I haven't been able to do anything to mess that up!

My willingness to help others has absolutely escalated the healing process, as well as learning to be vulnerable, which was a scary thing. However, instead of people running away from me, I found that being open draws people closer.

Once again, this last response is so instructive and so typical that it calls for less editing. Please allow yourself to identify with it as much as possible.

The shift into the awareness of being as God created me finally came. It took forty-six years to get to that point of surrender—a fact that I initially held against myself—but now I realize, Okay, forty-six years, so? I would trade forty-six years of my life for the last four of being happy, joyous, and free, and forget the rest. When people speak of the "good old days," well, okay, there were good old days, but so is today, perfect and wonderful right this moment, and I want to experience it like that. I no longer have to judge what it was like in the past.

Deciding to seek help was a huge step for me, a major, major turning point. At the moment I was ready, by no coincidence, wonderful, loving people came into my life, people who cared tremendously about me and my well-being, although I didn't realize it. They were real clear that my well-being was not being looked after by me. I called a drug addiction center out of state, and they told me there was hope and I could contact a local hospital. I thought my treatment needed to be private, fearing my career could be hurt, my business would fail, and everything would fall underneath me if people knew the extent of my damage. I called the hospital, withholding my name out of fear they would recognize me since my medical history was already in their computer because of my other illnesses. As an aside, it's interesting to note I haven't experienced any of those illnesses since then. Once you quit all the drugs and get back to a free life, you don't have all the medical drama. Finally, I was told that if I would not enter their treatment program, a psychiatrist would see me privately. She was very loving, very quiet, and after we finished our interview, she said, "Well, Scott, I think you're right at the edge. One more step and you're off the cliff, dead, so your timing is very appropriate. You're either going to die or step back and live your life." I realized, with greater awareness, the true degree of my addiction.

Therapy was very helpful in sorting out my intentions about recovery because I thought all I needed to control was the cocaine addiction; the rest were okay, in other words socially acceptable. I could see there was no difference between the drinking, drugging, power struggles, relationship dramas, and all the other things I was drawn to in order to avoid looking at myself honestly. She didn't focus on those because mood-altering substances were her specialty, and she was real clear that if I wanted to get better, I would no longer be able to use them. I was pretty upset about no mood altering, because I thought I was there only to get rid of the cocaine problem.

After subsequent group therapy and more bouts of depression when my father died, someone suggested I needed to deal with whatever was causing me to do all the drugs. I knew something was in the way and was very afraid to find out what, yet I wanted so desperately to be free of the anxiety and fear I had hoped drugs would solve. I knew defending against the drugs or stopping the behavior wasn't going to make me happy. Although I looked better outwardly—I looked "healed,"— nonetheless, I definitely was not.

Finally, I really got in touch with my feelings, which stemmed from the great fear I wasn't going to make it in this world. I had quit using addictive substances and was now affected by those feelings quite dramatically. I didn't act on them or create problems, but nevertheless, they were eating away at me significantly. Ultimately, I recognized the need for additional help. I needed to go into areas of guilt and distress I was holding back deep within me. Of course, I presumed fear had to be kept hidden, otherwise I would totally crumble and never be put back together again.

I spent great energy defending against drinking or drugging or not getting upset, which was part of my problem too. I became aware of the tremendous freedom in not defending a position because it might "get me." For instance, I was in the French Quarter of New Orleans recently, a location with more potential for temptation than anywhere else, but I felt no fear, threat, or need to defend. In fact, we went to a favorite bar to have an iced tea, and I realized how many hours I'd spent sitting there, totally inebriated and annihilated. There I was, still sitting on the same bar stool, not in a state of fear but in a state of peace, in the middle of the drama with people falling down outside the place, loud music, and drug deals going on. Some guy, really hurting, came up to me and started talking. He was me, ten years ago in that same bar, calling for love though not using those words. He was bouncing off the walls, but I wasn't threatened by that; for a moment we had this little connection, communicating peacefully about many things. He was a lawyer and I used to hate lawyers, but now, nothing he represented required defense. It was challenging for a person to reflect something about me, but I thought, Okay, I see what's happening here. I'm pissed off, but this isn't about you, I get to see about me now. What I used to defend against I now cherish as the road to take another look at what's holding me back from my freedom. Now I can sit on the same bar stool, enjoying it a different way through having someone come up to me calling for help, and being able to offer it—a gift to myself.

Clearly, upset is the unrecognized path leading to freedom, as when I hit bottom in 1994. That was only the introduction and significant things continued to happen, showing me it was okay to ask for help. During each period of introspection, I gained so much and the happiness broadened in my life. My uneasiness is the greatest road marker I could have. I don't have to be jumping and yelling and screaming, just being aware of a slight discomfort or a desire to defend; a turning away from, a lack of interest in joining are now blessings. It's a process that does take some time, but hiding is no longer appropriate behavior. My choice is to allow it to come up. I used to pray for easy lessons, fearing that "hard" lessons would be too much, but not anymore. It's the same thing about not having to defend. If I become alarmed even to the smallest degree, obviously I'm not wanting to join with an individual. The beauty of it is that all I really need to do is be willing to join with others.

My fear had been there would be some sacrifice required, and that everything in the real, practical world would get screwed up if I didn't manage it properly. Over the last several years there have been ups and downs, but they haven't been killers and have worked out just fine. My life now is about the development of trust. Now I have to decide, in each moment, to trust or to take control. It's my choice, and wonderful things have happened I never before imagined possible. If I seek peace, my problems will be solved and that includes the problems of the world. Now, they may not be solved the way I think they should be, but they will be solved—perfectly. The big one was when I decided God really didn't need my help in running the universe, that everything would be fine without my having to know how it worked and why or when. The trust now allows me just to "be."

I was hiding and repressing the whole, real me, and although sometimes I did a good job of acting, I knew it was a substitute. I wanted what is real about me to surface, which I was not doing in my addiction. It was my choice, at one time, to abuse, but no longer. The power of decision became mine again for the first time in many, many years, and from there I could choose to drink or drug again. I chose not to. It wasn't hard. In fact, every day showed me more and more how easy that choice was.

It is our most fervent hope that you have listened with all your heart to these stories of despair and confusion and are ready to write your own, for the last time. With a single, confronting event, some in our group were forced to see the hopelessness of their situations, while others took longer to reach their limits of pain. There is no right way to discover the pointlessness of our current situation, only that sooner or later we must admit that all is not well. How long it takes to come to this point is irrelevant, because as life begins anew, the unhappy past slides away and is no more. Please note this is not denial but the natural consequence of choosing a more authentic way to live now—choosing peace of mind.

This step becomes our turning point, as well. Here we recap all the hard-won wisdom expressed in the foregoing statements. As difficult as it was in some cases, everyone finally recognized the need to accept or embrace the disturbed or anxious feelings—the one choice they had steadfastly resisted. In my experience, almost no one understands what the word *acceptance* means. To virtually everyone, to accept means to resign one's self to a situation, to be finally overwhelmed by the feelings, to approve of the circumstance we have resisted, or to cast it forever into emotional concrete. Absolutely nothing could be further from the truth. To accept without resistance is the first step in the transformation process, in allowing our blocked energy to move once again. Blocked energy can be recognized as those areas of life where you feel inhibited, restricted, powerless, or your body feels tight or hard.

Some label the process of acceptance as embracing your experience, some call it allowing it to be, and others speak of pressing into rather than trying to separate from the feeling. By whatever name, the process required is to move from the thinking, intellectual mode to noticing just what these feelings are, without judgment or interpretation. I often ask a person to sit and be with their feelings, to give them room, to finally honor them and regard them tenderly. Sometimes someone will counter that they have done that and nothing was better. On further inquiry, however, it turns out that their version of "'sitting with the feelings" is really thinking about them, analyzing them, and trying to figure out where they came from, what should be done about them, who is to blame for them, and what should be their fate. Nowhere in that formula is there actually being with the feelings—the process is all in the head, with the energy as stuck as ever.

I remember a specific incident in my early days of learning

about feelings. I came in one day, feeling very upset about something—I have no idea what. I vowed to put these new ideas into practice and sat in my living room and surrendered into the feeling without resistance. In very little time, by being very vigilant about where I placed my attention, I was out of my head and into just feeling. All of a sudden, I experienced an inner sensation of a band of energy spiraling around me from my seat on the sofa to a foot or so over my head, with an accompanying sense of darkness turning into light. It took only a couple of seconds and as the energy shifted from dark to light, visually, it also shifted from heavy to light and the upset was changed into a sense of well-being. At once, an inner knowing clarified the sameness of these words—healing, forgiveness, transformation, alchemy, quickening. Our part of the transforming process is to be with the feeling. Then a built-in, what I call, "self-cleaning oven" in the very core of our being takes over. Correction is not our job, but there exists a faculty within us that does the transforming. It was astonishing to note how quickly the upset disappeared and how obvious was the path to peace. Remember, the process is easy; deciding to accept it is the only part that seems hard.

It is important to understand what is happening when we allow our feelings to be, rather than fighting and denying them. To use an analogy, when you put an ice cube into a pan, place it on the stove, and turn on the heat, the ice begins to melt. As any beginning science student knows, when heat is applied, the molecules speed up and the solid ice turns to liquid water. Have you ever met an ice cube that was able to revolt and declare it was not going to adhere to these physical laws and melt? Of course not. Ice cubes don't get to decide what will or will not happen once heat is applied. In the same way, upset feelings are like our basic life energy moving too slowly. When we decide to let them be, honor them, and join with them, we are "applying the heat" that comes from love, and no disturbed feelings can long remain when they are lovingly accepted. Our own energy quickens and the upset feelings turn into ones of well-being right before our eyes. Our upset truly is the raw material of our peace of mind. In every case, when all else failed, our participants employed this very process. They finally surrendered to the feelings, which then changed.

The great news conveyed in these answers is that, in all cases, the addictive behavior stopped on its own when the bound-up feelings were finally experienced, transformed, and allowed to move. When we stop interpreting what feelings mean about us and simply allow them to be, remembering we are just fine, they clear right up. When anxiety is diminished or gone, our behaviors change. Remember the train analogy: Cars go where the engine goes. Our behaviors become more appropriate, more self-fulfilling, more caring and loving toward others as we care more about ourselves. Loving unconditionally is our basic, most natural inclination. Self-expression is ultimately the expression of love, and we move automatically in that direction as we allow ourselves to feel, not resisting our ego, but ignoring it. All the assertiveness training designed to deal with overbearing individuals needs to be directed toward our own egos, as that is where we need the most practice in asserting our right to be.

Will you take the hands outstretched to you and allow this material to become part of your turning point? Notice that help was immediately available for everyone when they said, There must be a better way, and I don't know what it is—help that was recognizable and useful. They didn't have to go to the ends of the earth to find their answers, nor do you. Our answers travel with us wherever we go, and there are no exceptions. Don't try to make yourself the exception as that is merely a delay tactic.

Step 7:

Have you ever gone camping in the woods, where you made a great campfire and planned to cook a meal or two? Or maybe in your own backyard, where you planned a cookout? Imagine this situation. The fire reaches the perfect point for cooking and you and your friends all sit around it with the intention to cook your dinner; however, your food is still in the cooler. No one in his right mind would fault the fire and complain that it must be defective because dinner is not cooking, when the food is not even present. You must bring the food and put it on the fire if you expect the transforming properties of fire to operate on it. In the same way, the transforming property of love can only operate on those aspects of our lives that we are willing to bring to it. We must bring our hurt into awareness, and when we accept it with no regret or resistance, we are effectively bringing it to the agent for change within us. This transforming love is the very core of our being, however much it has been buried, denied, and disguised. And as with the ice cube, no stuck or hurtful feeling can long remain in the presence of the power of love, the only real power that exists. That is why the process works.

Now, please take some time to settle in, close your eyes, and put all your awareness on how you are feeling. Imagine that you are switching off the intellectual, analytical function and focus only on what you are feeling. Perhaps the feeling is localized somewhere in your body. Put your attention there and regard it tenderly. Imagine you are putting a spotlight on it. You may have a feeling of madness, of wanting to jump out of your skin, but stick with it and it will dissipate. If you are diligent with this process, you will feel a lightening up and a shift in energy. You can breathe more deeply.

Second, remember in an earlier exercise you were asked to notice all the things that you run or hide from, or dare not look at. The form that came up may have been a feeling, face, person, fear, an energy, or all of the above. Remember how you ran? Now, as a different and yet very effective way of moving that blocked energy, make the decision not to run again. Be very firm and authoritative with yourself about this. In your mind's eye, with your physical eyes closed, turn around 180 degrees and announce that you are not running any more! With your mind's eye open, stand your ground and look right at whatever is there as you turn around to look. You may find darkness, something evil, a family member or another person, a vague fear, a monster or devil, love, or yourself. The variations are endless. Whatever it is, do not take your mind's eye off it. Announce that not only do you refuse to run but that you intend to approach it—not with the intention to harm or threaten but to join with, to extend your hand to it. Keep talking to it and keep walking toward it. You will be astounded at what happens, and perhaps for the first time in your life, you will experience relief. Remember, what you accept you have power over. What you resist seems to have power over you. Will you honor yourself enough to take this step?

8. When did you discover all addictions could be addressed and released the same way?

The responses to this question were almost identical; therefore, only a few representative ones will be quoted. Our participants discovered, through their own experience, that every upset is approached the same way and that they dissipate the same way. And great liberation, feeling larger, and breathing easier was the result.

I went to Overeaters Anonymous, AA meetings, and codependent meetings to see what was out there in the form of group counseling. When I found the right group, their specific addiction didn't matter because I related with the people and found the issues were really all the same. I learned that getting outside myself and counting on something other than my own ego, letting God be God, helped me get stronger, more independent, and less reliant on my own knowledge. I was looking for answers in many areas, but it really came down to spirituality, God, love, relationships, and enriching my life with different types of people. Now it makes sense that anything can be an addiction, but I had no concept of that earlier. I'd say within the last two to three years, I've realized all of them get handled the same way, and that was such a relief.

The idea that all addictions serve the same purpose came out of the Course *study. The suggestion that all problems are the same but with many different forms was very, very important* to me. It was a relief to know I didn't have to attack these problems one by one and knock them down. Instead, there was one answer. There are two or three hundred twelve-step programs, and the idea of having to join all those would be pretty insane, but people do attempt that. Though it was not difficult intellectually to recognize one solution, internalizing and experiencing the eighteen-inch drop from the head to the heart was not fast. It took several years, but it did eventually happen. A marvelous book, written by one of the first one hundred sober AAs, suggests after much research that the answer to the permanent recovery of addictions is the same as we've discussed, the spiritual answer.

The idea of a common denominator to all addictions hit home in 1992, three weeks after Carol's workshop. I really got it! I was so happy because my analytical part previously thought there were thousands of problems and thousands of solutions, and somehow I had to figure them out to be happy! The idea of one problem showing up in thousands of different ways was such wonderful, good news! Wonderful because I could deal with one problem!

Alcoholism was very socially unacceptable to me and finally, I became so uncomfortable with it I had to find other things to distract myself. I still didn't realize what was behind all of them; the common denominator became obvious after I got involved with a number of groups. It was as if somebody suddenly turned the lights on and there it was. With the lights on, the idea of one solution to all problems came together at once. It was like working a jigsaw puzzle. When you get an idea of what the total picture is like, the pieces start to fall together quickly. Finding out that addictions are all the same and getting to the root of it all was refreshing and encouraging. I may not deal with it very well at times, but at least when I'm having a problem, I can start working on where it's really coming from. There was a lot of relief with that. All of a sudden there was some comfort in the discomfort.

I haven't fully come to the point, although it's inviting, of knowing that what drives humor addiction also drives substance abuse. It's difficult for me to come to a conclusion without working through it myself. I carry the residual effects of the terrible lie, "You're special," that mothers tell their children. That makes the world so impossibly difficult. I tend to think of myself as special, or my circumstances as different, and I don't know that I want to be lumped in with the emotionally addicted, especially. I can see the doctrinal pull to that, but I'm just not there yet.

Because we don't realize pain is the raw material for joy, we spend most of our time dragging garbage bags around and not looking up to see if healing could happen. I knew when I was doing the training in 1988, all addictions are healed the same way, but I lost it and went back into that diverse problem-solving, categorizing, putting-everything-in-a-cubbyhole state of mind. Only in the last two years has this become clear. With a sigh of relief I can allow feelings to be there without belittling them or me. It's just an awareness, and it all becomes a truly interesting adventure.

I went to one of Carol's seminars and remember sitting there, wanting to cry practically all day with the very meaningful, beautiful things she said. That was the beginning of realizing there's only one problem and one way of dealing with that problem, and then it was a matter of time to accept that. I presumed lessons were to be learned through pain. I thought you got that lesson over and over until you learned it. And one process, absolutely not! I always thought the process of learning was to analyze, to see the mistake one made, or to see the expectation that wasn't met by someone else, or perhaps to see where I was wrong in word or deed. I thought I had to analyze everything, adding to my knowledge, acquiring a bigger, fatter data bank, allowing me to look out there to see what was wrong, avoid it, and do it differently. A new technique was a better technique.

One addiction is not more special than another. Gradually, over the last four years I would say, it's dawned on me that the underlying motive for all addictions is the same and that they are healed the same way. I know this is not about promoting A Course in Miracles, *but I think that getting involved with it was the best thing that ever happened to me. It's such an easy, clear way with no gray areas in it. It teaches "this is how it is" for everything and everybody with no exceptions, rather than the idea that we handle drug addiction this way and alcohol addiction that way, as our society handles it. Our society doesn't ever address the actual problem.*

Until recently, I had never looked closely at addictions being the same, but when I did, it was so obvious I couldn't avoid it. As I learned to look at the source of the unacknowledged but socially acceptable addictions, as well as the familiar ones, it became very clear. I've had multiple addictions that sometimes can be switched, so knowing there is one way of getting rid of all of them is the best news I've ever heard. There's no need to battle or figure out which addiction is kicking in, since acceptance of any upset always dissolves it.

I had searched for answers in many areas, and as I read more of the Course, *it really dawned on me there was only one problem. Now I know when there is discomfort, I should deal with it rather than dissect it. I realize lack of forgiveness is it, period.*

These answers were particularly uniform. None in our group had an awareness earlier that all addictions are driven by the same inner experience and all eventually recognized the common underlying hurt behind them. Many of them commented on how clear and obvious their circumstances had become and how they marveled at their former inability to see it. As noted earlier, the ability to comprehend is directly related to the desire to do so! When any of us want to see the connection, we do. The majority also indicated great relief at the realization of one problem and, therefore, one solution for their addictions; they had tried so hard, without success, to locate the many different solutions, techniques, and strategies to handle their myriad problems. Many were very candid about their initial difficulty with accepting such a simple concept and some were doubtful for quite a while, but those who put the idea into practice were greatly rewarded.

Step 8:

We have learned to be ashamed of many of our past behaviors, and the guilt associated with them is the true source of our pain. Since this guilt must be relinquished for peace to return and addictions to depart, we will now take another step of the healing process. Practice acknowledging the following statements, or your own version of them, with your head held high and remembering your right to be here. It's helpful to speak them out loud and listen to the tone and strength of your own voice: "Yes, I have been selfish. Yes, I have been mean-spirited. Yes, I have been untrustworthy or dishonest. Yes,—fill in the blank. Yes, I have made mistakes. No, I am not a sinner AND I am loveable and deserving, I have a contribution to make, and I choose to live differently today. We fear the former statements are true about us and the latter merely a fantasy. The opposite is actually true and we need to practice making this reversal. Owning these statements from the past does not make you evil, shameful, or undeserving. They are descriptions of behaviors, not of you. They indicate blindness to the truth, rather than badness. Listen carefully: Your past behaviors, which have provided the excuse for your guilt, are gone! As you choose to be kind, compassionate with yourself and everyone else, and live as honorably as you are able, yesterday's mistakes are transmuted and are no more. Today's choice to be loving erases everything unloving through a process we cannot comprehend, but that does produce miraculous results. We have dominion over our experience through our ever-present ability to change our minds and start anew. You will be amazed at the relief you feel at saying the unflattering words out loud, rather than shrinking from them, owning your fears about yourself rather than trying to pretend and hide. Notice, also, how unfamiliar it feels to be your own best cheerleader and speak of your good qualities and contributions. Own the things you fear and salute your gifts, all in the same firm, positive manner. Just as it dawned on the members of our group, will you allow awareness and resolution to come to you? It may come with a flash of insight or in small increments. Whatever way, it will be perfect for you.

9. What was your experience after finally facing your fear and your equilibrium was restored?

Most of us have lived our lives with a certain quotient of fear. The only difference between us is the degree to which we have successfully deadened ourselves to it. As promised, when we actually do take time to be introspective, to feel our pain and recognize we cannot go on like this, to decide to be authentic rather than phony, our fear is quite literally transformed into well-being.

As we decide to accept our feelings, we add the component of love, not the romantic fantasy but unconditional compassion and regard. Acknowledging feelings without judgment brings our darkness to the light, fear to love, or pain to healing. More specifically, when we turn on the light of our true loving nature through the process of acceptance, the dark cannot remain. Imagine this situation. You are sitting in a dark room with many others. You have been sitting in the dark for so long you have forgotten any other condition is possible. Many strange and uncomfortable encounters occur as you stumble and crash into things because you cannot see what's in front of you. Time passes; you and your companions grow very weary of the problems and hassle stemming from living in the dark for so long. You gather together to figure out where the dark has come from or who is to blame for it, or to engage in many other theoretical exercises. All the while, there is a small awareness in your mind saying, All you have to do is turn on the light. All you have to do is love and appreciate each other instead of trying to figure things out. Our friends sitting in the dark ignore that message and decide to have a study group instead! And so they engage in endless, pointless discussions and employ countless strategies designed to make the dark go away, while steadfastly ignoring the one solution that always brings light.

At some point, it will finally occur to someone to heed the instruction to turn on the light, to love. Note these characteristics. The dark does not get to object. This is not a battle between light and dark. The dark is merely absence of light and when light is supplied, that is the end of the problem. Also note that only one person is required to turn on the light and everyone benefits. Nor does it matter how long everyone has been sitting in the dark. When the light is turned on, a new experience is at hand and there simply is no reason to ruminate on how dark it used to be. Now, finally, you are free to see! In the same way, your distress will always be eliminated when you choose to be kind to yourself, to regard yourself and others with love and acceptance. Refuse to listen to that tired, mean-spirited ego voice that keeps you in the dark. To what end? Just turn on the light!

I feel several things. In most cases, some absolute truths come to me and some shifts occur, not so much in my mind as in my heart. I'm more aware of moving deeper into a desire really to care for everybody. Sometimes I might immediately feel exhausted after an upsetting situation is brought to closure, but then I feel peaceful and calm, like I'm one with the whole world..

I feel I'm absolutely okay, totally at peace, and experiencing a sense of plenty. Everything is good right now, as compared to the old attitude, "If I can just do more, down the road there will be - - -." I definitely do not feel the same as before.

The other side of acceptance is never the same as when I went in. There's a sense of peace and a transcendence of the issue. I would never go back to living life unconsciously, from a place of mere physical pleasures, as I did before. I'm still not completely awake, but I now have a history of being unafraid of pain because I can trust I'm better off afterwards, looking at it and not running from it.

I feel different in that I'm closer to the answer; I feel better, at peace, restored. If the distress is with another person, I feel much more loving toward that person. As difficult as it might have been, the whole relationship generally changes. It doesn't always happen overnight; it sometimes takes time, but it's truly a gift.

I have all sorts of responses. Sometimes it's instantaneous release. Sometimes I hold onto upset and let go gradually, but always in the end, as soon as I let it go, there's a sense of peace, a rising up of happiness and joy. I see upset as an opportunity to heal. For instance, at any given moment I'm not just witnessing that experience of discomfort, but a long historical chain of feelings and situations. If I can look at that, I heal many other connections. My sense of self is always elevated and, in a linear sense, I'm further along the road, in a stronger place, a more whole place, and I don't respond to things that would have automatically pushed buttons several years ago.

It's very peaceful. I really don't feel upset very often any more, but when it comes up, I quickly recognize the feeling and think, Well, isn't this interesting? I wonder why I'm creating this and what it's about?

Well, everything just levels out, it's equanimity, and it's peaceful. No great big bells, whistles, sirens, no big bombs going off inside. It's just even.

Feeling what I'm feeling has been a huge challenge for me, but I have a much greater level of trust. I can come to a calm feeling, as opposed to a frenzied one.

As you recall from the responses to the first seven interview questions, peace of mind was a rarity in our group before they accepted the challenge of facing their fear. The disaster they had learned would befall them through telling the truth and allowing feeling, never occurred. Instead, there was much greater peace. Our participants now regard their ability to feel as a faculty that brings great reward. It allows for an experience of safety and contentment, or it provides the signal calling for a change of heart.

When I come out of a discomforting experience, I'm more. I don't know how to word that, but I'm more. The trees are greener, the sky is bluer. There's more of me present each time I go through it, and the more of me that's present, the more I can feel joy. Just more.

Discomfort now symbolizes that I'm holding onto an expectation or judgment about myself or others. Each time I come out of such an experience, this bag of expectations we seem to be born with is smaller. As I've been willing to go through the process, it's become a manageable little sack. And if I keep going, the remaining little bag will disappear. The total process is very, very helpful.

My sense of equilibrium, as I perceive it, comes after the fact. When I'm in the vortex of upset, the only thing I can do is bear in mind there is a solution for me, a place of safety, a good outcome, although I don't know where it is. It's difficult when I'm going through it, but coming out of it is a marvelous spot. I never come out at the same level. I come out improved, in the light really. It's an incredible experience and worth what I went through.

Somehow, I'm freer. For the first time, I'm experiencing worthiness and being good enough, even when I make mistakes. Right after a "big mistake," I think, So what? Who cares? Don't make the big drama," and I get to that place where there's no battle anymore. It's finally over, a non-issue. For another thing, when nothing is a hiding place, I can go deeper and freely make choices based on an inner guidance from the "real me," rather than pleasing other people. As to discomfort, it still comes in, but now I'm conscious of it—"Umm, guilt. There's that guilt" and know I don't have to pull the G card, so to speak. Let it be and it disappears on its own.

I return to a better place as I look at things and let them teach me about how I'm condemning myself. I'm still amazed at how practicing forgiveness, when I have a grievance with someone, always ends up in gratitude. I feel safer and more complete when I'm through.

Any time I've been able to get in touch with what I thought was the cause, and then face it, it was no big deal, nowhere near what I thought it would be. Once you face the fear, it's almost comfortable.

Mom and I had gotten into a conversation, which created a lot of tension. I was feeling really agitated, to the point that I went upstairs to my room and started crying. A bit later, I thought I heard Mom coming upstairs, so I immediately dried my eyes and sucked it all back in. Then that little voice came into my head and said, Look at what you're doing! So I went downstairs and let myself break down. She gave me a hug, and rather than something bad happening, that brought us closer. I was able to breathe, not feeling I was going to hyperventilate. I felt a whole lot better and Mom did too. It just feels good to let yourself cry.

The key was to face the fear of doing something and do it anyway. Then it was always beautiful, always better than I would have imagined. When I was in the fear, I could intellec-tually know it would go away, as in, "This too shall pass away," but that was not very helpful.

Fear was a marker for me, a red flag. The split second it occurred, I could think, Ah Ha! There's some forgiveness around this I need to accept. On the other side of fear I realize it's about forgiving myself. In my recovery, it was very important that I come to understand this thing about God, or Higher Power, and to understand I never disconnected from It. I experience that as the truth, recognizing that I can trust every moment of each day.

It's like a clearing. In fact, yesterday I cried to beat the band over someone hurting my relationships with my children. Now I feel much, much better, less threatened and bigger, as though before I had rubber bands around my whole self, holding me in. Through crying and screaming and feeling, some of those bands started to break. As a continuation of the process, certain people were placed in my path to tell me what I needed to hear. I needed to hear their words, as well as my words to them. I knew intellectually what I needed to do, but I couldn't. I was too closed off, too tight, too hard, and once I had the emotional release, I got softer. The result was physical exhaustion, which called for a nap, and then I felt normal.

What's been added is the realization that the "devils" were nothing but our perception. Everything we think about shows up "out there." We watched The Odyssey *the other night, and they knew this fact four thousand years ago. Why haven't we learned? Because we never question our culture's modeling. There's a resounding silence if you ask the question, "What's the matter with discomfort?" The idea that discomfort puts you in touch with hurtful beliefs puts a spin on a book that, formerly, I couldn't understand at all. It was about a well-known person in the New Thought movement; I was shocked because she seemed to have had a great deal of controversy with people close to her. It didn't make sense to me for a person who was supposed to know the truth to have all this difficulty. Now I'm learning that, until the discomfort comes out, you're not healed. I now have a whole different slant on the book; it makes more sense.*

I seem a little more centered or balanced, as if I've made progress, with more confidence and willingness to risk sharing with somebody. I'm no longer searching for people to fix, but they're coming to me. Rather than trying to fix them, I share my experience, allowing them to work it out for themselves.

I'm in a whirlwind of transition. I'm in a peaceful state, which doesn't feel normal, yet it's not alarming. Just unusual. I'm not accustomed to it, but I don't want to go back to the old one.

Until recently, I haven't felt right about being in a peaceful state.

There's a sense of well-being. I feel cared for, whereas before, I felt pointless, meaningless. My trust in the process has never been betrayed. My experience sometimes gets worse, but that's always a consequence of not doing this work, of thinking I can beat the system, or asking for help only half-heartedly.

I feel very, very good because my conscious awareness when I'm upset is, That's not me. I'm not a sinner. This is who I am. I'm okay. It never used to be that way. Then, I fell into long periods of distress about myself, call it shame or guilt or being down on myself. I don't go through that anymore. My trust is expanding, and I never get into a position I would want to escape from.

Oh yes, it's wonderful on the other side of fear. For example, at one point I was tremendously angry with the administrator at the VA Hospital where I was working. An event occurred that stirred up my anger so much I wanted to choke. It took about three days of introspective writing and meditating to get to the sense of insecurity and unworthiness at the bottom of all that. As I understood I had felt it necessary to be in control of the situation and let that go, I was more content, and the whole issue just defused and didn't bother me again.

A couple of years ago my wife was going through a lot of changes, and she was using me as a punching bag. My initial reaction was, What have I done wrong? It took several days to finally realize this had nothing to do with me whatsoever. It was coming from her. We confronted the issue, and it brought great understanding and peacefulness for me to be able to say, "I love you and I wish the best for you, but I'm not responsible for your happiness. That has to come from inside you." I had to let go my own sense of being overly responsible because that's what was making me uncomfortable.

It's almost like going up a set of stairs where I keep ending up on a different level. When it feels like I'm taking a little step backwards, that's fine, because the next step forward is a huge giant one and then I walk along again in regular steps for a while.

Peace of mind is greatly misunderstood. It is not a place of boredom, stagnation, or lack of change or challenge. It is a condition that allows all the variations of love mentioned above, a feeling of being "more" or "larger," a sense of greater comfort and trust, greater opportunity, more gratitude, safety, balance, aliveness, clarity, and the experience of moving forward or higher. The term *consciousness expansion* was not coined frivolously. It attempts to describe the myriad feeling states that occur when fear is transformed into love. It is particularly important to note that no one felt they had gone backwards or that their fear was justified. Quite the opposite.

These positive feelings may have eluded you until now, despite your misguided attempts to have them through trying harder and being better, or through engaging in aimless pursuits of pleasure or pointless accumulation. All this time, your fear, the raw material of your peace and contentment, has been misunderstood. Love and peace, patiently awaiting your return to sanity, are chosen from the inside rather than bargained for on the outside. All that has been missing is your willingness to be who you are, rather than pretending.

As I transcribed and edited these various conversations, I felt the energy of Beethoven's *Sixth Symphony,* the "Pastoral." The opening passage has a pleasant, sunny air about it, followed by gathering storm clouds, a ferocious storm, and the final return to peace and tranquillity. The stories presented here feel very much like that. Some lives seemed to start out just fine, or okay, or with some hope that the ways of the world would eventually work in their favor. They believed that living by the rules of "getting my way" would deliver happiness, as promised. With growing alarm, they discovered that it was not working out and that pain and feelings of entrapment were increasing.

Finally, as in the symphony, there is a great lashing out, a groan of despair as everything seems to fall into ruin, and all the pretense that everything is fine fails us miserably. We give up, dramatically or quietly, and when we do, the fog starts to lift. A tranquillity that was not present in the beginning has come upon us. Hear and feel in these words, not defeat or resignation but a new level of peace and certainty. Feel their strength of integrity and the dignity of authenticity, not the immaturity of denial and attempts to gain approval or to please.

Step 9:

Remember, these men and women are not inherently different from you or me. They decided to trust the process of honoring feelings and refused the invitation to make themselves wrong because of having them. Your decision to punish yourself or to allow your healing is forever up to you. Once again, remember the good news—the window of opportunity to change your mind never closes. Hopefully you have gained great insight from taking the suggestions in the preceding steps. They have led you through some internal practices designed to bring greater awareness of the actual problem and to erode the outer layers of denial. You have practiced stating aloud the accurate descriptions of your past unloving behavior, claimed all that is right and good about you, and allowed the comfort that comes from disclosing secrets to enfold you.

With this step, you are encouraged to practice taking action. There may be conversations that you are avoiding, decisions you are putting off, or activities in which you have refused to participate. Until now, you have convinced yourself that your excuses have been reasonable or necessary—not enough time, didn't know how, others wouldn't cooperate. Now you are challenged to face your fear and step forward into a task or an encounter you have heretofore resisted. Anything you choose will be fine. Even a very small step, when taken, can bring great relief and an experience of becoming larger, stronger, and more confident.

You may feel nervous and even pace the floor as you work up courage to take the necessary action. However upsetting it may be, acknowledge it and practice anyway. Ask for help in asserting your right to be here without apology. Facing your fears cannot be done theoretically or intellectually. You must confront the situation and move toward what you have, up until now, backed away from. We offer a guarantee—your fears will always melt as you proceed and you will wonder why you formerly thought this was such a big deal. You can't figure that out ahead of time. As the commercial reads, just do it! Our participants never experienced being worse off after taking their own courageous forward steps and neither will you.

10. How would you describe the quality of your mind or your thinking process, the inner landscape, when addictions and their cause are removed or reduced?

No one can live a happy, prosperous life when confused, disoriented, or depressed. The clarity of our thinking is paramount, because it provides the focus though which we create our experience on earth. We participate and collaborate in all the circumstances of our lives and no experience is thrust upon us, no matter how it may seem. Although that sounds extreme, it is nonetheless true. And thank goodness for that! If someone or something else is in charge of our lives, we might as well give up now. But if we are using a law we didn't know existed, and using it unwisely, we need to know about that sooner rather than later. When our minds are clear and uncluttered, we finally become aware of peace and all its treasure, which never left but has been rendered temporarily inaccessible. The confusion and clutter in our minds literally makes us blind to all the help available to us constantly. Now is the time to claim that help.

Recall that this book's primary thesis is that no matter the outward appearance of circumstances or the nature of addictions, they are all resolved the same way and the positive result experienced by everyone is the same. The details of the participants' turning points were different; however, the beliefs about discomfort, the unexamined assumption of unworthiness, and the healing resulting from facing the fear were identical. The answers to this question were, not surprisingly, very similar also. Almost everyone included the mental and emotional qualities of clarity, peace, and heightened intuition in their responses.

I'm a lot more peaceful, more confident and trusting, and I have a lighter feeling about crossing a threshold into new experience. The anticipation of an unknown result was a lot more severe than the actual experience. Becoming less preoccupied with my addictions didn't have the effect I expected. There was awareness and an opening to guidance that came along with it.

I'm more peaceful, with less negative chatter in my head. Actually, there are times when I don't have any chatter and wonder where it went. As for my intuition, oh, heaven's, yes, it increased tremendously! That's why my own writing venture sped up so. Once I get quiet, I have tons of material. I read the paragraphs on the computer screen and think, That's good! I don't know where it's coming from, but it's good! Also, I seem to be more sensitive to craziness; I don't want to be around chaotic energy. It's not that I judge it as bad, but I'm less willing to have my peace disturbed. I just enjoy the quiet and solitude.

Relaxed comes to mind. There's no strain whatsoever. I return to a state of peace, rather than having resentment about giving something up. The pressure's gone. The mind's urgency to move on to other subjects to keep itself busy relaxes. Oh yes, when I can get my addictions out of the way and get in touch with my intuition, certainly there is greater clarity on my view of the world.

First of all, my mind is a lot more peaceful and relaxed, not as cluttered. It's easier to come to answers and what appears to be the right thing to do when you don't have all that interference going on. It's hard to stay focused when you're constantly worried and preoccupied.

When all the planning, anticipation, and fear is gone, you simply find yourself in the instant and enjoying it, just resting in it. This busy-ness with the addictions or worrying about future events always clogged up everything, certainly creativity, getting in the way of the natural flow of whatever needs to be done.

Okay, first of all, it's calm; there's peace, a serenity, a faith. There seems to be more clarity, or knowing there's a big picture and it all goes together. Without question, I have more access to my intuition; answers and insights are definitely more available.

I don't know that I have a word for it, but I guess it's a settled feeling. It energizes every part of my life, internally and externally. It feels good and all-encompassing.

My mind is much more serene, more aware of nature and beauty. I'm staying aware, on an on-going daily basis that I want to connect and love. Absolutely, the oneness, which I can choose to generate, is there.

I'm much more at peace with myself and the world. The anger is gone, and when I think of judging someone, I'm reminded I don't want to do that. Also, I'm learning it's more important to be a listener than to talk all the time. Listening helps other people, because they need someone to talk to.

I'm truly more peaceful and certain, more secure, with the confidence that there is a higher order to everything; I'm willing to follow a plan that's bigger than mine. Also, I'm part of the planning committee, asking for what I want and how I want my day to go. Everything is no big deal anymore. I feel lighter, freer, and much happier than before.

Well, it's wonderful. My thinking is so much clearer. I don't muddle around and wallow in stuff. I recognize very quickly when I'm out of that peaceful state and am very clear about what's required to get back into it.

It's far better and clearer thinking than ever before. I have a lot more sense of purpose about wanting to be at peace with other people and wanting to help them, and I realize there isn't much here I want. This is not from the former place of wanting to isolate myself, but rather from recognizing the uselessness of most of what I have invested in. It has become irrelevant and uninteresting. That's very different!

Clarity comes to mind, as well as courage. I'm able to see the subtleties and the answers unavailable before. I can go forward because I'm no longer bound by the fears that kept me hesitant and afraid.

Clearer, more at peace, balanced, and trusting. When I get into free-floating anxiety from my own denial, I can spiral down into that, or I can remember about trusting. It's very important I go in my preferred direction of being happy, which trusting creates, and in my heart remember I'm okay and everything is just fine.

The two states of mind are so completely different, the only way I can compare them is this: The times of turmoil are like being in free fall, plummeting or hurtling through space, and the times of peace provide feelings of support and being grounded that language cannot describe. The experience is one of being unbounded because everything else is being trapped.

Without all the clutter there's more room for letting the truth come in. On a daily basis, I'm less frenzied, clearer, and more serene.

I had a fair amount of self-awareness before, but I've gone to another layer, so I have a lot more clarity. It doesn't necessarily mean that fear is entirely absent, but I'm able to name it. Also, I no longer feel I have to fix everything.
I now recognize what's going on when I'm upset and think, Okay, that's interesting. Next.

Much quieter, happier, and clearer. Without an internal block, I'm proceeding very mindfully, step by step.

I have many more creative urges, thoughts about painting or writing. Intuitive things just come. I experience a much richer inner world that expresses in many ways.

It's much easier to recognize when I am going astray in my thinking, going down some road that's not leading to happiness. When that happens, I realize I can immediately change the direction of my thoughts, whether it's been a minute, an hour, or a day. I don't have to wallow or stay in it. I am much more aware of my thinking process and of the power of my thoughts.

Oh, yes, yes, the quality is better. What first dawns on my mind is that when I used to be the savior—the gladiator for everybody else and wanting to be seen that way—I always had to come back to me and my inferior state. Now that I'm conscious of being worthy, I'm in touch with the real me and, by golly, I am a Son of God, a child of God! I'm going to live for eternity and am always in touch with that, no matter what I'm doing.

Occasionally, I still go from philosophical to self-important, although the older I get, the more I feel my need for things falling away. As a young person, I dreamt of an Armani suit; now I have a rack of them, and here I am in a free tee shirt and old blue jeans.

I feel a degree of comfort followed rapidly by the notion there is something wrong with me and I'm not entitled to experience peace. It's an interesting question because only recently have I experienced this contrast. I can sense moments of peace that I'm allowing to come into my life through acceptance, not questioning that I am an expression of God, which is an awesome thing.

Help is always available to those who ask, and claim that help, they did! Peace and calm rise up through these answers and you can discern the relief they all feel as compared to the old, addicted ways. Would we not all be willing to change our minds, to "get real," if we believed the rewards were so numerous?

Having peace, clarity, calmness, less pressure or busy-ness, and more intuition, energy, creativity, and awareness is no small matter. And no sacrifice is asked of us to have them; they are the gifts given to us in our creation. Are we ready yet to accept them?

Step 10:

How is the quality of your mind? Do you feel frantic or always on the backside of the curve trying to catch up, cluttered or confused? The most universal experience, when you are willing to follow these steps, is greater clarity. This is a far more valuable commodity than you might imagine. When your mind is clear, the elements in your life become obvious, simple to understand. The feelings of contentment and safety grow. You have more immediate access to your own wisdom. Loving intuition becomes your built-in guide. You no longer have to wonder about your direction in life, which in the past was fraught with doubt.

Have you ever experienced wrestling with a problem, trying to make something happen, and you finally gave up? Later, seemingly out of nowhere, came the answer. And often you are amazed at how simple, how easy the solution is. Where did that come from? From you, your own wisdom, which now is discernable when you are free of worrying, fixing, blaming, and accusing. What would life be like when you are in constant contact with that wisdom, rather than seeming to have none? Clarity and all its rewards are everyone's birthright.

Take some time every day simply to be quiet and undisturbed, even if only for a few minutes. Stillness is a necessity, not a luxury or a punishment, if you would be healed. Let all thoughts float by, put your ranting ego over in a corner of your mind and let it carry on before an empty theatre. Pay no attention. Know that being still is safe and that the insights you desperately search for, the experience you long for is only a breath away.

~ ❦ ~

11. How do you live your life now?

To come through a dark night of the soul and then return to business as usual would not only be insane, it would be impossible. You cannot change your mind about your goals and purpose in life, the way you wish to regard yourself and others, without upgrading the manner in which you address all the circumstances and situations in your life. Thus we now include very valuable pointers on how to inculcate new habits of thinking that one day will be second nature to you. The new ways of living and relating in this world will then become automatic.

I think the most dramatic shift in my way of handling situations is to attempt to respond rather than react. I usually stop, understand what I want to say before I speak, and try to feel where that's coming from. It's been a very positive thing in relationships because I am able to respond from a more reasonable position, one of seeing the love in the person and the fear that the attack is coming from, rather than getting on the defensive. It's really given me a better relationship with my children. I realize when discomfort does come up regarding them, it's something in me I need to work on. Those are always hard, as anything they do or say brings up a certain discomfort in me, stemming from my guilt about being an inadequate parent.

As a friend said years ago, "The important thing is the speed of forgiveness. How fast do you want to forgive? When are you going to let your shit go and get off it?" The speed of my forgiveness determines how quickly I will go to the solution.

Now I'm living my life more consciously, checking in daily because I'm still in the place where I sense "out of control-ness," and that's okay. I step along with the moments, and they're perfect however they are, mistakes included. They're about learning, and there's some fun, some adventure and mystery where there wasn't before. I have to be more of an observer of what I'm thinking, to be disciplined, and stop and inquire about my motivation or intention. Maybe an ego thought goes by and I have to let it go, simply observe it. My ego's still trying to say, "Out of control, out of control!" but the truth is I'm really not. I'm consciously aware that all is in divine order even when it might seem chaotic. What a relief!

Now if a person triggers some anger or an upset, I'm not making it be about them. It's about me, so I've got to stop, take a few minutes to go within. I realize they're just triggering it, whereas in the past I blamed them, they "made me" feel this way. It's amazing how much I've done that. Now I see through that projection and I'm not playing anymore.

I always used to say, "I don't know, I don't know what the problem is." I've found this to be one of my ego's games, because I do know. When we're at this discomfort level, we say we don't know where our guidance is, as we look for this bolt of lightning. We have guidance constantly in many, many ways; the discomfort is the guidance.

I live more intuitively, allowing the moment to be more what it is without being addicted to planning. I try to think of my real purpose. I'm here to love without any idea how the form of an event is going to show up. Lately, my life has been totally unpredictable and if something changes my plans in the middle of the day, I think, Oh, this is an adventure! For instance, I have my day planned out, then five changes may occur, and I really stay at peace about that. The most wonderful things start happening; if I had tried, I couldn't have planned it more perfectly. The chance of meeting this person, or running into that situation, or having that event happen is one in a million and exactly what I needed and asked for that morning. It's amazing how this happens over and over. Peace through letting go and not planning is so much more attainable than all the work I did before.

I'm not sure, except I have more control over what or how I feel. I enjoy my life, what I do, where I am, and my friends. If both my internal and external atmosphere and environment is because of what I'm thinking, I have it pretty good, and I'm very grateful for that.

I find myself going with the flow a lot now. By that, I mean I don't resist going on an errand or taking on a project that makes no sense at the time. I get more satisfaction out of any experience, knowing that no matter where I go, I'm exactly in that place for some reason. I'm allowing myself to go wherever I feel compelled, getting more in touch with my intuition, developing and trusting it. That's probably the strongest thing for me. More than ever, I'm wandering around, not aimlessly, but following the cue of whatever in the universe is pulling me. While I'm "over there," all the other issues are working out. I used to work deals very hard, thinking I was going to put it all together, and when I reached an impasse, I would go on vacation to Europe or somewhere and, miraculously, all got taken care of. I recognized then there had to be something to going with the flow and that same pattern now seems to be expanding.

I don't feel I have to explain or make excuses anymore, rather I say so when I don't want to go someplace or to do this, and I hope they understand. Ironically, it works out better for others, too.

However, there's still a part of me that sometimes thinks, It's too good to be true—something on the other side of that door is going to drop. I will get cut down a few times or have a bad day, but it's not as frequent or intense as it used to be. I don't think I could run to the old addictions even if I wanted to, like smoking a cigarette and enjoying it. It's as if I have an innate response system that's protecting me. My whole makeup has changed. It's a natural progression, whereas before, I had to pay attention not to do something.

Even with the consciousness of what works, at times I still fight it. For instance, just in the last three days, I've had some physiological discomfort with menopause, and there has been an unsettling inside me. The first day, I fought it almost automatically; interestingly, my first inclination is still to fight any kind of discomfort, especially if it comes from a place I'm not expecting. My first impulse to fight reminds me I've still got a way to go. I have to catch it on a conscious level and remind myself, That's not helpful, relax. Sometimes I can do that in five seconds or a minute, and sometimes it takes me a day and a half. However, the good news is that what used to be a month-long struggle has shortened so much and that feels good.

I still have my own journey, but I'm excited about it. That's the big difference. I know I'm not "baked" and don't think I ever will be, but it's exciting and fascinating to watch how my mind wants to trick me. I'm my best guinea pig. I'm amazed, too, that sometimes I think I should be further along, which is just another little trap. We set all these traps and then try to avoid them. I think it's a hoot!

If I'm doing something that makes me uncomfortable, most of the time when I'm sane I'm able to stop, to go inside if neces-sary. About 80 percent of the time I find myself in a wonderful space, but for 20 percent I want more. Then I give my dog a big hug or sit and close my eyes, sometimes using special music, sometimes reading, and it clearly shifts my mind and I'm quiet. I'm guided exactly. On the front of my computer I have a lot of inspirational sayings and I often focus on those to return to peace. Whatever I do always works. It's not a denial thing, but if I do deny, I don't worry about it because it's always going to come back up. There will always be something or somebody to show me an old pattern I haven't dealt with.

Surrender and the accompanying shift results in a happier inner climate, very much so. For me, it helps to have a partner who's also operating this way because if we weren't both doing this, each in our own way, we wouldn't be able to live together. My former husband was a saint because I was the bitch from hell. I wouldn't be here if every single aspect of that relationship and of every other one hadn't happened. Everyday, I remember that if things don't come out the way I want, there's always a reason, so let it go. I'm not fighting it anymore and it's so easy.

I'm still hanging out in the no-man's land of developing aware-ness, but I can see the edge in front of me, the end of the road. The idea of feeling feelings is newer, but it's so clear I know there's nothing else; there's nothing tentative about it. To use a sporting analogy, which is absolutely absurd because I'm not a sports fan, is that what I see in front of me is home plate, the line around the batter's box, and there's no fulfillment outside that box. It's not so much knowing I have to participate, it's having some understanding of what participation means. I haven't participated much, but I know there is nothing else but that.

I sometimes feel there are still "demons" out there. For instance, if I take my boat out without the registration, I fear I'm going to get put in jail. It's all those fears about doing something illegal, which other people seem to do without having any problem. But I'm much more at peace knowing that everything, including how I want to feel, is up to me, not someone else. Sometimes, I get so uncomfortable, I tell myself, This is stupid; I don't want to do this. Then it seems to disappear, because I realize it was an illusion, something I created in my own mind. I almost gave up watching the news because all those things I saw seemed to run many different feelings through me. Now I think, Well, it must be for a reason, some unfinished business I have to work through.

I study the Course because it keeps me in tune, usually reading before I go to bed if not in the morning. I don't have nearly the anger I used to have. Once in a while I get a little bit angry, getting dragged into it when I hear my son talk about work, but if I reflect on everything as perception—everything I hear is my perception or a mirror of myself—my life is so much fuller, richer. I'm retired and I've never been busier in my life. Now I realize I can do anything and we're having a great time.

Now I consciously take the step of remembering that, in order for a little mishap to dissipate, I've got to put into practice what I know is true about who I am and live in the now, instead of running away from who I fear I am and not feeling. Especially recently, when distress comes up, I take a step toward fear and join with it. It's been hard for me because I'm a bit too analytical. I've always tried to figure things out, so I have to practice differently now and try not to analyze something to death.

Well, let's say this. I have some spiritual tools now. There are moments when I forget about them or have a tantrum or experience some pointless thought about myself. For instance, as I'm driving, I remember an experience I viewed as painful, and suddenly I realize I have spiritual tools. I specifically elect to open up my spiritual toolbox the same way as, formerly, I elected to look at the array of things I could hide behind. When I forget my spiritual tools, anger is the easiest and "safest" hiding place. I can take that off the shelf, making me feel very powerful with a big adrenaline rush, and frighten or stun people around me. At least I have that perception, whether it's true or not. I must realize that's an absolutely conscious choice. I've reached up on the shelf and taken down a bottle called anger and opened it up. Now I don't feel compelled to do that as frequently to be safe. For example, in a recent situation with some personality conflicts, I elected to close my eyes for a second and ask the Holy Spirit to come in and calm the situation, and it happened. I don't remember to do that as frequently as I'd like, but with practice I'll use it more. I think I have a lot of lifetimes to practice.

I take more risks. I always felt I was pretty authentically me, but now I'm even more so. When pain comes up, and it does with some regularity, I acknowledge it with, "There you are again." For example, on Mother's Day I recognized I was going into my funk thirty minutes into it. I got into pain really good for five hours; I decided to wallow around in it, stay with it, not do anything different with it, and it dissipated. I'm real clear pain is coming from me. Real clear! I still have this little chorus that occasionally says I'm not okay, not worthy, not good enough, not pretty enough, not smart enough, not anything enough.

I would say the speed and regularity of becoming aware of it has improved 1000 percent. That much! That five-hour upset could have been a five-month one earlier, and things that used to bum me out for a day are five minutes now, only tiny little upsets.

Absolutely, with no question my goal is to be who I am and that is a great adventure; I'm willing to allow myself time to develop.

When I look back, I realize I was born angry. In a rage, actually. So now when I look at my father, I can say, Yeah, all that makes absolute sense, whereas nothing made sense before. I would like to say I was willing to experience this before because I was having the pain anyway, but that's not true. I wasn't willing to listen. Then I reached a point where I was willing to make use of the pain, as I call it, to gain the truth rather than constantly re-experiencing pain. We've all been living with pain all our lives and it's time to use it as intended, which is to bring us back to the truth of who we are, instead of constantly experiencing it. Then I don't have to live in it, and I certainly don't have to die in it. Now I'm more able to let it go, saying, "Well, that's okay. It will be what it will be, and my only job is to keep letting it in, inquire about what it feels like and, therefore, tell me what I believe.

I really do want a new purpose and attitude. I've made that decision, and I'm trying not to care what the outcome is. I try to give up arranging and rearranging the exterior, although I've not mastered that by any stretch of the imagination. When I get centered, accepting my own divinity, forgiving myself, and understanding there was never anything wrong with me, the rest falls into place.

The way I try to live my life, and I think I do a fairly decent job, is through acceptance and forgiveness. Things come up, and I've long since learned not to spend any time analyzing them but to accept them. I remember once when I was angry, yelling at the car in front of me, and halfway through the sentence, I ended up yelling at the person I was really angry with. I've found, with acceptance, there's no need to sit and search for what's being reflected to me, because it just appears. At which point, forgiveness is natural and gratitude is a happy experience.

I'm releasing the fantasy of romance and sex and the world's opinion that everybody needs a partner. I let whatever emotions are there come up, and the less analysis the better, which eases things. I actually have gotten to the point where I don't even ask what is being reflecting in an upsetting situation.

I can feel that addiction become less important or valid and I don't wonder where it's going to end. Being open when an emotion comes up is important, and telling one other person confirms I'm not hiding it. Then it dissipates. When your intimate life is your addiction, you're constantly defending it, as compared to its being a natural part of any given day. You can't enjoy anything while you're defending against losing it. You can't have fear and joy. A relationship is enhanced when that clingy, needy stuff is gone because it permits so much more honesty, more relaxation, and much more appreciation for the ease and flow of it all.

You know what? I'm not really involved with any goals or activities. I honestly do nothing and it's wonderful. I don't orchestrate my life anymore. We do very short-term things, deciding we would like to do something, and if it works out, fine, and if it doesn't, that's fine. We don't have a lot invested in the outcome of anything, and I don't plan for the future. I get up every day, let it unfold naturally, and it always works out fine. People think that's crazy, but that's exactly how it works.

My life is wonderful. I am so peaceful. I don't feel a drive. People say, "Well, Karen, you have to do something." Well, no, I really don't have to do anything. Occasionally, I will get a feeling I should be doing something productive, and within about ten seconds, that second voice says, Oh, no, you don't. You've been there, done that. You don't have to do anything if you don't want to.

Keeping our own peace of mind is the best thing we can do. I don't attempt to fix people anymore; the really nice thing is that by staying in that frame of mind, just being where I am, I have had people say to me, "You know, I listened to you talk about things and poo-pooed it." And six months later, they come back and say, "Darn it, everything you said was exactly true. I got a lot more from you than I ever wanted to get. I didn't want to have to start looking at my stuff." But they end up in the middle of it, saying they just absorbed a lot without even realizing it. I don't believe any conversation is casual. There's always an underlying purpose, and I don't have to know what it is or orchestrate it. If someone asks, I'm happy to tell him what I know, and if they think its "hoo-ha," it's okay with me. It's a wonderfully easy way to live and I think that's what we're supposed to be doing here.

Oh, my gosh, functioning now is awesome, as I design and create as co-Creator. I must be most cautious in saying this, because anyone who doesn't know me, clearly would think I had gone into the Bible-thumping, holy-roller religious realm, but this truly isn't the case. I invite Spirit, the essence of my spirituality and the knowing I'm always taken care of, to set the tone for my day, to ask for whatever I want, and to take me where I'm to be. I say what I need to, and for the most part, when I catch myself having an irritation, I choose an immediate response: "No, that's not what I want to send out. I don't know the circumstance. You decide for me." And I get to have an awesome, peaceful day. That doesn't mean there aren't days when things seem not to work out, aren't exactly what I would have chosen, but it gives me another opportunity to choose between being peaceful or twirped. If it hadn't happened many times, I probably wouldn't be able to do it as well as I do now.

When I got to sit on my fanny for nearly a year in a wheelchair, I began to appreciate everything in my life, who I was, my skills—awesome skills of how to take care of myself, believe in myself, and do whatever was required to get through the moment. All of that came with me. I think it's about becoming more real. If I feel compassion for someone, I display it. If I don't give a damn, I don't pretend anymore. If it doesn't fit, it doesn't fit. It's taken years to come to that place where I don't do things out of guilt or obligation. I'm truly more peaceful and certain; I really feel the security, the confidence, and know that there is a higher order to all of this.

Just staying comfortable, taking it a day at a time, and staying with whatever I'm doing, not worrying about what anyone thinks. I have always loved physical, hard, manual labor. Last summer I worked on my uncle's farm; he wanted me to watch his grandkids for a while and I didn't want to because I wanted to be outside baling hay, doing hard work, drilling myself into the ground. Now this summer, I'm totally content watching two kids and having a leisurely day outside on the swing set, not feeling I need to work myself to death.

During my first semester in college, I was always doing something—writing, swimming, going to class, or working, but yesterday I was lying on my bed, remembering my constant writing and realizing I didn't feel like writing then. I felt very content; then the old voice came: *Wait a minute, Megan, you always want to write. Shouldn't you be writing?* So I opened my journal, wrote three sentences, and then just put it down and relaxed, so my need to push myself is softening.

Most of the time, I live my life without stress. Working in mental health is trying to save people and there is a tendency to imply, "I'm okay, but you're not." Now, number one, I keep totally away from all the old psychology. I find all my clients open to getting into their spiritual content, by which I don't mean asking them if they are Catholic or Baptist, but inquiring into who they really are. I want to join in sharing with them what I know, that every answer of who they are is already within them; it doesn't come from outside. My role in all this is loving them, helping them to see who they really are, helping them to grow so they can consciously know, " I'm not who this one says or that one says. I'm not something bad because I lost a boyfriend or a wife or a husband or whatever. Life is within. Now I know it's there!"

My life is completely different from what it was four years ago. I enjoy people, I enjoy myself, and I enjoy most of the things I encounter today, whereas I was having a terrible time when I finally decided to do something about my addictions. I had already gone through a lot of problems, and life was not very pleasant then, but today it's very peaceful most of the time. That's not to say there aren't bad days, where some are diamonds and some are stones, but even the stones are not as rough and big and difficult to cope with as they were. On that same thought, there are times when uncomfortable things are almost welcomed, because I know getting to the root of what's causing a problem will expand to even greater freedom.

Number one, pain doesn't come up very often because, for the most part, I live from my wholeness and strength of knowing who I am. It's not an ego sense, but it's knowing my source is love, joy, and peace. When I come from that, my experiences are completely different from those that come from feeling "less than." I'm very blessed with so many relationships that are whole and wonderful and I'm grateful every day for them. I want to bless them all, out of my gratitude.

    Now, if discomfort does come up, I obviously believe something about myself or another that's not true, that isn't coming from wholeness and peace and joy. When that happens, first of all, I have to be willing to let this come up, see what I've let drive me, bring it to the truth, and let it go. If I can look at a person's behavior as a call for love, and not as their doing something awful, I can recognize I have that same call. Then I can ask for healing for both of us. I used to feel attacked or separated if someone didn't agree with me or if discomfort occurred. This is a totally different way to live because I'm seeing equality, joining with and wanting the best for everybody, so the separation is not perpetuated but healed. Now my lessons are very gentle.

I have faith in the universe's investment in me, that I'm loved and cared for and important. When I grab the shitty end of the stick, that's not bad luck but an opportunity for God to show His love. I love the expression by a certain wonderful, enthusiastic speaker, "God has a picture of me in His billfold. And He also has yours."

    I compete differently now, going from winning at another's expense—the "in order for me to do well, someone has to do poorly" scheme—to everybody getting a blue ribbon. And I'm perfectly happy. I've managed to remove myself from trying to identify winners and losers. The rarest person you can find is someone capable of great admiration without a tinge of envy. I like that, and my goal is to increase the admiration and decrease the envy. Many have been the times I've thought, Well, you son of a bitch, you've pulled off a coup. That could have been my coup. Or somebody wins the lottery and I think, I've used those numbers before. That could have been me just as easily. Now I hear the wise part of me say, That's not your purpose, not your circumstances. Enjoy what you have. That's theirs, and it's perfect for them. It would not be perfect for you. Now, when people have their coups, I'm prepared to admire their accomplishments without feeling diminished. That's been a real breakthrough, because I've been a secret envier.

Remembering God absolutely has a daily place in my life. Every morning and sometimes during the day or evening, meditation allows me to connect again from a place deep within me, which I find necessary. Some call it prayer, and I don't know whether that's different or the same, but it allows me to be still, quiet, and reconnect with who and what I am. I believe my Creator wishes to communicate with me in that way, wishes me to know I am loved. All I need is to be still and allow awareness to occur, which it does. When I want to go into a meditative state, it's a stepping back, a making room for the experience and it's wonderful! My life is focused around that meditation; I haven't missed a day in at least a year, and there's no need to miss one. What's so important to realize is that the time taken for meditation, which I might earlier have called a waste, collapses time in some other area. So all of sudden, what I thought wasn't enough time is the perfect amount of time because I'm not in charge of arranging my day. The planning is there to some degree, but I'm really not in charge. Life is a much more relaxed enterprise, and letting up on the throttle has created a huge reservoir of happiness.

The experience of remembering, in my daily activities, that I'm not in charge is necessary for me to reconnect to something bigger and greater, more wonderful and loving than anything the little "I" can make up. I was "God" for a long time, so my day begins with remembering my ego is not God. My ego isn't necessary for my survival or anyone else's; I can either choose it or to be at one with my Creator. My meditation always gives me the feeling of safety, comfort, and joy.

*More and more I'm recognizing whenever there's discomfort, I'm
the root cause. Nothing I see or experience out there is causing
it. When I recognize it rising, or that I'm in the funk, there's an
awareness that I can't cure it or change it on my own, that my
job is basically to say a little prayer or talk to the Holy Spirit. I
give it up and say, "Holy Spirit, I obviously can't do anything
with this. I give it to you to transform it, to change it from a fear
thought to a love thought." I may have to do that several times
and it may take a day or two, but it's a constant process.*

*Usually I can look at discomfort immediately as an opportu-
nity to heal, and I always eventually see it as one. When I
recognize I'm holding onto pain, if I can't look at it that moment
and laugh at it and let it go, I might play with it a little, asking,
Why am I holding onto this? What am I getting out of this
drama? I recognize that if you want the pain to end, you have
to let it go.*

*God, Holy Spirit, spirituality, all of them are connected. Not
having to live my life feeling alone turns on the biggest light for
me and has to be the one biggest secret I wish everybody knew.
And they can; we're all the same. We all want that acceptance
and love. Once you understand you are love, can have and give
love on a daily basis, it's pretty terrific.*

*I relate to my body with much balance, a real key word for
me now. I feed it spiritually and intellectually, as well as physically, every day. I eat when I'm hungry. I work out when I want
to but certainly not every day anymore, and wow, I don't fall
apart! I didn't turn into a four-hundred-pound blimp. I'm still the
same person, and it's so much easier. The balance is there, and
I think that's the key.*

*I haven't been sick in so long; I used to have colds and other
ailments I don't have anymore. Very rarely do I hide out in food
or working out. I still have my boring days where I might eat a
little more than normal, but everyone does that. The point is, it's
not addictive anymore. The most important element in a body
being beautiful is coming from within to the outside. I'm loving
myself, listening to my inner voice and my intuitions coming
from the holiness in me, my spirit. I'm not perfect yet, missing*

my intuition sometimes, or the ego slips in and confuses me. I'm human, but overall, I'm getting very good at hearing and actually following through with my inner voice; whether it's with a creative endeavor, reading, seeing a movie, or going somewhere by myself. I never knew I ignored it so much before. I would say that loving myself enough to honor my desire and hear my true self, is where I'm finding my value now. Not in the body at all.

Step 11:

Collectively, our group's comments on how to live could be a book in itself. From their wisdom, which they have internalized or are in the process of doing, are derived the principles listed below. Living according to these principles will heal the hurt we currently experience and would have prevented it in the first place, had we been willing to listen. As with all aspects of love, living these ideas are both the means and the end. These responses are particularly noteworthy in their absence of blame and in their inclusion of others in the healing process. As we become less fearful, all the people around us become better and more loving in our sight.

1. Be willing to listen, instead of assuming you already know it all.

2. Stay open rather than always being on the defensive, and respond rather than react.

3. Own your discomfort and learn from it, rather than blaming others.

4. Realize your discomfort is triggered rather than caused by outside events or people.

5. Give up your "position" and get to a place of forgiveness quicker.

6. Live consciously and mindfully, as the observer as well as the participant in your life.

7. Give up control and expectations—surrender.

8. Live intuitively, follow the heart, and use guidance in making choices.

9. Take more risks; have more adventures.

10. Find things to be grateful for.

11. Tell the truth about what's going on with you, live authentically, get real.

12. Challenge the ego voice.

13. Wish everyone well and presume they are valuable.

14. Seek a spiritual life; make time for introspection, prayer, meditation, and connecting with your God.

15. Practice faith, love, compassion, and acceptance.

16. Practice what you know, use the tools consistently.

17. Embrace pain quickly; don't run or hide from it.

18. Recognize the omnipresent choice to change your mind.

Sometimes as a first reaction, we fight against a feeling or situation or changing our mind, but it doesn't take nearly so long to come back to awareness and decide to practice what we know works. We have been long enslaved, hypnotized by our ego minds, and learning how not to listen to it takes a while. Even if you feel you have only a dim awareness of another choice open to you, you are making tremendous progress. Imagine fast forwarding to the last day of your life. You ask your ego for your reward for so diligently punishing yourself, denying yourself, making fear-inducing choices all your life, following its directive that life will get better "later." Well, "later" has finally arrived. You wait eagerly and the ego's response is, "You were really stupid for listening to me in the first place. There is no reward for hating yourself and holding yourself back. You've wasted your life. Too bad!" What a ghastly scenario! Don't wait until the last day of your life to decide you deserve better. Put these ideas to work in your life now!

12. What would be your advice to anyone willing to listen?

Most of us have learned by this time that giving others advice is futile. Nor is it our job. My partner, Robert, is fond of quoting, "You can't answer a question which has not yet been asked." To presume that we have others' answers is arrogant. Everyone has his own answers; they are merely fogged over with the confusion of fear in all its various forms. I have often said I am not interested in spending two seconds trying to convince someone of the validity of these principles, but I will be there 200 percent for anyone who asks for help in applying them in their lives. I remember, in the early days of my explorations, how I had to work up enough courage to ask friends and colleagues for their feedback about various aspects of my being. Egos, by their very nature, are fragile, and the veneer of our civility is very thin. When our images are not upheld, we feel very attacked, believing we are those images. We are not! We are invisible spiritual beings, and learning that is what this dialogue is for.

As was suggested in the previous list of principles for living successfully, be willing to listen to the advice that follows because it comes from experience, not theory, and with love and a desire to speed you on your way to peace of mind.

The universal piece of advice is, have the courage to ask for help and do not try to figure out what "help" is supposed to look like.

Just continue the journey. Don't give up if you come against obstacles and you haven't found your way yet. If you're searching, it has to come. My favorite saying in the whole world is "The teacher will appear when the student is ready to learn." That got me through so many times of trial when I didn't yet know the answers and was struggling. That's a hard place to be sometimes but be reassured help appears. That's the truth.

Re-examining our take on discomfort would be a huge thing. The way we usually interact with each other is not helpful, so getting it that all feelings we have are fine would expedite our learning process. Through my profession, I spend a lot of time helping adults accept their feelings. I usually go through the children to get the adult's attention, using that path to work with the adults so they can learn to offer acceptance back to their children. So, when children do express emotions and feelings, the adults won't respond with, "Stop that, that's bad." Perhaps it's not said in those words, but that's what's conveyed. They may actually say, "If you're going to have those feelings, go to your room. I don't want to see it." We receive so many messages indicating that our discomfort is irritating not only to ourselves but to others, and that it's bad, so don't have it! I see parents distracting children from their feelings all the time. They grow up and then we have these little drug prevention programs—programs to teach teenagers not to use the distracting drugs. I'm thinking, Hello. Hello. Does anybody get it?

Second, it would be helpful to look at the notion that resistance brings change. We have a strong belief that if you want something to change, you drop a bomb on it, you've got to fight it. As long as we hold to that idea, we can't explore the possibility that acceptance brings change. Sometimes I'll find myself being forceful and resistant, too—"Just make 'em move! Give me that phone!"—as if that makes things happen and that you'll be run over if you lay back.

The first piece of advice would be to look honestly at the belief system you've lived under all these years and recognize it doesn't work. It's never served us well; it's never had what was best for me and mine, as a purpose. If you can recognize that, you find you have nothing to lose by being willing to look at it differently. Learning to let go of your agenda and expectations of everything and everybody and wanting peace in your life are giant leaps for anyone to make. The underlying cry in all of us *all the time is wanting that peace. We don't actually want the bigger house, the nicer car, and a bigger paycheck. We want peace in our lives, and if we honestly ask for that, not caring what form it comes in, that request will always be answered. We don't like to trust, but we're always answered. The universe hands you peace when that's what you truly want more than anything else. After that, it's a piece of cake.*

My intention, although I don't necessarily spell it out to friends and clients, would be to ask, "Would you like to find out who you really are, so you can dispel those notions about what you are not? Would you like to go on that journey?" If a person doesn't entertain that question, then I help them begin by having them talk about themselves and ask, "Is this really me?" It always amazes me how we can invent so many different ways to escape from who we really are. The life we live is an absolute fake, having to be "somebody" to impress others and trying to fit ourselves into some mold we think is a requirement. That's a terrible, terrible burden!

The only thing I would ever say to someone—stay present and in the moment and look for ways to find joy and gratitude—is so simple it's almost hard to do. We look for our rewards, set up our agendas, think about our accomplishments, and if we could experience a few days of not setting up anything and allowing each day to unfold, what would that feel like? Be willing to flow, to learn there is a much gentler, easier way to live, and it's about letting go of plans and agendas. Wishes and desires don't control the outcome or the necessities getting done.

Being present is when the heart and mind are congruent. When you have conflict between what you think you need to be accomplishing in the world and what your heart says to you, then I say, "Hey, buddy, you need to chill out for a little while." While there are incongruencies in your life, allow them to be made known to you, write about them, face them, so you can come to peace about them. Decide on the goal you want and who you want to listen to. If you choose anything other than the peaceful way, you can guarantee to experience the lack of peace you've chosen and created, and that's okay. A lack of congruity between your heart and soul and the intellect is the essence of the cause of addiction. As long as those are in conflict, you are in conflict.

I would say, "I know that despite all my perceived errors, deficiencies, and mistakes, there's still a perfect creation under here, and I know that about you, also. That's the person in you I'm wanting to communicate with, from that person in me." Merely choosing to see the good, without giving advice, totally disarms the other person.

I would tell them we're equal and that a loving teacher exists within us all. When you go within past that fear, there is such light and joy and beauty that unerringly, unfailingly guides you through any of your relationships, through any of your life experiences. When you can access that, you don't need anyone to give you advice because you have your Guide within that will always help you. When you face those demons, they dissolve, and right behind them is the truth about who you are.

My important missing piece has been not really being 100 percent for God. I would say refocus and pay attention to the spiritual part of us, accepting the equality and divine nature of everything.

What would I say? I've thought about that lately. First, I would say, through whatever means are at your disposal, to think about the possibility that you are a direct creation of a power greater than yourself. I would then encourage anyone to contemplate the "being" aspect of who he is. We are recognized as human beings who perform as "human doings." I'd suggest giving consideration to the first point—that we're human beings—and to pursue to the best of their ability what that means to them. If asked, I would tell them what I did, how I got to where I am, give them a brief description of my life, and offer a means of taking advantage of the detours I traveled so they don't have to. If they choose to take detours, that's fine too, but there is a shorter way. I would further say, to anyone who asks, think about ways of truly loving yourself, and that does not mean pursuit of pleasure but of unconditional positive acceptance. That's about as simple as I can put it.

What I count on to keep me safe is paying attention to who I am spiritually. That is the only point. The invisible is all that's real. Nothing here keeps us safe, nothing! As I said yesterday to someone who was very sick, "Could you embrace that clogged sinus and upset stomach and see them as friends trying to let you know how you need to love yourself?" Rather than fighting against what we have judged to be wrong, put your arms around it, honor it, and embrace it because it's like a whining, crying child that will respond to that love. That is the most meaningful thing you could do with something you think is wrong with you.

Spend twenty minutes a day in reflection or prayer, so that in spite of all the craziness going on, you have at least twenty minutes a day to reflect calmly on who you are.

I would say that if you take care of your Self—that's the big S self—everyone else will follow. Those words are very easy to hear, but the application is a little more difficult. Please find other loving individuals to model self-respect for you, to support you in it, to listen to you, guide you, answer questions, or just to be in the same space with you. I would just want to hold them, as I really feel that holding tells them how precious they are, reflects how precious and innocent they are. In my mind, I tend to put everybody back into a baby's body in order to recognize they're still perfect.

My learning came through associating with those who were practicing the same things I wanted. It's that same old twelve-step process of finding a sponsor who has what you want, and this group had what I wanted—peace. There are no words available for the gratitude I have for the experience of the last couple of years, for the people who have been around me, who've loved me through everything and taught me how to love myself again.

There's just no way to express it, and I wish everyone could feel that much gratitude. Just ask for a hand. Just ask, in your thoughts, and it will appear. You don't know whose hand it's going to be, but someone will appear. I have gotten very conscious about what I ask for now, because I've learned every single one of my thoughts is a prayer. Every time I ask, I get what I want. If I don't like the way something is turning out, I need to change what I'm asking for. It's different, but it's fun.

My friends and associates are in very different places regarding their discovery of their feelings, making it clear I have to let everybody be wherever they are. My job is to help a person in whatever way they need it, not in whatever way I think I have to have it. I started with complete unwillingness to look inward, so I'm aware of a person's reluctance and avoid pushing for anything. If they don't ask for advice, I still see them as fine in my mind. However, if someone asks for help, that's a different story. Then I can clearly let them know there is another way to live.

Number one, don't feel guilty about your addictions. Guilt never serves any purpose to anyone at any time. Accept and let go of whatever emotional buildup is there. With addictions, it seems when the rug is pulled out from under you, there's always something hiding there. For instance, if you're addicted to food and it's not available, the cover of our disguise is quickly pulled off and the upset hidden there revealed. Simply accept whatever emotions are there. The process is natural, so no thought need be given it.

I would say, if we're talking about addictions and patterns, they all stem from fear. They are all a call for love and attention that we try to get from other people. In fact, the attention we're not giving ourselves is what's really lacking, as opposed to someone else withholding it from us. If we can focus on learning to love and recognize ourselves and give ourselves the attention we deserve, then everything will come to us. It's hard for people to see us when we're not expressing our truth, but hiding behind our facades instead.

My advice depends on where they are at that moment, because when I'm going through my stuff, sometimes I don't want someone quoting the truth to me. I don't want to hear it. Also, with some people, the minute you talk to them about God or Holy Spirit, they turn you off. However, I try to help them see they need to look at their own contribution to the scenario, when it seems that someone is doing something to them. If they can hear it, I'll suggest they might choose to see the situation differently or from another point of view.

I think the primary step in getting beyond addictions is to recognize you have them. That's the shocker. Everyone's in denial because they think the problem is outside of themselves, believing something is affecting them and they have no control except to rail against it, or tell twenty people and let them fester too, to justify it.

If you tell someone, "Whatever you're thinking is what's manifesting in your life," some people will not even continue the conversation. So I tend not to get into a discussion unless the person is more receptive. If the asking for advice is genuine, I would say I have learned a lot from the concept of mirroring. I try to invite them, with whatever comes up, to ask themselves, What is this mirroring? What am I thinking that looks like this? I'd like to help make them aware that there's no need to point the finger at somebody else, that the person or situation that's triggering the discomfort is showing them something they think about themselves. We have all the power, if we choose, to really learn it's not the other person causing our problems.

What I've learned the most about, and want to feel more, is that I am good, a holy child of God. I don't feel that all the time, but somewhere I know it, and when I don't experience it, I have judgments about myself for that. Letting go of judgment is at the top of the list. As I recognize the circumstances in my life are related to judgments I have about myself and realize they aren't true, I've found upset goes away. I didn't believe it could disappear so quickly, but it can. I still can't figure out how transformation can be so fast and easy.

First of all, I hope I would be aware of where I am at the moment of the question, because if I'm in my "in charge," egoic frame of mind, my answer will be how to fix this person, rather than how to help. Assuming I'm not in a state of fear myself, I can allow the question to be asked without my having to have an answer. Words don't necessarily communicate what someone is really asking, so the question might not need to be answered. What's called for is for me to put my arm around that person and to be at peace myself, to demonstrate I trust this Creator we're talking about, allowing that everything is the way it ought to be.

The degree to which an individual wants an answer is the same degree with which they will understand what I'm communicating. If they really are calling for love and I'm offering that, and they truly want to receive and be aware of receiving it at that moment, then they will. Sometimes I battle with words and a few things come out backwards, but the person understands I'm coming from a place of love. Sometimes, someone will indicate that they didn't like something I just said and that's fine. If I suggest forgiveness is an important issue and they indicate no interest in what forgiveness means, or block that conversation and say they're not really ready for that, then perhaps they didn't really want another way of looking at their situation. They actually wanted me to buy into their drama, and my job is not to do that.

A very dear friend, in whom I see so much of myself, is in AA, and even though he's not drinking, I've noticed whenever he wants to talk about something, he'll start to get upset and then say, "Nothing's right or wrong, it's just the way it is. I'm where I am and it's fine." And he'll totally do what I've always done, analyze it until he forgets what he's even talking about. Sometimes I'll mention little things, directing it more to myself, hoping he'll hear it for himself. Right now, he doesn't even realize he's holding back, and I let him be with that because he's not ready to hear my suggestions to him. If he asks for advice, then I'll tell him. Otherwise, I think my advice is not to try to analyze or fix him. I guess, just be kind to yourself. Give yourself a break. Don't be afraid of what you feel, and don't worry about why you feel that way. Just face it. Ask yourself if you are hiding because of what someone else thinks, because that doesn't matter.

I always tell anyone there's one problem, one solution. It they're calling me for help, calling for love, that must mean I'm calling for help and for love. I'll put the cards on the table and tell them I'm hurting as much as they are, so let's get together and allow the Holy Spirit to answer our joint question. Now we share a common goal, and the Holy Spirit can answer that common need because we don't have separate interests. After I respond that way a number of times, everyone knows what my answer is going to be, so they don't call back.

Wow, I don't know. I'm not in the advice-giving business, but if you held a pistol to my head and I had to give some, I would say that the two things I have discovered as a result of my journey are: the price of being right is grossly, tremendously overrated and surrender has been vastly underrated, demeaned, and undervalued.

Well, telling people to come to faith is foolish advice, because they won't. I would say love your brother as you love yourself, the golden rule. Find a way to see how anyone you deal with is as perfect for his or her purpose as you are for yours. He may be displaying characteristics we shrink from, open sores, or whatever, but find that way. Seeing that everybody has a purpose is the ultimate egalitarian view of your fellow man.

I just have to laugh because nobody pays attention. The only answer is to practice forgiveness. There's really nothing else to say. I'm willing to forgive. Have a nice day.

Many of us have suffered under the misguided notion that correction, primarily of others, was our job, and that those who do not follow our advice are being deliberately perverse. Actually, if we are focusing on their problem and all they should do about it, we are being singularly unhelpful. If we jump in and rescue them, prevent them from experiencing the natural consequences of their decisions and behavior, we are not in the least helpful. We are catering to our own need to reduce conflict, to preserve the status quo at any price. Often we want others to "get fixed" so our discomfort level will be reduced. Most of our reasons for wanting to help and give advice are very self-serving. We don't want our routines and our own hiding places to be disturbed or revealed.

Please notice that the primary "advice" given by our group is to begin to live a more spiritually aware life. That does not necessarily mean a religious life. We are inherently Spirit, essence, boundless, and free. Therefore, this world, this time and space dimension with its focus on things material and limited, seems foreign to most people, when they allow themselves to notice it. Addictions prevent our noticing because we don't know what to do about that discovery. Living a more spiritual life is simply admitting it feels better to follow our own inborn, loving inclinations. It is more rewarding to be kind, which does not mean weak, to be grateful, to ask for help, to realize our interdependence with each other and with the God within.

As mentioned earlier, we are interested in solutions, not problems. Giving advice usually focuses on the problem, in complete unawareness of the immutable law that what you give attention to, you will have more of. In deference to that law, and with the intention of working with it in a truly helpful way, we are asked to listen, to remember all that's right and good about those we would advise, and remain steadfast in our awareness that they can and will, ultimately, choose again, with very different results. When they choose to focus on the solution, rather than on the problem, is up to them, not us. Simply wish them well and know that no problem will remain unresolved, no matter how impossible it currently appears.

Step 12:
Follow the above advice, which is to honor yourself, take time for yourself, look for all that is right about you, and get out of

the advice-giving business! Take time to list ten things that are especially great about yourself. Notice if you are uncomfortable with that or if you feel it to be arrogant, not appropriately humble. It is not humble to put yourself down; it is ridiculous. It is hurtful and serves only your ego's purpose, which, you remember, is not in your best interests. You are not urged to consider yourself better than others, but you are asked to see yourself as equal to everyone else. Declare to yourself that you sit on the front row, as a world-class citizen, along with everyone else. Hear this closely! If you do not consider yourself good and valuable and equally entitled to a happy life, no one else will either.

13. What is your current opinion of addicted persons now that you have changed your mind?

Before you begin this section, you might find it interesting to re-read the responses to the second question—our participants' original reactions to those with addictions. For the most part, they didn't know or care much about them. Their cavalier attitude has shifted from "this is not about me" to one of compassion and understanding. We would all do well to follow their example.

It's much gentler, always about another choice, but each person has to embrace that choice himself. There's nothing I can do or give them other than to see the truth of their perfection. If I can do that for them, I need to make sure I'm also doing it for me. It makes it much easier not to judge or be harsh or vindictive. There are no similarities whatsoever between where I've been and where I am now, which is pretty unbelievable.

I think everybody's addictions are a choice, not some outside, evil force that's descended upon us. Addictive behavior is the result of a mistaken way they perceive themselves, the way they're thinking. I regard them as unfortunately choosing a path that's not bringing them much happiness, choosing incorrectly rather than being inherently wrong.

They're reflections of myself, of course, and we can all heal together. I know I see addiction as a cry for love. Having an addiction to victimhood is the same as having an addiction to a drug, just a different form, and one is no more valid than another. Probably about 99.99 percent of the people on the planet are addicted to an assortment of things. I don't see them as any "less than" but as "equal to" and loving. Definitely a far cry from earlier days!

I used to believe these people were unfortunate victims of circumstances or mistreated by their parents. Now I think we're all one, all equal, and peace and harmony will come only as they find what to let go of. I see myself in them and I see them in me, and I'm not just saying that in a trivial way. They're not sick or emotionally disturbed. They're nothing but best friends, unaware rather than weak.

I think we really are all addictive. If we could only get that, we would reduce the amount of books and therapy to nothing and be a lot happier. Also, sometimes I realize I'm still hiding out and wanting to see differently. When I feel part of me in someone else who's obviously addicted, I know I need healing.

How I regard the situation is that everybody is addicted. Everyone falls into that category. I realize we all use addictions of some form to hide from what we fear we are, the monsters we fear are the truth of us. There's no reason to judge addictions or to see one as any different from another because they're all the same.

I feel it's a societal thing we're all going through, and it's certainly not about derelicts.

Well, back then, when I was in the addiction, I thought other addicted people were weak but I had control. It was only on learning I didn't have control and was probably an addictive personality that I wanted to get rid of it. I read a few books that scared me about how addiction grows and grows until it takes over 99 percent of your life. I decided I didn't want any part of that and would do whatever was necessary not to lead that type life.

I remember the teaching about not going to heaven alone and having to take your brother along. In order to do that, you have to see him as perfect. I'm working to see the addiction as only the ego in him talking, only his fear or where he thinks he has control. It's not about pity but seeing someone else's problem as a teacher for me, a mirror being held up to see if I'm through mine yet.

I'm reminded of something I read this morning, which I thought was very good. It's as if an addiction bears false witness to who we really are; it shows us we're trying to look for who we are and trying to solve a problem that doesn't exist. Addictions are meaningless. It doesn't mean we're bad. I don't judge those who are addicted because I don't judge myself. As I view someone who has an addiction, most of the time, my willingness is to love and not judge. More and more, I can feel my success with that. As I see them, I see myself, and I never would have thought that before. I always thought I could see others as jerks and myself as perfectly okay, but that's not true at all. It doesn't work.

Related to your question, I used to be concerned with the Christian aspect of AA meetings because at their conclusion, they say the Lord's Prayer, which I saw as elitist. I thought it might possibly run off my Jewish, Buddhist, and Muslim friends, as well as people like me who have abandoned structured Christianity. The end of the Lord's Prayer, "Lead us not into temptation, but deliver us from evil," I always thought that was so odd and I felt resentful about a God that would do such a thing. Emmett Fox's book, The Ten Commandments, described perfectly what that prayer means to a recovering person— permit me not to judge—referring to my former behavior that I disapproved of and now saw reflected in my brothers. That was fabulous, absolutely right on the mark for me, so I embraced it. It certainly is apropos to this question.

I have a lot more compassion for addicts, a lot less sense of separation from them, that they're beneath me or somewhere I haven't been.

I can see when somebody is preoccupied, and I've tended to be more compassionate. I've opened my heart to them, wanting them to know they are good, a holy child of God; because I know they're hurting and fighting against something, too.

Well, that's definitely the question for me. I'm realizing I'm at a point where I can't stretch the boundaries of the novice category. It's no longer a question of not judging other people as wrong; I have to want them to know they're right. There is no other option that can possibly be successful, no neutral place, no no-man's land between hatred and love, and no fence to sit on. That has become real at the gut level.

An example has just happened regarding my ability to see addiction differently. We were in the Bahamas with a person who has a very compulsive, addictive personality. Even as I noted those characteristics, I simultaneously saw more of the person than I was formerly able to see, this wonderful, loving, kind person, at times scared and calling for help. The fear was not a big focus; I saw it and knew it was there. Before, however, the addictive personality is all I would have seen and pointed out to you. It didn't bother me, and I didn't get tangled up in it or judgmental about it.

I want to reach out, and I'm a little hesitant about what that actually means. Two things occur. The first is, if asked or if appropriate, I would let them know it doesn't have to be the way it currently is, followed instantly by trying to recognize they are children of God. I haven't quite reconciled those two, as it's just occurring to me. Sure, I still react with judgment sometimes, but

I'm aware of that reaction, knowing it's not appropriate and that they're just fine. What I'm seeing is merely a physical thing at this moment. They are manifesting certain things I have empathy with, and my concern is to direct that empathy in the right way, in the way that doesn't try to fix it.

It's been very easy to get away from judgment by recognizing people with addictions are in the very fearful place where we've all been and that's why they exhibit the behavior they do.

I truly have come to see this is part of their purpose or path, and I don't need to know what that is. I will support and love them. I don't see them as being wrong, just playing out their purpose.

In all honesty, things still get triggered within myself about addicts. I definitely am no saint, because I still make judgments but am consciously aware of it. Stopping those judgments is a main, big difference from before. What's left is observing them, understanding them, as opposed to judging. The other way felt very separate and disconnected, but this way doesn't. I can see their addictions, have compassion, and still feel connected: "Wow, we're all in this together, and I know what she's going through, and hey, who am I to judge?"

Formerly, I had to hide how I saw the "addicted." They were weak and I was weak, and it was a big, frantic turmoil! Now, I recognize how they so want to be loved. So, wow! Now when I see people who have addictions, whatever their form, I'm able to love them.

I love them. In fact, I love them so much I started working with addicted kids because their hurt is so obvious, and they're so up front about it. Their candor provides a place where I can hook in and tell them, "You're loved anyway, and this isn't who you are. This is simply a way you're finding what your views are." I have noticed, in my groups, almost all are recovering from chemical addictions or victimhood, and I think it's wonderful.

For the most part, I'm able to see nonloving behavior, or

behavior stemming from addictions, as a cry for love and not directed at me. For a long time, even as a little kid, I felt everything was directed at me. This weekend, someone was really, really angry with me, and I had to keep reminding myself this was his pain. He's welcome to it, and it's not up to me to fix it. I don't need to change me to fix his pain, which was part of my earlier addictive process. He's a friend, I love him; he can be upset as long as he chooses, and that's okay. And I'm a good person.

I always stress, with everybody I talk to, we are not different at all, no matter what color, age, socioeconomic background, or type of addictions. We're all exactly the same, all made of the same stuff. I wear mine this way, and you wear yours that way. I've never really had animosity toward people who were in pain and addicted, except my own kids. I used to want to kill them, but now, they're getting the same respect I give the rest of the world. My attitude toward the addicted is the same as toward those who don't consider themselves addicted. As far as I'm concerned, we all use something to keep ourselves away from God. Period.

The first thing that comes up is an awareness, a noticing, if you will, that somebody's got an issue, they're in a certain spot. Without feeling sorry for them, I understand that's where they are at the time. This noticing is almost a signal that trips and, first, I notice myself judging. Second, I pivot from that point, not being sorry for them because that puts them in a lesser position, and realizing that's where they've chosen to be just as much as where I've chosen to be. Basically, I try to send them love in the appropriate manner, from the basis that if they have chosen to be where they are, then I accept them where they are.

I look at them, see them in their addiction, and know they are going to stay in it until they're ready to come out, and that's their right. I try to let them know in some way, this is where they have chosen to be. They're coming from the same tremendous place of fear I used to come from, and they can remain there as long as they want and be loved just the same. I don't look down on them, but I don't buy their drama anymore, not a bit. I might even wind up telling people, not point blank or crudely, that it's okay for them to do what they want, but I'm not interested in the details. I'm interested in where we go from here, and when you decide you might want to change, whoever you need will be right in front of you. I try very much not to get involved in their horror stories because that's a diversion, and I don't need to go there.

To some extent, there's one part of me that still feels a bit of sympathy for their situation, with perhaps a desire to reach out and be of some assistance, if that's possible. On the other hand, part of me knows I can't fix them, although I would like to reach out, grab them by the scruff of the neck, and see if I couldn't shake some of that denial loose! In the final analysis, I know they're really all right anyway, and sooner or later, in their own time, they're going to get through whatever they're dealing with.

Actually, the closer they get to whatever experience can wake them up is okay. If I distract them from their fear, which sometimes I can do, that interferes with their getting clear about their issues. Remembering not to play God is real important for me. Sometimes we get close to the breaking point and don't go into it because we're still afraid it will be too overpowering. Then we need somebody to say it'll be okay, giving us a little more strength to push in there a little harder. It's for me to be at peace, and from that, they gain some confidence, some trust that it will be okay.

There's a street person who has taken up quarters at a very busy corner close to my office. About fifty feet back from that corner he sits underneath an oak tree with all his possessions, mostly plastic bottles and things, and every time I drive by, he's there. I have a choice about how I want to see him. I could see him as addicted to victimhood and guilt and lack, at the very least, but I have decided to see him as just fine. He's under a wonderful tree and doesn't seem bothered by the police or the government, so he has his space. One day, after going by there many times, I pulled over and asked if I could give him a couple of dollars. Since he was a heavy-set, older person and not moving quickly, he took his time coming over, and the traffic stacked up behind me. I was fine with that, and as he finally came up to the car, I extended my hand and even went a little further because he wasn't going to make that final grab for the money. I felt good about giving it to him and think we joined for a moment. I've seen him on that same corner since then, but I don't feel compelled to give him any money. If I feel so directed, I will, but he's fine just where he is. I'm not the Creator, not in charge of the universe, but my job is to listen and I will do what I'm told. If that's to give him two dollars, I'll do that, and if it's to keep on driving, I'll do that. I want to be open to listening, to quiet my own mind, to hear my directive, and to see his situation as other than tragic. In most cases, someone who is down and out is probably closer to waking up than many of my other acquaintances who haven't got a clue and aren't even looking for one. Most people I know are in denial about their lives, trying to make the dream a little better, and that's okay. When they show up for me to learn about my own forgiveness issues, I'll listen. This happens so gently that I'm very appreciative of all of them. Many people in recovery groups think that seeing those who are down and out is a reminder of how terrible it would be to go back to their addictive state. It certainly can be a reminder of the consequences of that choice, but that wasn't a sufficient reason for me not to do it, and it isn't enough for them either. I don't defend against any lifestyle, and I'm not in charge of anyone's drama or their path, so I allow everybody to be where they are.

And so we come full circle. We have been silent, respectful witnesses to an awesome event—the resurgence of the loving, eternal human spirit. Through these pages, we have accompanied our friends on their journey, which is still in progress, from self-centered unawareness to a place of much greater peace and compassion. We have watched with some as they endured harrowing physical pain or had their life-long dreams dashed in a single traumatic instant. For others, it was more the "death of a thousand cuts" where relentlessly, despite their best efforts, things simply would not work out. And all had their times of wrenching heartbreak and despair. When all else failed, they took the only path to peace—they gave up, and brought their fear to love and their pain to healing. And now, with much lighter hearts and a sense of purpose, they continue their journeys toward even greater awareness. They beckon to you, saying, "It's all been worth it and you, too, can escape the lure of addictions." Now, will you join with them?

Conclusion

When I was growing up, my favorite place was in the water. Any water would do—swimming pools, rivers, creeks, ponds, or gutters along the street awash with spring rains. We loved to go out to our favorite river where there was a large waterfall, at least from our child-sized perspective, and drench ourselves under it. Now for a parable. It would have been very peculiar if, while standing under that waterfall, we had begun to ask, plead, or pray to get wet! The decision to stand under the waterfall guaranteed that we would be deluged with water. In the same way, the decision to claim our value and to focus on the good in ourselves and in others guarantees that peace and abundance and clarity of thought will be ours, and quickly. Water automatically possesses certain properties such as liquidity and wetness; we don't have to invent them. In the same way, life has properties of prosperity, joy, peace, and safety built in that are not of our making. How ridiculous we would have been to sit by the side of the waterfall, watching the tumbling waters and praying to get wet and be delivered from the heat and dust. No sane person would do that. Anyone watching the water who still complained of the heat didn't really want to get wet, because jumping in was all that was required.

If we are sitting on the banks of a potentially fulfilling life, but refusing to jump in, then we have to own up to the fact that we are choosing not to participate. No one prevents us from diving in. Some of you may protest that others are holding you back. It's time to give that one up and acknowledge that sitting on the sidelines is our first choice or we would already have jumped in. Could it be that we are afraid or offended by the process of jumping into life? And what is that process? It is the decision to love, to bless, to regard everyone and everything that comes into our awareness positively and without condition, whether they are physically present or not. If you bristle at that idea, that's fine. It is simply time to realize that we jump into life by loving and supporting everything without regard to excuses, upbringing, or other conditioning. If we choose not to stand under the waterfall of abundance that is being showered upon us, then we must admit we prefer something else even more. That's okay because, as with the waterfall, the blessings continue to shower. Both water and blessings know there is not a problem, and if we step away for a little while, they continue to pour and are inexhaustible. The waterfall is not confused, nor does it question its existence, and we will never be punished or condemned for shifting our attention from it momentarily. We simply must be clear that foot-dragging about accepting our good is the cause of our pain, not what is happening to us. This pain then prompts us to find distractions, which are called addictions if they are socially unacceptable, compulsions if they are less threatening to others, and laudable and desirable behaviors if our culture has arbitrarily agreed they are.

The happy experience of life is not complicated, mysterious, or secretive. It does not ask for sacrifice or punishment or that you earn your right to it. It is available all the time to everyone. Our only confusion has been about how to participate in life, thereby accessing all that is our birthright. The answer is choosing to engage only in loving, supportive, encouraging thoughts and actions. If you choose otherwise, by your own free will you *temporarily* close the door to all the goodness available for you. It is there for everyone—life has no favorites.

If we are addicted to anything, it is to our "right" to judge and condemn, and we are very tenacious in our belief that judgment is helpful and will keep us safe. You certainly may indulge in judgment, but you will never fully experience the joy of life by so doing. Many of us procrastinate in clearing our minds of old resentments, judgments, and opinions by asking for a guarantee that life will work out and be fulfilling if we have only loving thoughts. Or we insist that other people or situations prevent our change of heart and mind and must change first. That is clearly not true and merely an excuse to delay our homecoming. Only with commitment and courage do the doors begin to open. And the good news is that you need make only the smallest gesture toward seeing yourself and others from a different perspective to begin to experience the flow of life.

For instance, a dear friend was experiencing a very difficult time in her life a couple of years ago. Everything seemed to be going wrong. Her recalcitrant, soon-to-be-ex-husband was being greatly uncooperative, her mother had recently died, and she was concerned about her teenage son and his activities and friends. Her business was not doing well, and she believed her friends were disappearing in droves. A short while after we discussed her situation, she was attending our weekly class and noticed a new person there, without a book and sitting alone. She moved next to the woman and asked if she would like to share her book. They remained together for the duration of the class, and as a result of that very small gesture, my friend's life began to clear up. The light came back into her face, and every "impossible" situation has turned around in her life. We don't need to know the mechanics of how our situations will be resolved, only that they are when we indicate even the smallest willingness to reach out and be helpful and kind.

In summation, here is life at a glance, given to free everyone from the tangled confusion about what addictions are, where they come from, and what to do about them:

1) We are in the habit of choosing ego thoughts—judging, being right, impressing others, getting approval, saving face, avenging ourselves, focusing on the forms of people or events, hypnotizing ourselves about our inadequacy, and separating from others.

2) This choice, whether we have been aware of it or not, is the choice to sit on the banks of life rather than participating, because participation in a fulfilling life calls for blessing, being of service, honoring ourselves and others, appreciating, and acknowledging the inherent worth and goodness of everything. The choice for nonparticipation always brings pain, and we adamantly refuse to see this connection. We want so much for our fantasy about "how life is supposed to be" to succeed that even when the evident failure of our plan smacks us in the face, we engage in massive denial. We know in our hearts that our plan will not work, and yet we are very willful in refusing to accept one that does. And so we sit on the banks of life's river, stubborn, unrelenting, and praying for deliverance from the heat and dust. The ever-available option remains open while we reassess our choices. Our joint purpose is to help you make the right choice sooner.

3) We conveniently forget we made this choice to stay on the bank, rather than participating. When we forget we can choose, we forget we are powerful and feel, instead, small, separated, and ineffective.

4) As we continue to focus daily on our ego thoughts and the pain they produce, we think our two choices are to medicate our pain or to deny it is there in the first place. Those two choices are really only one choice, since neither brings joy. They merely forestall the inevitable.

5) No one is wrong for having delayed making the right choice, even for a long time. Notice that the waterfall is in no way disturbed by your refusal to stand under it. There is no condemnation, only a continuous outpouring. And so it is with us. The great outpouring of love continues and is always available no matter how long we procrastinate. Every moment can be a turning point as we keep changing our minds and choose to participate in a happy life.

6) Participation refers less to actions and accomplishments as it does to establishing a partnership with yourself, to

adopting the attitude that everything is inherently good, although fear may have obscured that to those determined to see only form. The one final and lasting solution to the problem of addictions, guaranteed to be successful, is to trade in the habitual sense of worthlessness for an equally habitual experience of joy and certainty. We have a spiritual problem, not a behavioral problem. We have denied our spiritual heritage, and it is this for which we long. We cannot "scratch the itch" until we surrender to our true desire to love and be loved unconditionally, rather than to spend our lives running and hiding from the truth of our goodness and value, the truth that lies unknown beneath our fears.

Most of us have not yet comprehended the monumental needless suffering that can vanish in an instant if we would be willing to open our minds and hearts and begin to question. Our biggest problem is not questioning the validity of the ego's voice, that endless critical and fear-inducing inner chatter that drones on relentlessly. Why are we so slow to question it? Because it is our beloved child. We made it up, and we are frantic for it to succeed, even though at our expense. We need to see that egocentricity and pain are an inevitable package; the very construct of the self-image, which we ask to save us, is the culprit. The more faithful we are to our egos, those precious little inventions we so desperately want to be right, the more impoverished we become. "Saving face" has been more important than solving any given problem, and we have listened to those ego voices even as they plunge us into the depths of despair. What loyalty we are capable of, what determination, in the face of truth, to forge ahead trying to make our way work!

You might say, we are addicted to not doing our part, coming up with long, ingenious lists of "why we can't." The fact is we can, whenever we decide it is important to us to do so. And until we do, we will continue in that vicious cycle of pain, denial, and medication or addiction. All that you are asked to do is to reconsider your position. If you are not experiencing joy and abundance, you need to change the focus of your attention, not do penance or engage in self-recrimination. The water doesn't mind if you have been sitting on the bank a little longer than others have. You are always welcome whenever you decide to jump in.

Here is a very simple two-step procedure: First, recognize that upset feelings are perfectly legitimate; they are merely warning signals indicating we are out of alignment with our true, loving, outpouring nature. Second, correct the problem they warn us of. We are being unloving to ourselves and others. We have total and absolute choice about the decision to love anyone, including ourselves, no matter what has occurred in the past. This is a current decision and is easy unless we listen to our ego commanding us to judge and hate, based on the past. Thus our short-range goal is to accept the feelings without judgment, and the long-range goal is to think and choose in such a way that these warning signals become unnecessary.

Remember, we have complete power to think as we choose and to question everything. As we take charge of our beliefs, recover the power we pretend we gave away, and choose to change our minds about how we regard everyone and every-thing, upset feelings disappear. Then the question of what to do about addictions disappears as well. Consider these ideas a challenge to all institutions and individuals. If you choose to dismiss them out of hand rather than experimenting, then you must acknowledge that you prefer to remain part of the problem. All addictions, socially acceptable or not, contribute to conflict in the world at large because they maintain inner conflict on an individual basis.

We have pretended we are not sufficiently powerful to make another choice or to establish another habit because we are afraid of our power. We are afraid that if we acknowledge our power to change our minds, we are in some way accountable, and will draw punishment down upon us. But our pretense of powerlessness is *already* attracting punishment. Our primary focus has been on the solution, not the problem, in honor and recognition of the fact that you always have more of what you pay attention to. Who wants more of the same addiction, impoverishment, pain, and loneliness? Who really wants to continue the closed loop of fearful thought, pain, need to medicate, increased fear, and more medication? Some people, perhaps; but if you have found this book, you have already decided to make a drastic change of allegiance. Don't be afraid of your power. It is a friend now ready to help in every possible way. Our power and ability to focus awareness wherever we choose is of enormous and utmost importance.

Finally, our primary addiction, compulsion, or habit is living an unexamined life of guilt and smallness, the unchallenged guilt that steals into our minds and robs us of all peace. The secondary addictions are all those substances, behaviors, and points of view that derive from the basic, unfounded premise of being guilty. Many hundreds of different addictions, and only one cause—it's time to give it up!

Life never resists, it simply flows. We can focus that flow through honoring all created life, including ourselves, or we can have our noses in a dismal, third-rate novel of judgment and pain. It's always our choice, and there is never any punishment or withholding from us for reading that pathetic novel right up to the last page. We are always beloved children of the universe, and always held in the heart of God as unique, necessary, and precious beings. Choosing to accept this truth is always up to us, and our moments of choice are endless. Very few of us were blessed with aware, enlightened role models. May we begin this millennium anew and become the role models we did not have, thus ending the reign of terror, the downward spiral to addictions that begins with repressing our feelings. And as we part, know with certainty, life can always have a happy ending!

A workshop, which is the basis for this book,
Healing the Hurt Behind Addictions,
is available on audiocassette.
(Recorded live)

See How "Life Works"
with C. Howe and Associates!

For more information about this book,
the LifeWorks audio and video tape series,
workshops, or speaking engagements, contact:
Carol Howe and Associates
P.O. Box 151456, Altamonte Springs, FL 32715
Phone (407) 339-8866 Fax (407) 339-8071
www.carolhowe.com
carol@carolhowe.com